MW01634691

HOME MOVIES

MARTIN KNELMAN

HOME MOVIES

TALES FROM THE CANADIAN FILM WORLD

Martin Knelman

KEY PORTER BOOKS

© 1987 Martin Knelman

All rights reserved. No part of this work covered by the copyrights hereon may be reproduced or used in any form or by any means — graphic, electronic or mechanical, including photocopying, recording, taping or information retrieval systems — without the prior written permission of the publisher.

Canadian Cataloguing in Publication Data

Knelman, Martin
Home movies

ISBN 1-55013-049-8

1. Moving-picture industry — Canada. 2. Moving-pictures — Canada. I. Title.

PN1993.5.C3K44 1987 791.43'0971 C87-094692-7

Key Porter Books Limited
70 The Esplanade
Toronto, Ontario
Canada M5E 1R2

Cover Design: Marie Bartholomew
Typesetting: Velum Print and Graphic Services Inc.
Printing and Binding: John Deyell Company
Printed and bound in Canada

87 88 89 90 6 5 4 3 2 1

For my parents
and their only granddaughter,
Sara Ouellette Knelman,
whose birth on June 28, 1979
pre-empted the author's attendance
at the world premiere of Meatballs

and in memory of Claude Jutra (1930-1986)

Acknowledgments

This book evolved from a series of lunches with Anna Porter, and things eventually reached the point where either Anesty's had to change its menu or I had to write the book. The Canada Council and the Ontario Arts Council provided generous assistance, and I'm grateful to John Gray, Christina McCall and Brian Moore for supporting the project. A number of friends in the film industry told me all kinds of things against their better judgment, luckily for me. Charis Wahl was my editor, as usual; Linda Book took the author's photo, as usual; and Charles Pachter's Moose Spot provided the perfect image to sum up my thoughts about the Canadian film industry. My editors at *Toronto Life*, especially Marq de Villiers and Stephen Trumper, were stoical about the disruptive effect this book had on my work for the magazine. My wife, Bernadette Sulgit, scribbled things in margins from time to time, and my son, Joshua Knelman, put the whole experience into perspective for me by discreetly asking how much I was paying Mrs. Porter to publish this book.

Martin Knelman

Contents

Opening Shots

Canada has had a love-hate relationship with Hollywood since the early days of movies. People who grew up in what they regarded as a provincial backwater, feeling as deprived and as desperate for excitement as the young heroine of *My American Cousin*, could sneak off to the movies and catch a bit of American glamor and sophistication. And like the girl in the movie, Canadians were always of two minds about the glimpses of American life they saw on the big screen.

America as seen from this side of the border through the open window of Hollywood could be envied or could be despised, but it couldn't be ignored. And right from the start, those trying to create Canadian alternatives found themselves confronted by the overwhelming factor of what playwright John Gray calls "the American hallucination in Canada."

Throughout this century Canadians trying to carve out a small part of the entertainment world for themselves have gone through endless stages and variations of a bizarre and elaborate ritual: dancing with Hollywood. At times, the dance has been a kind of flirtation waltz; at times it has been a dramatic tango charged with the theme of renunciation. Resenting Hollywood has been almost as great a Canadian compulsion as emulating Hollywood. Canadians feel incredibly flattered if one of our films is well received by Americans or nominated for an Oscar. And incredibly hurt and angry when Hollywood overlooks us, again, or takes us for granted. Pierre Berton actually wrote an entire book bemoaning the misconceptions about Canada contained in Hollywood movies.

For those in the movie business, Hollywood was many things. It was a role model for how Canadian movies ought to be made; or it was a warning about what could happen if you went about making movies the wrong way. It was the symbol of success or the symbol of false values. It was a place you went to test yourself against the most talented people in the world; or a place you had to stay away from if you wanted to maintain your integrity and purity of heart. It was the place you went to prove something to the folks back home. It was a hopelessly domineering partner who would try to make you change the flags and the dollar bills in your own country. It was a benign partner who would give you money to enable you to make the films you dreamed of doing the way you wanted to do them. And finally it was the place people went when they wanted to pretend to be someone else, and a place from which they would eventually return when they were ready to be themselves again.

As for the resentment, there were some good reasons for it. Until Garth Drabinsky came along, it was considered normal for the largest chains of movie theatres to be controlled by foreign companies. By not only taking hold of a large and powerful chain of theatres in Canada but also becoming a major player in the United States, Drabinsky almost single-handedly reversed the brand of Hollywood cultural imperialism that had seemed to be one of the irrefutable facts of life for Canada—although his complicated partnership with the Music Corporation of America raised puzzled questions about who was taking over whom.

But owning theatres is one thing; producing movies is quite another. Even before talkies came in, Hollywood had established its grip on the Canadian theatre market, and an attempt to establish a feature industry in this country was crushed as a result of pressure from Hollywood.

For decades Canadian filmmaking was largely a matter of documentaries in the National Film Board style. When a feature-film industry did finally develop, through government subsidy, those films often couldn't find audiences because the system of film distribution and the theatres themselves were controlled by Hollywood.

In 1967 the Canadian government committed itself to establishing a feature-film industry, and began dispersing funds through its new creation, the Canadian Film Development Corporation (which in 1983 was transformed into Telefilm Canada). The government also offered tax incentives to investors in Canadian movies.

But Canada's new film industry was plagued by problems. For a period a lot of movies were doomed because they weren't as slick as Hollywood movies and didn't have Hollywood stars in them, and so couldn't get into theatres controlled by Hollywood.

And then there was the notorious era of Hollywood North, when Canadian movies were mostly bad imitations of Hollywood movies, with Canadian cities disguised as American cities and with has-been American actors in the cast. Emulating Hollywood, it turned out, had its down side. The industry ground to a halt in an atmosphere of shame and recrimination.

During the 1980s Canada developed new ways of dancing with Hollywood. The idea was to make films that could be shown on TV, to keep creative control in Canada, and to use Hollywood as a financial partner to get the films made and shown. This plan resulted in success stories as varied as the late-night cop show *Night Heat* and the two *Anne of Green Gables* films. It also resulted in a number of successful, low-budget feature films—including *My American Cousin, The Decline of the American Empire* and *I've Heard the Mermaids Singing*—that won acclaim both at home and abroad by taking paths that were distinctly off-Hollywood.

Canadians changed their image of Hollywood to suit their needs. What never changed was that Canadian movie people continued to be obsessed with Hollywood, whether the obsession was positive or negative. Whenever Canadian movies were made, they were made in the shadow of the American eagle, or of the MGM lion, or of Mickey Mouse.

Day in and day out, year after year, the dancing pilgrims left and came back on the five-hour nonstop flight between Toronto and L.A. Above all there was an unmistakable sense that if you were in the game of making major movies sooner or later Hollywood was the place you had to go—even if the movie was about a Canadian who goes to China.

Hollywood was mostly not interested, and when the movie was finally made in 1987, it was made, rather surprisingly, with very little help from Hollywood. With hefty backing from Telefilm Canada and a coproduction deal with the Chinese themselves, *Bethune* was produced by two Montrealers who hoped it would stand as proof that Canadian moviemakers don't need any help from their American cousins.

That was a questionable, highly risky thesis—as well as a tricky new step in Canada's ongoing dance with Hollywood.

PART I

DANCING WITH HOLLYWOOD

1

The California Connection

Picking up a rental car at the Los Angeles airport and getting on the freeway, an unsuspecting Canadian embarks on an experience that in our naïveté we might call heavy traffic. But Joan Didion, in *The White Album*, explains: "Anyone can 'drive' on the freeway, and many people with no vocation for it do, hesitating here and resisting there, losing the rhythm of the lane change, thinking about where they came from and where they are going. Actual participants think only about where they are. Actual participation requires a total surrender, concentration so intense as to seem a kind of narcosis, a rapture-of-the-freeway. The mind goes clean. The rhythm takes over."

And according to architecture writer Reyner Banham, "The freeways become a special way of being alive. . . . The extreme concentration required in Los Angeles seems to bring on a state of heightened awareness that some locals find mystical."

Cruising the freeways may be as good a way as any of getting your sociocultural bearings. Southern California is not only the land of sunshine, palm trees and movie studios, not only the testing ground that gave the world hot tubs, sensitivity training, Jesus cults, frozen yogurt as a way of life and Ronald Reagan. It's also the last frontier, the place where the land stops, where Joad in *The Grapes of Wrath* wanted to get to, where unsettling numbers of latter-day gypsies, some of them very rich, prefer to live in rented houses, the quicker to make their getaways. People worship cars because they spend preposterous amounts of time in them.

Southern California looks like paradise — and a wealthy paradise at that — but it bears the burden of an overwhelming sense of cultural inferiority, which not even the openings of two major museums of modern art within a year can entirely erase. "Out here we don't go to the theatre much," I was told by a sophisticated easterner who moved to L.A. for the pleasure of gazing at the sea and feeling the heat of the sun in January, "but we go to a lot of movies."

The implication is that when you live among the heathens you should keep track of what the heathens are up to. Even with its huge population Los Angeles retains the mentality of a frontier outpost, always apologetic about failing to keep up with its betters. Canadians, who are used to living in a country with a national inferiority complex, feel right at home in L.A., where half the people you meet seem to be embarrassed they're not in New York. People flocked to southern California for the sun and the sea, to get away from the Depression, or to break into the movies, often with a curious sense of having done something vaguely disreputable, all the while putting down the very pleasures they sought.

"The thing I don't like is that everyone is very hedonistic and materialistic," confided a friend from Winnipeg who had a wonderful time discovering California high-living. "There really isn't any intellectual community to speak of," a literary man said sadly, sipping vintage wine and watching a spectacular sunset from his terrace.

Like television and comic strips, Los Angeles, the heart of the movie world, is a phenomenon to which everyone can feel culturally superior. The movies began as a tawdry entertainment form — crude flickers for the uneducated mob to gape at — and there's still an element of that in the way the big movie companies operate. Those who made it were gypsy entrepreneurs, refugees from the garment industry or the junk business, and they had a comic anxiety about giving their product respectability and legitimacy.

California is regarded with suspicion by the rest of the country, like the black sheep of the family who ran away from home and did something outrageously unconventional. But now the black sheep is the most successful member of the clan — the state keeps gobbling up more and more of the U.S. population — and is writing new rules for establishment decorum. If California were independent, it would be the eighth-largest industrial power in the world; its gross regional product is exceeded by only thirteen countries.

L.A., the world capital of glittery fantasy, is an entertainment-industry town the way Pittsburgh is a steel town. The focus of conversation tends to be the latest regime at the major studios. Everyone tells entertaining anecdotes with frequent punchlines, as if auditioning for a guest spot on *The Tonight Show.*

Among its other impressive claims, L.A. happens to be the fourth-largest Canadian city in the world, with about a million pilgrims from the North. They're not all in show business; it only seems that way.

Mary Pickford, a girl from Toronto, became known as America's sweetheart in the days before the screen learned how to talk; and Aimee Semple Macpherson, the pop evangelist, once called California "God's great blueprint for man's abode on earth."

There were scores of other pilgrims, from Walter Huston, Mack Sennett, Louis B. Mayer, Marie Dressler and Norma Shearer in the early days, to Lorne Greene, Lloyd Bochner, Dan Petrie, Norman Jewison, John Vernon, Monty Hall and Christopher Plummer in the Eisenhower era, to such relatively recent arrivistes as Geneviève Bujold, Margot Kidder, David Steinberg, Ivan Reitman,

Michael J. Fox, Helen Shaver and Donald Sutherland.

What made this group distinct from other émigrés in Hollywood — the Europeans like Marlene Dietrich, Greta Garbo, Fritz Lang, Liv Ullmann, the British such as Laurence Olivier, Charles Laughton, Merle Oberon, Alfred Hitchcock and Vivien Leigh, even the recently arrived Australians like Mel Gibson and Peter Weir? Why, the very fact that the Canadians weren't easily identifiable as Canadians. The differences between them and native Americans were so subtle they could pass for Yankees — and often did.

Canadians were considered so nonthreatening and, well, invisible that a TV mock-documentary, *The Canadian Conspiracy,* treated the Canadian invasion of Hollywood as a joke — with the humor coming from the assumption that only American paranoia could see it as anything but benign. This award-winning film, written and directed by Robert Boyd, presents Canadians the way Orson Welles presented Martians in his notorious *War of the Worlds* broadcast, and the way Joe McCarthy treated the international Communist conspiracy. What makes these new intruders so dangerous is that they look and sound just like Americans. Yet they are actually ruthless aliens from the North, spreading their subversive attitudes through a "harmless" form of popular entertainment.

One by one, the operatives — Margot Kidder, Anne Murray, Dave Thomas, Eugene Levy, Leslie Nielsen, Monty Hall, David Steinberg, Rich Little, Raymond Burr, Morley Safer, Ivan Reitman, Doug Henning and Lorne Michaels — deny there is a Canadian conspiracy to sabotage the American way. But a deadpan narrator rattles off the indictment and shows details of a plot going back to Mackenzie King and Mary Pickford. Eventually the investigation leads to Mr. Big; Lorne Greene, who operated a school of broadcasting in Toronto circa 1950, long before he became America's favorite patriarch on the long-running hit show *Bonanza,* is exposed as the centre of the ring. When cornered in the deep end of their California swimming pools, Hollywood Canadians deny they've even heard of Lorne Greene. Yet few are willing to explain why it was so easy for them to get their Greene cards.

These days Canadians in show business don't need green cards because they don't exactly move to L.A.—they half-move to L.A., splitting their time between southern California and Canada. Air Canada and Ma Bell are the big winners. Among those who keep at least one foot in L.A. while continuing to reside in Canada are Al Waxman, who plays the boss of Cagney and Lacey in the CBS television series, and Garth Drabinsky, who continues to buy up theatre chains in the United States and has a complicated, ongoing, corporate relationship with Universal, a giant among the Hollywood majors.

Inevitably some people tire of commuting and decide, somewhat apologetically, to move their families to L.A. and take up residence there. The high-profile émigré of 1987 was Jon Slan, who hangs out in Hollywood to hatch the deals for such projects as his *Philip Marlowe* TV series or his forthcoming *Alfred Hitchcock Presents* series for Universal—even though Slan's company, Paragon, has its headquarters in Toronto. Slan may have the distinction of being the only person ever to hold office as chairman of Toronto's Festival of Festivals while living in L.A. A running joke among Slan's friends is that Drabinsky, with whom Slan has crossed swords several times, agreed to let the film festival use Cineplex Odeon theatres only on condition that Slan leave the country. Slan, for his part, maintains that the move is only temporary; he and his family plan to return to Toronto after two years or so.

The show-business Canadians of southern California cross paths regularly at lunches and cocktail parties, at speeches and seminars organized by Telefilm's L.A. office, at the annual party thrown by Norman and Dixie Jewison at their Malibu beach house, or at such gala events as a dinner at the posh L.A. restaurant Le St.

Germain to mark the opening of Stratford's U.S. tour. (Ontario Premier David Peterson was among the contingent that flew down from Toronto for that weekend in November 1985, and he took the opportunity to promote not only Stratford but Ontario as a film production centre.) California Canadians tend to share a certain giddy feeling, almost of being born again.

Paul Mazursky, a writer-director who moved to L.A. from New York in the early sixties and now satirizes the California high-life from the inside in such movies as *Down and Out in Beverly Hills*, has this theory about what makes people in southern California a bit nuttier than people elsewhere in the United States. "If you have sunlight all year round, your brain gets baked. Someone comes along and says, 'Look, if I rub your forehead and feed you carrots, it will make you a sexy person.' And if you've been living in the sun too long, you'll believe it." Mazursky expounded this theory beside his swimming pool.

That theory applies beautifully to some of the Hollywood Canadians who've shed their skepticism along with their inhibitions under the influence of the California sun. What they find exciting about L.A., besides the climate, is the naked ambition, the rampant free enterprise, the unqualified, self-promotional optimism of all the hustlers and would-be creative geniuses. You rarely hear anyone whining about Canadian cultural identity or the shortcomings of the CBC. Pilgrims from the north shed their cultural insecurities along with their winter clothes. In the rush of optimism, they may even believe this is the only place to put together the movie about the Canadian who goes to China.

For decades various Canadians had been cruising the L.A. freeways trying to find a way to make a big movie about Dr. Norman Bethune, the romantic, enigmatic Montreal surgeon and crusader who rebelled against the medical establishment and upper-class WASP Canadian society and became the most revered martyr of the Chinese Communist Revolution. Among those who had become obsessively involved with trying to make this movie were screenwriter Ted Allan, who had been Bethune's disciple and biographer, producer John Kemeny, actor Donald Sutherland and two of the most prominent Canadian directors working in Hollywood—Ted Kotcheff and Norman Jewison.

Canadians come to Hollywood to carve out certain myths. A favorite, the myth of boy tycoon, was more or less created by Ivan Reitman. Few Hollywood Canadians have risen with his spectacular rapidity. Only a decade ago Reitman was an impecunious, independent producer-director hustling to survive. But that was before *Animal House,* which put Reitman into a Bel Air mansion along with his wife, a charming French-Canadian former actress named Geneviève Deloir, and their children.

A scrawny, toothy kid from Czechoslovakia who came to Canada at age four, steerage class, and began his movie career as a boy-mogul at McMaster University in Hamilton, Reitman quickly earned a reputation for entrepreneurial genius. But his interest in raising the level of movie art seemed at times minimal.

In 1969 Reitman made *Orientation,* a fresh, casual, student short about freshman initiation. He followed that with *Foxy Lady,* a low-budget campus sex spoof. At twenty-three Reitman was engagingly blatant about his priorities; he told interviewers that his main objective was to make a bundle, fast. He also had a certain relish for notoriety; at McMaster he produced a film, *Columbus of Sex,* which was seized by police and resulted in Reitman's being fined $300 for making an obscene film. For a time he gave up directing and turned his energy toward becoming a producer of schlocky movies for the exploitation market. Among his productions from 1973 to 1977 were *Cannibal Girls, Death Weekend* and two David Cronenberg movies,

Shivers and *Rabid*. (*Cannibal Girls* was written over a weekend by two of Reitman's friends and collaborators, Dan Goldberg and Len Blum, shot in ten days and sold to Samuel Arkoff of American International Pictures.)

By the mid-1970s Reitman was regarded by some observers as a symbol of what had gone wrong with the Canadian movie industry. He had also become, at a preposterously young age, the only producer in the country who regularly turned a profit. Then Reitman went to Hollywood and (in collaboration with Matty Simmons, founding publisher of the *National Lampoon* magazine) produced *Animal House*, a grabbag of raunchy sketches about frat-house high jinks, circa 1962, featuring in its cast a young comedian named John Belushi. *Animal House* grossed $200 million and transformed Reitman, rather hilariously, into the latest reincarnation of Irving Thalberg.

Reitman wanted to direct as well as produce, and he got his wish with *Meatballs*, a high-calorie, low-nutrition, summer comedy about shenanigans at an Ontario summer camp. Unlike Reitman's other post–*Animal House* films, *Meatballs* was actually a Canadian production. Unfortunately, the financial statements were of much greater interest than what was on the screen; you had to be willfully infantile to enjoy it. But *Meatballs* was a big winner at the box office.

Afterward came the military comedy *Stripes* (the most likable of Reitman's films, though it wasn't a huge hit), *Ghostbusters* (one of the biggest box-office winners in Hollywood history) and *Legal Eagles* (Reitman's effort to break away from sophomoric humor and make an adult movie). It starred Robert Redford and Debra Winger, and it wouldn't take Sherlock Holmes to deduce that all did not go well. In an interview with *Vanity Fair*, Winger remarked unceremoniously, "I've never worked with such pigs."

When it comes to the myth of the writer in splendid exile,

there's no one who can touch Brian Moore. To get to his Malibu home, you head westward out of L.A., then turn north at the Pacific Ocean and just keep going, past the tacky drive-in restaurants by the sea, onward through the chic beach colony along the road to San Francisco. Staring at the facades as you zip along, you might well ask, Who would want to live right next to the Pacific Coast Highway? But walk through one of those doors and you enter another world. The highway noise is drowned out by the roar of the sea, and a spectacular stretch of sand is warmed by the California sun. A movie director buys a house there after scoring a big hit. It's a place where you can live as if you've dropped out without actually dropping out.

Malibu is show-business heaven—but not exactly the place you'd expect to find the author of *The Luck of Ginger Coffey* and *Catholics*. Serious writers are expected to live in slum garrets or roach-infested Paris hotel rooms, at least until they become rich and famous. Then they are allowed to live in fancy pads in great metropolises. But not in an isolated movie-town retreat forty miles from L.A., which is itself, by common consent, culturally nowhere.

Moore lives there (with his second wife, Jean, a former TV commentator from Nova Scotia) in the tradition of Irish literary wanderers from James Joyce to Samuel Beckett and Brendan Behan. It isn't only Ireland (to which he makes an annual pilgrimage) from which he's exiled. Moore is also an exile from Canada, the country of his citizenship, where he lived for about a decade.

At sixty-five, Brian Moore is a faintly impish-looking man with a cheerful disposition, punctuated by a sarcastic Belfast tongue. If you were particularly anxious to irritate him, you couldn't do better than to suggest that it must have been the movies that lured him to California. Moore moved there in spite of the movies not because of them. He came for the sun and the sea, and because he had trouble getting down to work in New York. But now he writes screenplays when he's between novels. He's working as executive producer as well on a forthcoming Canadian movie version of his novel *Black Robe*. And finally, after three decades of false starts, his first novel, *The Lonely Passion of Judith Hearne*, has been filmed, with Maggie Smith in the title role of a neurotic Belfast spinster living alone in poverty and in a state of increasing personal disintegration.

Serious novelists like Moore are relatively rare in the land of surf and sun, but almost every second person you meet is working on a screenplay, or claims to be, including a number of Canadians. Bernard Slade, a former actor from St. Catharines, Ontario, who eventually made it big on Broadway with *Same Time, Next Year,* spent a lengthy stopover in Hollywood, where he got established writing for the TV program *The Flying Nun*. Slade has a thesis about the attitudes that set Canada apart, culturally, from the two countries that have dominated it. In England, according to Slade, you're known by your best work. In the United States, you're known by your last work. And in Canada, you're known by your worst work.

The Canadian screenwriter who struck it rich most flamboyantly in Hollywood is Tom Hedley, the former Toronto magazine editor whose major claim to fame is that he wrote the movie *Flashdance,* which has added $5 million or so to his bank account. Hedley now resides in a walled property in the Hollywood Hills and drives a white Cadillac once owned by Elvis Presley.

According to Hedley, Canadians who become successful after leaving the country are hated by those who stayed home. But that doesn't mean they would be welcomed back, he told journalist Ian Brown. "You come back, and they say, 'Oh, he came back. He's just another loser like the rest of us.' "

No doubt many people still dream of making it big in movies and moving to Hollywood, as Hedley did, but almost the first thing Arlene Sarner did after enjoying a fairy-tale success with her first script was to move back to Toronto, her home for most of her life.

Before going to Hollywood, the biggest thing that happened in Sarner's writing career was a 1979 *Toronto Life* cover story on books. After that she wrote a few other magazine pieces, had a couple of bad experiences at the CBC and hooked up, personally and professionally, with New York journalist Jerry Leichtling. Together they wrote *Peggy Sue Got Married,* a kind of *Back to the Future* for grown-ups, which was on the verge of being shelved when Francis Coppola came along and made it.

So why move back to Toronto just when everything seemed to be coming up roses? Because Toronto has people who aren't in show business, a subway and streets where you walk and hear people talk. Yes! Peggy Sue got married, won the Hollywood lottery and moved back to the future.

Ken Finkleman, one of the few Canadians who went to Hollywood as a writer and wound up as a director, acted out the myth of prisoner in a hell on earth. Finkleman, the younger brother of Toronto broadcaster Dan Finkleman, earned a track record writing the script for *Grease II* —which was why Paramount hired him to write the script for *Airplane II.* Just before shooting was to commence, the director became unavailable. Finkleman was astonished when the studio asked him to step in; after all, he had never directed anything, and this was a multi-million-dollar movie from a major studio. A Paramount executive prevailed on him to let the studio test his directing aptitude. After a few hours of moving cameras around, he was deemed to have passed the test. And so he directed *Airplane II* and, after that, *Head Office,* a satire he had written about life in a major corporation. But Finkleman despised L.A. and its folk customs, and after *Head Office*—which was not a happy experience—he moved back to Toronto to continue his writing career. Not long before packing it up, Finkleman told Ron Graham of

Saturday Night: "I'm here to make money, not to express myself, but living in an atmosphere that you're rejecting all the time can make you feel dead."

Daniel Petrie created the myth of the veteran who has been in Hollywood so long that it's too late for him to go home even if he sometimes longs to do so. Petrie is still a Canadian citizen four decades after leaving Canada. He expressed his impulse to come home, in symbolic form, by making a movie about his roots. The Hollywood films Petrie has directed, such as *Fort Apache: The Bronx*, tend to be identified with a star or a writer rather than with him. But in his 1984 movie *The Bay Boy*, produced by John Kemeny, Petrie finally told who he is and where he came from.

The movie isn't strictly autobiographical, but a number of details are close to the story of Dan Petrie's boyhood. The hero is a sixteen-year-old boy from Glace Bay, played with quiet and likable authority by Kiefer Sutherland in his first major role. The story is set in 1937, and like the young Petrie, Donald Campbell is a dutiful "good son" in a Scottish Catholic family touched by tragedy. His family and the nuns at school expect him to become a priest, but the boy, in the midst of a sexual awakening, is heading in a different direction. The movie tells the story of his decision not to become a priest.

The Bay Boy is a flawed movie — its thriller mechanics don't carry much conviction, and Liv Ullmann is jarringly wrong for the role of the hero's mother — but it's fascinating as a piece of autobiography. The father on the screen (Peter Donat) is, like Petrie's father, a businessman who lost almost everything in the Depression. And the family in the movie has endured sorrows like those experienced by Petrie's family. Petrie's young alter ego has a retarded brother who dies in the film, and his mother is haunted by the memory of a daughter who died earlier. The literal truth was different. In Petrie's family one sibling died of a ruptured appendix the year before Petrie was born, and a twenty-year-old brother died of encephalitis when Petrie was five, but what stayed with him all these years was a great subject — the pressure felt by a child who has to make up to his parents for the loss of other children.

The role of unofficial godfather in Hollywood's Canadian film club is played, to the hilt, by Norman Jewison. This point was recognized by Air Canada in a full-color ad that has been appearing recently in glossy magazines. With palm trees and ocean sunset in the background, a jovially smiling Jewison, recently turned sixty, sits in shirtsleeves in a director's chair proclaiming, "Only one frequent flyer program stars in my California Connection."

Jewison is a raspy-voiced, silver-haired scrapper from the Beaches area of Toronto who made it big in Hollywood, first as a director of live TV variety shows featuring the likes of Judy Garland and Harry Belafonte, then as the director of such entertaining mainstream movies as *The Russians Are Coming, The Russians Are Coming* and the Oscar-winning *In the Heat of the Night*.

For the past decade Jewison has been living mostly in Canada (he and his wife, Dixie, have a farm in Caledon East, north of Toronto, and still maintain a house in Malibu). As he puts it in the Air Canada ad, "I came home to Canada in 1978. In search of my roots. I shot *Agnes of God* in Quebec, Montreal and Toronto. In film, timing is everything. It's the same with airlines. I'm probably one of the most frequent flyers on Air Canada flight 791 to Los Angeles. I call it the 'California Connection.' It's the only morning nonstop, plus I get Aeroplan miles. I know all the flight attendants. I think I can almost fly the plane."

Jewison may be a patriotic homebody who likes making his own maple syrup at his Caledon farm, but he hangs onto the perks of Hollywood success while living a long way from Hollywood. Even when he works in Canada, Jewison continues to make Hollywood films — *Agnes of*

God starred Jane Fonda, Anne Bancroft and Meg Tilley, and the soon-to-be-released *Moonstruck* stars Cher and Nicolas Cage. Still, Jewison is eager to play a leadership role in the Canadian entertainment industry. He used a young Canadian, Leon Marr, as apprentice-observer on *Best Friends*, and felt proud when Marr went on to direct *Dancing in the Dark*.

But Jewison's impulse to be the matchmaker marrying off Hollywood gloss to Canadian culture went awry when he tried to make a film of *Automatic Pilot*, Toronto playwright Erika Ritter's lively comedy about a stand-up female comic with a disastrous love life and a gift for talking dirty. Throughout the writing of a first-draft screenplay, their relationship got testier and testier, until Ritter's temper boiled over one day in Jewison's office, and he responded by turning to his assistant to say, "Cancel lunch." It was his way of telling Ritter he was ready to move on to a second draft with another writer.

Since moving back to Ontario, Jewison has been a conspicuously good citizen, serving on the boards of the Stratford Festival and the Festival of Festivals. But his biggest effort has gone into spearheading the establishment of the Canadian Centre for Advanced Film Studies, which is modeled on such organizations as the American Film Institute and the British Film Institute. With a little help from such friends as the estate of E.P. Taylor, the Bronfman family and the Ontario government, the centre will begin operations near the end of 1987.

Jewison is partly responsible for a surprising new trend in the air traffic between Toronto (or YYZ as it's designated in airline lingo) and Los Angeles (or LAX as its main airport is known). In the past few years, coming home has become as powerful an imperative as getting out used to be. For Gordon Pinsent, the actor-writer-director from Newfoundland, the ultimate step in Canada's flirtation waltz with Hollywood was the one that brought him home again at last. Pinsent decided to move back to

Toronto from L.A. in the mid-1970s because, as he explained at the time, "Nobody wants to be a tenant forever. We all want a place of our own. In Canada I feel like a landlord."

On the first Sunday of February 1987, the launching of Pinsent's Newfie home movie, *John and the Missus*—a parable about the crucial importance of hanging on to one's own identity by clinging to the patch of ground one has always regarded as home—became the occasion for a great outpouring of emotion about coming home, showbiz style. The premiere was a $200-a-head benefit for the Canadian Centre for Advanced Film Studies. But if you took your clues from the speeches, you might have thought you were at a revivalist meeting of born-again zealots.

The most rousing speech came from Christopher Plummer, a classical actor who wasted no time putting miles between himself and his home and native land three decades ago. Plummer is known for his disdainfully raised eyebrows rather than for heartfelt emotion, but on this occasion he held the audience spellbound with his dramatic, ironic account of how those who had run away from Canada, himself included, had been seduced.

"We forgot what fun it was to fight for dear old art on our own front lawn," Plummer declaimed. When the Canadian film industry began, "we came home again, riddled with guilt. But the great big movies we finally got to make here for world consumption were a bit derivative. There wasn't much of us in them. We forgot how to be original. We forgot who we were and where we came from.

"That is one of the things our centre can fix. It can help us rediscover ourselves and prove that we do have something to say—that we're interesting because we're so damn complicated. That dilemma of us is funny, it's touching, and it's worth holding on to. It's part of what makes us different, unique—us."

Like a preacher working the congregation, Plummer built to his final glorious revelation of spiritual purpose: "From now on, we're not going to hide behind our borders. We're going to abide by the unwritten artistic law that we show ourselves as we are to the outside. We've got to shake off our fears, let our imagination survive. . . . As from today, we're not going to run away from home no more!"

Hallelujah! The assembly of the faithful gave the actor a rousing amen, a chorus of the elect proclaiming with one thundering voice, "Cancel our reservations on the California Connection."

Plummer invented a new myth for himself—the repentant sinner who escapes damnation in Hollywood by being born again in Toronto, the man who marvels that once he was lost but now he is saved. Generations of Canadians who dreamed of making it big had gone to Hollywood believing it was the promised land. Now one who had been there was telling them it wasn't that at all. Hollywood, the way Chris Plummer saw it, was merely the devil's playground.

2

Hollywood North Follies

The notorious symbol of Canadian movies at the peak of the imitation-Hollywood tax-shelter hysteria of the late 1970s was a film called *Circle of Two*, produced in 1979. Typically, it was made in a Toronto disguised as someplace else. Typically, the two stars — the late Richard Burton, playing a sixty-year-old painter, and Tatum O'Neal, as the sixteen-year-old girl who falls in love with him — were imports. So was the director, Jules (*Never on Sunday*) Dassin. And, typically, the money was raised from ordinary, slightly upscale earners who wanted to get in on a trendy investment.

Circle of Two sounded good in the prospectus, and 570 units were sold at $10,000 a crack, for $5.7 million. Although the movie never reached North American theatres, it was sold for release in Brazil, Iceland and Mexico, and you may have caught a fleeting glimpse of it one night on the CBC. But the drama on the screen was less compelling than the aftermath, which has dragged on for years in the courts. In 1983 solicitors for a group of 240 investors issued a statement of claim seeking $34 million in damages for breach of contract. The defendants included the Film Consortium of Canada, a company owned by the producers of the movie, William (Bill) Marshall and Henk

Van der Kolk; David Roffey, one of the highest-flying film financiers of the era; and Morguard Group Ltd.

In 1979, seventy feature films were produced in Canada (compared to ninety-five in Hollywood) but more than half of them were never released. Abuse of the tax-shelter law became a national scandal, and the bubble burst. Only small portions of the astronomical sums invested in those movies were visible in what was shown on the screen. Huge fees were paid to producers, lawyers and brokers. When asked why certain producers seemed interested only in very expensive projects, a cynical insider explained: "If the budget is less than a million dollars, it makes it very hard to steal a million." In 1982, only twenty-seven feature films were produced; the dentists and lawyers had jumped ship and put their capital into mining stocks.

The reason for the boom-and-bust was simple. The federal government attracted investors to movies by offering a hundred-percent tax write-off. Investors flocked to movies, glad to have their money sheltered, but also hoping for a future profit. Too often the future profit failed to materialize, and so, even though they had the advantage of tax relief in the short term, the investors lost money in the long term. In those days the federal law specified that to be eligible for the tax write-off, a movie could not have preproduction sales of distribution rights. That turned out to be a huge mistake. Most films are much easier to sell before they're produced than afterward. When the laws were revised in the mid-1980s to facilitate a new wave of TV films, "pre-sales," as they are known, were made compatible with tax write-offs.

Those with long memories had a sense of déjà-vu about the boom-and-bust of the late 1970s. This wasn't the first time Canada's movie industry sputtered and died. The story of how it evolved during the 1920s and 1930s, before the National Film Board was even thought of, was told in the intriguing 1974 documentary *Dreamland*. History repeated itself in a more spectacularly gruesome way after Ottawa set up the Canadian Film Development Corporation (CFDC) at the end of 1967 to stimulate a new feature-film industry. Amazingly, movies did get made; unfortunately, they were often the wrong movies, made by the wrong people.

In the late 1960s and early 1970s, during the early phase of the Canadian feature-film industry, a number of talented directors emerged, and everyone talked about movies as a director's medium. There were breakthrough pictures like *Goin' Down the Road* (1970), *Mon Oncle Antoine* (1971), *Réjeanne Padovani* (1973), *The Apprenticeship of Duddy Kravitz* (1974), *Les Ordres* (1975), *Why Shoot the Teacher* (1977) and *J.A. Martin, photographe* (1977). But the marketplace, dominated by U.S.-controlled theatre chains in collaboration with Hollywood studios, made it difficult for small independent films to reach the public. Some of the best people found it impossible to do the work they wanted to do, and they began to feel the industry was collapsing under them. It wasn't enough, it became obvious, to have a few talented people along with technicians and a government sugar daddy. The missing element, the theory went, was the high-powered producer.

The late 1970s spawned a new breed of producer — the tough, shrewd, showman-entrepreneur who put the whole package together and created that most prized of all movie entities, the deal. In Hollywood, the studios were relying more on independent producers, and in Canada, where there were no studios, the independent producer was the only game in town.

It was perhaps a measure of the cultural climate in Canada in the late 1970s that when a full-fledged feature-film industry blossomed, the one genuine star it created was not Canada's answer to Chaplin or Garbo or Fellini. No, the true star to emerge from Hollywood North was a crafty back-room boy and veteran of the Ottawa political machine, Michael McCabe, the man who made producers king.

As executive director of the CFDC from 1978 to 1980, McCabe maintained as high a profile as any performer or politician in the land. His detractors said he didn't care about Canadian cultural expression, that he had no commitment to native talent, that he neglected Quebec and that he wouldn't recognize a good movie if it were sent up to his room on a platter by room service. His boosters claimed he was exactly the brash, fast-talking wheeler-dealer needed to put Canada on the map of the movie world, where what counted most were nerve, confidence and gambling instincts.

One thing McCabe's fans and critics agreed on: he single-handedly revolutionized the Canadian film industry and put his stamp on it. His style was hardly that of a civil servant of the old school, and part of the shock he generated could be attributed to the dramatic contrast between McCabe and his predecessor, Michael Spencer, a white-haired, distinguished-looking fellow whose demeanor seemed to have been learned from old British films about the aristocracy. McCabe, who looked as if he'd taken tutorials from his old friend Bill Marshall, the producer, in how to look impudently disheveled, had a sort of chatty, saloon-style ebullience.

McCabe believed his mandate was not to turn out more dull little films about losers in the backwoods — no Canadian equivalent of Swedish art films for him. Rather, his mandate was to turn moviemaking in Canada into a profitable operation. Since it was impossible to do without major foreign sales, that meant making movies people all over the world would shell out money to watch. If the only way to do that was to make "Canadian" movies on home turf with Hollywood stars and frequently even with Canadian cities disguised as American cities, well, so be it.

Typical big movies made in Canada for the international market during the McCabe era were *Murder by Decree* (or *Sherlock Holmes Meets Jack the Ripper*), with Christopher Plummer and James Mason, produced and directed by Bob Clark; *Running* (a mixed-up boy from Middle America pulls himself together by running a marathon at the 1976 Montreal Olympics), produced by Robert Cooper and Ronald Cohen, starring Michael Douglas; and *Nothing Personal*, a dim-witted comedy with Donald Sutherland and Suzanne Somers.

Among the producers who became the high-fliers of the industry under McCabe were Robert Lantos, a young Montrealer who would be one of the few to survive the crash of Hollywood North; Garth Drabinsky, who would soon abandon production and become the giant of the exhibition side of the industry; Harold Greenberg, chief executive officer of Astral Bellevue Pathé, which controlled the widest-reaching communications empire in the Canadian film world; and Bill Marshall, who had been executive assistant to David Crombie when Crombie was mayor of Toronto, and who had founded Toronto's film festival in 1976.

Greenberg, who had the fortunes of Peter and Edward Bronfman behind him, came to movies via the photofinishing and camera business. His main concern was to produce movies without the risk of losing money, and no one ever accused him of getting carried away with love for the art of the director. A typical Greenberg project was the ludicrously inept *City on Fire* (1979) with Montreal standing in for a midwestern American city that goes up in flames.

Bill Marshall came out of the slums of Glasgow, but he was not the Second Coming of John Grierson (the visionary Scot who founded the National Film Board); in Marshall's view Grierson made earnest little films that no one would pay money to see. With his leather boots, blue jeans and silver lapel star that announced, simply,

MARSHALL, he liked to come on more like a cattle rustler than a movie producer. Along with Henk Van der Kolk, his partner for a time in the Film Consortium of Canada, Marshall established himself as a power to be reckoned with. Their one clear success was the surprise hit *Outrageous!* (1977), with Craig Russell as a homosexual hairdresser who breaks into show business—produced for less than $200,000. But the budgets of their next films —*Wild Horse Hank, Circle of Two* and *Mr. Patman*—were more than ten times that amount, and they never had another hit. Now all that remains of their empire is the ongoing courtroom saga of *Circle of Two*.

Like the hero of his 1978 box-office winner, *In Praise of Older Women*, Lantos was a young, aggressive Hungarian refugee who had wound up in Montreal. Unlike the character in the story, and unlike fellow producer John Kemeny, Lantos didn't come to Montreal direct from Budapest. He spent his childhood in Uruguay, where his father was in the textile business. At McGill University he took classes from, among others, poet Louis Dudek and National Film Board founder John Grierson. He had a brief career in the tabloid press, and he distributed porn films before getting into production.

In Praise of Older Women, based on the novel by Stephen Vizinczey and directed by yet another Hungarian refugee, George Kaczender, got mostly terrible reviews in Canada, but it put Lantos on the map. Before the film was even finished, he engineered a splashy layout in *Playboy*, and when the Ontario censor asked for a two-minute cut, Lantos whipped up a controversy and used the publicity to sell the movie. The film cost $1.3 million and grossed $20 million.

Certain other movies, produced by Lantos and his partner Stephen Roth, were not successful on any terms. *Suzanne*, directed by Robin Spry, reached a peak of inadvertent comedy when Winston Rekert as a mean jewel thief dangled a necklace in front of the heroine while trying to hump her on the floor—prompting Jennifer Dale (aka Suzanne, aka Mrs. Lantos) to ask, "Uh, couldn't we do something else for a change?"

But *Suzanne* was a masterpiece compared to *Your Ticket Is No Longer Valid*, based on the Romain Gary novel of the same name and directed by Kaczender. British actor Richard Harris played a business tycoon of a certain age facing a double crisis: his financial empire is crumbling, and he is becoming sexually impotent. This is the movie that contains that classic line, delivered by a wise doctor, "Do not underestimate the value of a partial erection."

Harris and Lantos did not get along, to put it mildly. The way Lantos told the story in an interview with the trade paper *Cinema Canada*, Harris took the role mainly for the money, hardly bothered to read the script and totally sabotaged the movie, which was never released in North America.

When Harris came to Toronto to star in a stage revival of *Camelot*, he heard about the Lantos interview and decided to give *Cinema Canada* his version. According to Harris, Lantos was primarily interested in using the picture to establish his wife, Jennifer Dale, as an international star. Harris watched in dismay as his hopes for the movie dwindled; afterward he tried, without success, to buy it back and have it re-edited.

"My relationship with the director [Kaczender] was fine," said Harris. "He came to me one day pale and shaking. Lantos had accused him of betraying Jennifer Dale and favoring Richard Harris. . . . Lantos came to my room one day to talk about the script. I was at the time separated from my wife, Ann, but she'd come to see me for the weekend. The hotel had winding stairs to the bedroom. Lantos heard some noise and accused me of having somebody up there listening to our conversation. He said the atmosphere wasn't congenial to a discussion about the script because of that. I called to Ann, and she came out, and I introduced them. It was an alarming outburst."

When the picture (under a new title, *Finishing Touches*) was screened in 1982 for members of the Academy of Canadian Cinema prior to balloting for the Genie Awards, the audience was in an uproar. It wasn't just a few subversives at the back who were snickering; scores of academy members screamed with laughter while Harris did his damnedest to rally his slumbering penis to its former glories. Despite the buzz it created—one excited spectator phoned her friends and loved ones and implored them to rush down to see it—this movie failed to win any Genies; there wasn't a category for accidental comedy.

Hollywood North itself had become an accidental comedy. Who could help giggling when people who had always felt precluded by circumstance of birth and citizenship from contact with the great and famous suddenly had to make stars feel at home? With the likes of Ellen Burstyn, Vanessa Redgrave, Robert Mitchum and Ava Gardner in their midst day after day, Canadians became like a nation of klutzes preparing for a very important dinner guest, going all out while knowing in their hearts they weren't going to fool anybody.

When the production of *Circle of Two* had to shift briefly from Toronto to New York, Air Canada refused to give a first-class seat to Richard Burton's dog, a Mexican mongrel named Lupe. This action threatened to cause an international incident when it was revealed that Melina Mercouri, whose husband, Jules Dassin, was the director of the movie, also wanted to take her dog on the New York trip. A rival airline proved more open-minded than Air Canada.

It was, of course, the function of stars to behave outrageously. On the day of his arrival to film *Surfacing*, a misguided adaptation of Margaret Atwood's novel, Timothy Bottoms forcefully voiced his discontent in the lobby of the Windsor Arms Hotel in Toronto, then went to the airport without even checking into his room. (His brother, Joseph Bottoms, stayed on even after Tim was replaced.)

Some of the American stars didn't know much about Canada. Shelley Winters arrived in Montreal during a July heat wave for the filming of *City on Fire*. She was wearing a fur coat over a tent dress, and explained she had been warned Canada was very cold. Winters was so anxious to avoid succumbing to the Canadian elements that when she went to expensive restaurants she insisted on having the air-conditioning turned off. Other customers may have been annoyed, but they mostly kept quiet. After all, it wasn't the place of a Canadian to tell off a star.

In 1977 a full-page ad in *Variety*, the American show-business weekly, announced a major movie. "It is with great pride and pleasure that we announce the acquisition of screen rights to Margaret Laurence's world-acclaimed novel *The Diviners*," the ad trumpeted. The accompanying photograph showed Susan Clark, a Canadian actress who had gone to Hollywood and appeared in a number of movies and TV shows, in a cryptic, aggressive pose meant to suggest the fierce determination of the New Woman. Clark, who was to play Morag, Laurence's heroine, was shown with her legs spread while seated on something you couldn't quite make out—perhaps a throne or maybe a toilet—and smoking a cigar. Coproducers Judy Steed and Joyce Wieland, along with associate producer Charles Pachter (better known as a painter), announced they would start shooting the movie in the spring of 1978, with a release date the following winter. But the movie was never made, and in 1987 Atlantis Films announced with great fanfare its plan to film *The Diviners*.

Mind you, the original producers sold eighteen investment units at $50,000 each for *The Diviners*. But Steed and Wieland kept running into brick walls. They hired, and then fired, Eric Till as director. They hired Margaret

Atwood to write a screenplay — then dismissed her. They listened to people who told them that in order to get U.S. distribution they should cast Lily Tomlin in the title role, and change the locale to somewhere in the United States — which had been done in *Rachel, Rachel*, a 1968 movie based on Laurence's *A Jest of God*, starring Joanne Woodward and directed by her husband, Paul Newman. And for a few weeks they even seriously considered the advice of some Hollywood oracle who told them what they ought to be making was not a movie but a pilot for a TV series. In the end, the movie petered out, and for a while the CFDC was left holding the rights to the novel.

One of the few directors who managed not only to survive Hollywood North but even to carve out a career and a reputation was David Cronenberg, who became a name to be reckoned with in Hollywood while remaining in Toronto. Indeed, by 1983 Cronenberg had attained such exalted auteur status that he was given the singular honor of a complete retrospective at Toronto's annual film orgy, the Festival of Festivals.

The retrospective traced Cronenberg's progress from awkward, experimental student (*Stereo, Crimes of the Future*) to cult object (*Shivers, Rabid, The Brood*) to bankable major-studio commodity (*Videodrome*). Cronenberg has been attacked for his alleged depravity, most notably by Robert Fulford in a *Saturday Night* column, which, according to Cronenberg, got him evicted from his apartment. But he doesn't always deliver the cheap thrills some people hope for; he can at times be as solemn as Stanley Kramer.

On the occasion of its retrospective, the festival also published a book about Cronenberg's work, *The Shape of Rage*, featuring solemn, quasi-academic analysis by seven critics as well as a fawning interview. Sample insight: "Cronenberg's work represents a search for wholeness, first by articulating the absence of wholeness, and then by beginning a process of restitution, or reconstitution." Sample interview comment: "So *Shivers* and *Rabid* actually express a form of social alienation because the consciousness that is imagining them has the sense of being an outsider, and consequently there is a slightly paranoid attitude towards society." Shall we repeat that slowly for those taking notes?

The festival even announced a bonus. On closing night, as a late-night extra, the festival would have the world premiere of Cronenberg's new movie, *The Dead Zone*. Since closing night corresponded with Yom Kippur (the festival had switched its opening night to accommodate those marking Rosh Hashanah), the programming was wonderfully appropriate. We could break the fast and munch popcorn while taking in the newest work of Toronto's own Jewish horror king, a man who once remarked, "I would much more likely be put in jail for my art than for my Jewishness."

But three days before the scheduled premiere, Paramount boss Frank Mancuso pulled the plug. The studio expected the film to be a box-office winner and didn't want to take a chance on getting bad reviews six weeks before opening. Paramount tried to pacify the angry mobs with a consolation prize—the Canadian premiere of *Daniel*, based on E.L. Doctorow's fictionalized look at the case of Julius and Ethel Rosenberg, American Jews who went to the electric chair in 1953 for passing atom-bomb secrets to the Soviet Union. What a Yom Kippur special—the ultimate Jewish horror movie.

The Dead Zone, based on a Stephen King occult thriller, demonstrated Cronenberg could make a slick, smooth and respectable mainstream film, given a $10-million budget and a Hollywood star (Christopher Walken as a young man who acquires psychic powers after emerging from a five-year-long coma).

But Cronenberg's biggest breakthrough came three

years later with *The Fly*—a darkly funny, gross-out parable about disgust, a Hollywood production filmed in Ontario. This movie isn't campy fun like the 1958 cheapy that inspired it; Cronenberg's 1986 version is more unsettling, and you can't shake it off. He was lucky enough to have Jeff Goldblum in the role of the obsessive scientist who invents a machine to teleport matter and tests it on himself. The picture incorporates themes and elements from Cronenberg's early films, only this time he gets it right. The picture was a hit, and many North American critics chose it as one of the year's best. By then Cronenberg had gone from young Turk to elder statesman. He'd become a Hollywood name without going to Hollywood—an almost unheard-of feat. The rise and fall of Hollywood North hardly affected him because his movies were never part of the syndrome. Rather, they were, well, David Cronenberg movies.

Other talented directors were not so lucky. They had to sit by, along with talented actors and writers who were also being neglected, unable to do work they wanted to do, and might have been proud of. In the giddy, banana-republic ambience of Canadian cinema, circa 1979, writers, directors and actors were less important than the doctors, lawyers and accountants who were getting their feet wet as investors. And the hustlers and dealmakers, whose aesthetics were formulated between courses at expensive restaurants, made movies that featured third-rate, has-been American actors and Canadian cities disguised as Somewhere Else.

Late in the proceedings of *Mr. Patman*—directed by the British John Guillermin from a script originally written by Philip Hersh (whose name was dropped from the credits after a dispute with the producers) then rewritten by Tom Hedley—there was a disconcerting moment when a merry troupe of misfits and runaways, led by Mr. P. himself (the American actor James Coburn), decides to take off for

California. When it's suggested they might miss the winter, we become aware this is the first indication we've had that they live in a northern climate. Could it be Sweden? Nope. No one here speaks Swedish. The audience is forced to apply a rule of thumb: if you can't tell, it's probably Canada.

At the beginning of the movie, when there should be some information about where we are, there's a street sign or two that might enlighten those intimately acquainted with Vancouver. But the sense of place is left deliberately vague. If the movie were specifically located in Vancouver, the producer might fear that a good American release and American TV sale would be jeopardized—as if any mention of Canada was a kiss of death for audiences who would otherwise line up to see this movie.

A year or two earlier the producers could have shot the movie in Vancouver (to qualify for Canadian tax-write-off privileges, get government assistance and escape the jurisdiction of American unions) and try to pass off Vancouver as Seattle or Portland. But cultural nationalists had finally shamed McCabe into announcing that Canadian cities could no longer be disguised as American cities in CFDC-supported movies. So there was only one way out: fudge it.

Occasionally an expensive movie with an American star would actually be set in an undisguised Canada, but this didn't necessarily result in either art or authenticity. In *Silence of the North*, directed by the Canadian documentarian Allan King and filmed from northern Alberta to Toronto, Ellen Burstyn played a Canadian pioneer woman of the wilderness, Olive Frederickson. The movie turned out to be an expression of Burstyn's power and bad judgment.

The way Burstyn played her, Mrs. Frederickson, who had written a best-selling book about her life in the North, was so overwhelmingly heroic and saintly that she was barely human. Deep inside the Northwest Territories, she has to take care of an infant while her husband makes a futile attempt to trap muskrats. Then her hut is attacked by a bear, and she ruins her hair while trying to shoot it. The supplies run out when the temperature hits forty degrees below zero, and Olive is reduced to brewing spruce-needle tea.

But do we see Miss Ellen Burstyn putting on a cranky face? We do not. She just keeps looking at an old framed photograph of her mother for inspiration, and making quietly profound observations about life. Burstyn turns Olive into the most dedicated movie wife since June Allyson waited patiently, sniffling by the fireside, while James Stewart went missing in *The Glenn Miller Story.* And when her husband dies and then the child he never saw also dies, she attains martyrdom.

Perhaps an honest, exuberant movie could have been made about a woman making a life for herself in the Canadian wilderness, but *Silence of the North* wasn't it. The movie had nothing to fall back on except Richard Leiterman's stunning cinematography; a sequence of the ice breaking up on the Athabasca River recalls Pudovkin, the great Russian director of the 1920s. Nobody involved, not even King or producer Murray Shostak, could thwart Burstyn's iron will, so she got her own lunkheaded vision on the screen.

It was as if the Katharine Hepburn character in *The African Queen* had been played straight instead of for comedy. Burstyn had come to Canada, a grande dame colonizing the hinterland and bestowing her grace on the humble natives. Leiterman and King caught the breakup of the ice in a northern spring, but they couldn't crack the deep freeze of Burstyn's radiant, noble smile.

Reaction to the results of McCabe's policies was predictably divided. Show-biz entrepreneurs tended to be wowed by the fact that there were dozens of big-time, Hollywood-style movies being produced in Canada—

movies such as *Agency, Nothing Personal* and *Final Assignment*. Culture-watchers turned pale and remarked that McCabe had sold out, turning Canada into a dumping ground for second-rate American movies.

During this period, promotional hype took precedence over film art, and "Canadian movies" vied for a place on that list of double-barreled phrases—such as "designer jeans" and "educational TV"—ridiculed by satirist Fran Lebowitz on the grounds that one word of each phrase contradicts the other.

At the Cannes Film Festival, offerings were presented under the slogan "Canada Can and Does" but skeptics muttered, "Canada does but shouldn't." One headline in the Toronto *Star* over Sid Adilman's report from the 1980 festival was "Canada a Laughing Stock at Cannes." In the *Globe and Mail* Jay Scott remarked: "For *Fantastica* and *Out of the Blue* to have represented Canada in the main competition is so egregiously embarrassing that many people were asking seriously if the festival, pressured last year by the Canadians, had decided to wreak revenge by programming two terrible Canadian films in spots where they could not be missed."

There were feelings of betrayal in these and other reports. The CFDC's latest slogan—"Great pictures, Canada's got them"—became a bitter joke.

Once the glossy, "international" movies with American stars, set in Nowheresville, became a national scandal and an international embarrassment, it might have been expected that the people responsible for them would have admitted they'd made a mistake. But no. Instead they latched on to a new idea.

The trouble was not the quality of the movies, they explained, it was the hostile press. If reviewers would only get into line and sing the praises of the new Canadian movies, why then the industry would be in fine shape.

Miraculously, in this depressing climate, a few people

managed to do honorable work: *The Grey Fox, Les Bons Débarras, Ticket to Heaven, Heartaches, Les Plouffe, By Design.* But unlike the Australians, who became known for their successes while keeping their numerous flops quiet, Canadians became known for their bummers.

What came of it all? A few disreputable people made some money and rode high for a year or two on their own delusions of grandeur. At the peak of the lunacy, a telling bit of graffiti was reported by a visitor to the women's washroom of the Courtyard Café, symbolic home of the industry: "Beat me, fuck me, make me write bad cheques."

The flowering of a schlock-movie industry did fulfill the Canadian need for self-denigration. Pierre Berton had complained indignantly in *Hollywood's Canada* that Hollywood movies were filled with shocking misconceptions about Canada. But once Canada started turning out glitzy movies of its own, the insults we had endured from Hollywood seemed petty mischief. When it came to trashing the Canadian image, it turned out nobody could do better than Canadians. What linked these movies was a certain subliminal message: nothing of any importance ever happens in Canada, so let's pretend we're not in Canada.

You might expect producers to be passionate devotees of movies, but few of them demonstrated any overwhelming respect for the talented directors, actors, writers and crafts people who were ready and willing to be given a chance. They thought they could outsmart the audience; instead they made Canadian movies notorious around the world.

To some observers, the great Canadian movie scam of the late 1970s seemed like a farce at the time, but only now that it's safely in the past is that most peculiar chapter in this country's cultural history about to be presented to the public as a farce. Coming soon: *Hollywood North,* a wickedly satiric comedy about those giddy, bad old days, when sleazy producers living on outrageously inflated salaries rode high at the Courtyard Café; when preposterously bad movies were fronted by has-been American stars in Canadian cities disguised as American cities; when Bay Street opportunists skimmed off the investment cream through scandalously fat finders' fees; when eager investors, rushing to get in on the glamor, were taken for a bumpy ride.

To be produced by the respected Peter O'Brian, *Hollywood North* is set in 1979, at the peak of the tax-shelter movie madness. It's the saga of a young producer whose capital comes from the family chicken business, and who has himself just produced a pure turkey—a horror movie more horrifying than anyone intended. Especially horrifying is the reaction of the investors—a group of eager doctors and dentists sucked into this project through a passionate belief in tax deductions.

The producer is obliged to come up with another movie, but fast, which will incorporate enough of the aborted horror movie to get the investors off the hook. (To comply with the tax regulations, it has to be started by December 31.) In desperation, he takes on a script based on a novel set in South America. He has to shoot it in Toronto in the winter, and he can't afford a studio, so the crew's energy is spent keeping snow out of the shots.

To those who followed the last rise and fall of Canadian feature films, this movie will seem like pure documentary. But luckily the follies of that era could at last be viewed as a period piece. By the mid-1980s the Canadian film industry was ready to be born again.

3

Up the Bayou Without a Paddle

By 1983, the year *Louisiana* was filmed, Hollywood North had reached the end of its boom-and-bust cycle. The Canadian movie industry was about to turn into the Canadian TV industry. Voilà. The government had introduced a new Broadcast Fund, and turned its film-financing arm, the Canadian Film Development Corporation, into Telefilm Canada. To tap the fund, a producer had to have an agreement from a Canadian broadcaster to show the film in prime time. This requirement neatly side-stepped one of the most embarrassing problems of Hollywood North—the fact that many of the films produced with the help of public subsidy couldn't get distribution and never reached an audience.

The new false messiah for the moment was pay television, whose debut on the Canadian airwaves was rather naïvely looked to as the salvation of a sick industry. To get their licenses, the pay outlets had to promise lots of Canadian content; and to get that Canadian content, they would have to make deals with film producers.

Even before the Canadian government shifted its subsidies to TV films, John Kemeny and Denis Héroux—producing partners with an impressive track record—had cooked up a huge deal involving three properties produced simultaneously as theatrical films and television miniseries. The three involving coproducing partners in

France were *The Blood of Others*, an adaptation of the Simone de Beauvoir novel; a sequel to *Les Plouffe*; and *Louisiana*, a *Gone With the Wind* clone based on a popular French novel. Kemeny and Héroux divided their work, and *Louisiana* became Kemeny's baby.

The *Louisiana* deal was complicated, but a huge part of the $13-million budget came from TV pre-sales. To honor their commitment to invest in Canadian production, Jon Slan and Dr. Charles Allard of Superchannel—who had regional licenses in, respectively, Ontario and Alberta—decided to get massively involved in one deal with top producers rather than spend smaller amounts on a number of deals. Superchannel was a partner in all three Kemeny/Héroux hybrids, and put up $1.5 million for *Louisiana* alone.

Producing a two-hour movie for theatres and a six-hour TV miniseries simultaneously would be a treacherous business, everyone knew. A movie has one kind of rhythm and a TV series another. A series is by nature episodic; each installment has to have a dramatic shape of its own. (The long version of *Louisiana* has characters who don't even appear in the movie version.) In Kemeny's eyes, the solution was to regard the scripts for the two projects as separate adaptations. Certain scenes were shot two ways.

One of the oddest things about *Louisiana*, given its subject and setting, was its Canadian I.D. Under the rules that determine whether a production qualifies as Canadian for tax purposes, there's a big bonus for having a Canadian star. Thanks to her Lois Lane roles in the *Superman* movies, Margot Kidder was the most popular Canadian girl in Hollywood since Mary Pickford. So it was almost inevitable that if a major movie about a southern belle was going to be made by Canadian producers—albeit with French coproducing partners—Kidder would play the heroine.

Through most of the filming, Kidder barely spoke to Kemeny, who had moved to Hollywood on the wings of his success with *The Apprenticeship of Duddy Kravitz*. Yet the flamboyant, outspoken actress and the solemn, cost-cutting producer with the thick Hungarian accent were partners in a shotgun marriage dictated by the rules of the Canadian film industry.

A tall, gaunt figure with receding gray hair, Kemeny has a perpetual look of worry. After fleeing Budapest during the 1956 uprising, he had landed in Montreal with a wife and child. He spoke neither French nor English well enough to get a job in the film industry, though in Hungary he had been involved in film distribution.

He was working as a dishwasher on the night shift at a Montreal club when the mob moved in and killed the manager. Clearly, it was time to get back into the film business. Kemeny found a woman at the NFB who spoke German, a language in which he could carry on a conversation. She took him to meet Pierre Juneau, who was then running the place, and Juneau agreed to give him a job: stapling and photocopying in the basement. By staying after hours to use the equipment, Kemeny learned enough to work his way up—to assistant sound editor, assistant picture editor and eventually producer-director.

Among the NFB movies he produced was Margot Kidder's debut film, *The Best Damn Fiddler from Calabogie to Kaladar,* directed by an eager young cousin of Lester B. Pearson, Peter Pearson, who had graduated from the Rome Film School and who would become a key figure in the Canadian film industry. But Kemeny's big one was *Bethune,* on which he collaborated with Donald Brittain. Kemeny's films consistently won prizes, but by the time he went to Cannes in 1969 as the producer of an undistinguished NFB drama, *Don't Let the Angels Fall,* he was disenchanted with the board. Things there seemed too complacent, and he had achieved everything he felt he could do within a government bureaucracy. He was ready to get out on his own.

Kemeny spent the early 1970s testing his wings as an independent producer, working primarily on educational films. He also began working with Denis Héroux, then a young French-Canadian director, later a producer in partnership with Kemeny. In 1974 Kemeny scored a breakthrough when he produced the movie version of Mordecai Richler's novel *The Apprenticeship of Duddy Kravitz.* At a cost of less than $1 million, it became the first commercially successful English-Canadian production, a marvelously dynamic and enjoyable movie generally regarded as one of the three or four best ever produced in this country.

Duddy Kravitz was a genuine hit, but instead of inspiring more independent production, it provided a ticket to California for the people who pulled it off and wanted to work with larger budgets and less risk. Kemeny moved to the Columbia lot in L.A., where he became an independent producer with a multi-picture deal. He made three movies for Columbia, two of which were enormously profitable: *White Line Fever* and *Ice Castles.* The third was a Canadian fiasco, *Shadow of the Hawk,* from which the distinguished director Daryl Duke was fired in the middle of the shoot in Duke's own hometown, Vancouver; the film wound up as fodder for the drive-in circuit.

While based in L.A., Kemeny continued to produce Canadian movies, including *Les Plouffe, Atlantic City* and *Quest for Fire,* with his partner, Denis Héroux. These movies won awards but sometimes had little to do with Canada. *Atlantic City,* selected by the National Society of Film Critics as the best movie of 1981, was filmed in Atlantic City. It featured American stars Burt Lancaster and Susan Sarandon, working from a script by New York playwright John Guare under the great French director Louis Malle. The movie was dreamed up to comply with conditions that might have been invented by a satirist taking aim at Canada's shaky film industry. A director with French citizenship was needed to take advantage of Canada's coproduction treaty with France. Malle was approached because he not only was from France but had experience working in English and a classy reputation as well. He was asked to come up, fast, with a movie that could be made quickly, starring Susan Sarandon and some unnamed bankable American actor. Lawrence Nessis, a former Winnipeg rabbi turned high-flying Vancouver film financier, had the investors all lined up.

But it was July, and in order to get the investors tax breaks for the current fiscal year, the principal photography for the movie would have to be started by the end of the year and be completed by February. Malle called his friend Guare, who said he'd been reading something about Atlantic City, which reminded him of stories he'd heard as a child. The next day the two of them went to Atlantic City and began talking to people. And so a Canadian movie was born.

And *Quest for Fire*? A funny thing happened on its way to Hollywood. It turned into a Canadian movie—well, half-Canadian anyway. Jean-Jacques Annaud, an Oscar-winning director from France, had been working for years to launch his dream picture—an epic about prehistoric man. In the summer of 1980, he finally had everything in place. A major Hollywood studio, 20th Century Fox, agreed to finance this risky, high-budget epic. After months spent choosing the actors—who had to be unknowns to give the project authenticity—and traveling all over the world selecting the animals, Annaud was ready to begin shooting in Iceland with a mostly British crew. Then came the strike of the Screen Actors' Guild—and the picture had to be shut down.

In the face of the strike, there was no way any American company using SAG actors could go ahead. But *Quest for Fire* was harder hit than other movies shut down by the strike because of the problems associated with casting animals. Annaud knew that although he could get new actors if necessary he wouldn't be able to get the animals back. It had taken a worldwide search to find and train these animals, which were in quarantine and had to be either used or released. *Quest for Fire* seemed doomed.

That's when John Kemeny got a tip from his old friend Sherry Lansing, at that time the new president of 20th Century Fox, with whom he had worked in the mid-1970s at Columbia. According to Lansing, Fox was looking for an independent producer to pick up *Quest for Fire*. The studio had already spent more than $2 million on preproduction — not to mention the effort of getting the animals — and was anxious to recover it.

Kemeny had an idea. It was just possible, he thought, that the production could be changed around enough to qualify under the terms of the same movie coproduction agreement between the French and Canadian governments that had worked for *Atlantic City*.

Coming to the rescue, Kemeny was able to make a tough deal with Fox. The company wouldn't see any of its preproduction money until Kemeny and his investors had recovered their money. (This was one reason why, when distribution rights were auctioned off, Fox outbid everyone else for North American rights.) Most of the British crew were replaced with Canadians. One leading player, Rae Dawn Chong, whose father is half of Cheech and Chong, happened to be Canadian anyway.

Much of the location shooting was shifted to Canada — the Alberta Badlands, the British Columbia rain forests and Lion's Head, Ontario, in the Bruce Peninsula. The actors worked naked, wearing only skins and furs, and on some days spent seventeen hours standing up to their necks in freezing swamps.

Was it worth it? Well, the movie won a great many awards and did well at the box office, even if there were a few scoffers like Pauline Kael, who joked that it was the kind of movie spectacle that made you wish you could recognize famous faces under the makeup.

John Kemeny came away from *Quest of Fire* drenched with prestige, but he knew the times were changing.

That's why he and Héroux put together the three projects meant to be feature films and TV series. *Les Plouffe*, directed by Gilles Carle, was a marvelous movie with a strong sense of Quebec social history, but the version shown on the CBC was destroyed by wretched dubbing with no French flavor. *The Blood of Others*, directed by Claude Chabrol, a veteran of the French cinema, was the kind of washout that makes people who've just seen it want to change the subject.

As far as the Canadian status of *Louisiana* was concerned, the person who loomed largest was Margot Kidder. To have their movies certified for tax-write-off privileges, producers needed Canadian stars, and since there were so few Canadian actors around whose names had box-office appeal outside Canada, those few had considerable clout. Not surprisingly, Kidder got asked to appear in a lot of Canadian movies.

Her background could hardly be more Canadian. Her father was a mining engineer who worked with explosives. Margie, as she was known then, was one of five children, and the family moved from one scuzzy small town to another, from Yellowknife to Labrador City. The lesson she learned from her childhood was that you have to rely on who you are and what you can carry with you. Reading became an obsession and an addiction. At seven she was reading forbidden books under the covers; at thirteen she was reading Leonard Cohen and fantasizing about having an affair with him. As a teenager she was shipped off to Toronto's Havergal College, where she earned a reputation as a troublemaker who, in the lingo of report cards, "can do better."

There was still a trace of the brilliant, bratty underachiever in Kidder. After Jewison cast her in *Gaily, Gaily*, Kidder's Hollywood movies included *Quackser Fortune Has a Cousin in the Bronx*, *The Great Waldo Pepper* and *Sisters*.

Kidder had a stormy Hollywood career. She made a

number of movies she despised, such as *The Amityville Horror*; she married several times and had a daughter by novelist Thomas McGuane; and from the enormous fees paid to her for the *Superman* movies, she won financial control of her own life—what she says is known in Hollywood as "fuck you" money, because it gives you the freedom to say no. And she bought her own Tara in Marina del Ray.

"It's nothing to be proud of," Kidder says offhandedly, "but I've done movies I didn't care a damn about. I got sick of reading second-rate scripts and then having to charm or convince or sell myself on something I had less than a total commitment to."

Did Kidder have the slightest idea what she was getting into when she signed to do *Louisiana*? She had had a number of bad experiences with Canadian productions—producers who behaved like con men, directors who couldn't communicate, contracts that were full of holes, deals that fell through just before the cameras were supposed to roll. More than once she'd vowed not to do any more Canadian movies. But the pulp energy of *Louisiana* seemed seductive. How many times would she get a chance to do the life story of a southern belle?

No one could deny the story had epic sweep, tracking Virginia Tregan from the mid-1830s to the post–Civil War period, through an exhausting variety of lovers, husbands and children. In the course of a typical day's shooting, Kidder would go from girlish young belle to strong-willed, hot-blooded old renegade—and back again—with the help of latex wrinkles.

Kidder did the best work of her career in *Heartaches*, working with the Toronto director Donald Shebib, best known for his gritty, low-budget 1970 fable about two Maritime drifters in the big city, *Goin' Down the Road*.

Shebib had spent several years developing the script for *Heartaches* with screenwriter Terence Heffernan, and he felt it was a dream project. Inspired by *The Bottle Factory Outing,* a novel by the English writer Beryl Bainbridge, the story is about two female misfits from a small Ontario lakeside town who get thrown together on their way to Toronto. They wind up sharing a decaying apartment, working together at a factory and trying to sort out each other's messy lives.

For the part of the dreamy, pregnant runaway, Shebib was delighted to have the gifted, but little-known American actress Annie Potts. For the role of the loud, pushy klutz, he was less than delighted to have Margot Kidder. But he knew he needed her.

Shebib — who is known not only for his prodigious talent but also for his grouchy disposition and habit of complaining to whoever will listen — resented the idea of having a star. He wanted someone fat and unknown, and as unattractive as possible. Only half-jokingly, he kept saying he wanted Miss Piggy. Margot Kidder, on the other hand, was thin and famous and, in her own unorthodox way, attractive. She loved the script, she was determined to do it and Shebib was powerless to resist. Her name made it possible to raise the money to make the movie.

Even before filming began, *Heartaches* proved a prophetic title. Shebib had already had his share finding a producer. First the money was there, then it wasn't. The starting date had to be postponed several times. Kidder had a name big enough to nail down those elusive investors, and she came on like gangbusters after Bette Midler and Stockard Channing had turned the part down.

Kidder saw in Shebib not a moody genius but an appalling boor. His opinion was that she couldn't act. The director and the star spent vast sums of energy bad-mouthing each other. It was like a Canadian replay of Carole Lombard and John Barrymore in *The Twentieth Century.*

Heartaches proves that good films do not necessarily go hand-in-hand with everybody getting along and being polite. *Heartaches* is lively and engaging. It has such a winning spirit that even when it goes terribly wrong, as it does in places, it never loses the goodwill of the audience. It has characters you can laugh at and root for at the same time.

Robert Carradine and Annie Potts are both likable in an understated way, but *Heartaches* is Margot Kidder's movie all the way. Her Rita, the epitome of cheap glamor, is a great comic creation. She wears jeans, a cowboy jacket with gaudy beads and a T-shirt that proclaims her fondness for *"les hommes."* Her hair is frizzy yellow patches of chaos. She's always chewing gum and talking too loud. Rita walks like a truck driver, and comes on so strong that she scares people away even as she reaches out to them.

Margot Kidder had her own dream Canadian movie — a dream she nurtured for several years before she came to the painful realization she'd have to let it go. It started at an airport in the late 1970s when she bought a copy of *Lady Oracle* because she needed something to read during a trip to Vancouver, and Margaret Atwood's comic novel was the only item in the airport bookstore that appealed to her.

"I planned my death carefully, unlike my life . . ." Almost from the moment she read the opening sentence, Kidder felt this was it: she had found the role she was born to play. She had read Atwood's poems and earlier novels, and a few years earlier, she had been set to play another Atwood heroine. But *The Edible Woman* changed hands and went through several scripts and the heads of movie companies played musical chairs and canceled their predecessors' decisions, until it got lost in the shuffle.

The subject of *Lady Oracle* is the trash imagination, and the story rings more than a little true for Kidder. "*Lady Oracle* relates to being a Canadian and stuffing your skirt in your snow pants before you left for school, and going to Brownies — and all those little things that were part of our upbringing," Kidder observed. "The heroine has, as I did, two personalities. The kids at my high school in Vancouver knew me only on the outside. But I had inside me another personality, this person who read a lot of poetry, and listened to Tchaikovsky, and contemplated jumping out a window. I had a great romantic sense of life. Someday I would fall in love, my prince would come, he would be an artist."

Lady Oracle became an obsession, as if in some crazy way it would redeem all those mediocre movies that Kidder had done carelessly and casually. The process of negotiating for the rights she found almost intolerable. When things got tricky, Kidder went slightly berserk. "At one point I just wanted to call Atwood and scream, 'Just sell me the book, I have to have it!' " After trying outside writers, Atwood and Kidder tried to do a script together. Intending to produce and star in the movie, Kidder spent hundreds of thousands of dollars developing the property, but it didn't work. They had to give up. For Kidder it was a crushing blow. So she went back to working on other people's projects and building up her "fuck you" fund.

Many of her more extravagant adventures were financed by the *Superman* movies. The Hollywood insanity that those movies represented gave her, from time to time, the urge to flee—which she did at various times and in various ways.

Here's her description of working on *Superman II*: "It was *Looney Tunes* time. I was being driven in a Jag to the set every morning where someone did my hair and someone gave me coffee and I read *The Great Shark Hunt* and wrote a couple of letters—and for this I was being paid $100,000 a week for the first six weeks and $150,000 a week after that. I began saying to myself, 'Wait a minute, I'm losing my sense of reality.' So I left for Morocco saying, 'This is immoral and sick. I have to quit acting.' I was going to take this van with Maggie, my daughter, and see the world. But we had to cross most of the countries off the list because they were having wars."

Margot Kidder had endured rough shoots before, but even by the twisted, cloud-cuckoo-land standards of Canadian movies, *Louisiana* was a nightmare. The sheer heat of a southern summer made the cast and crew edgier than ever. The film was shot at Nottaway, a spectacular plantation where David O. Selznick had tried to shoot *Gone With the Wind* (he was turned down on three separate occasions). In keeping with historical authenticity, the plantation had no air-conditioning, but someone had sneaked a swimming pool into a corner of the grounds. Kidder's costar, the English actor Ian Charleson, put modesty aside to enjoy a quick skinny-dip while Kidder sweltered under several layers of skirts, hoops and crinolines.

Within this overheated Babel, film technicians in jeans and T-shirts barked instructions at one another in French and English, while a group of Texas tourists in polyester leisure suits were taken around by a Nottaway guide. The extras were lined up on the stairs and overflowed into the basement, all sweating in their oppressively weighty tuxedoes and ball gowns. Most of them had been waiting through hours of heat and boredom for the few minutes they'd be needed for the grand ballroom sequence.

The shoot was not just tense and difficult; it was a floating disaster. The weather seemed to have a personal score to settle with Kemeny. First there was a near-hurricane, which struck hours into the first day of shooting. Then there was the movie's most temperamental star, the Mississippi River, which flooded a $500,000 set, a replica of an 1830s village. Two alligators set up house in front of the picturesque church, and another moved in behind the barn.

Kemeny had human disasters, too. *Louisiana* was an

official international coproduction, and the coproducers were from France. For that reason the film had a director from France—Jacques Demy. But Demy found himself in serious trouble early on, and it came as no surprise when he was replaced with Philippe De Broca, another acclaimed New Wave director from Paris.

Kidder was one of the few who had the contractual right to refuse overtime work, and she began exercising her right to say no in order to get time off for her exhausted makeup lady or limousine driver, who didn't have the right to say no. One morning, after refusing an early call on the grounds that she needed her sleep, she was heard noisily roller-skating outside Kemeny's room.

Louisiana was the kind of movie on which everything that could go wrong did go wrong. As his troubles mounted, Kemeny pushed everybody around him to the limit. By the time De Broca arrived from Paris to begin his salvage operation, many among the cast and crew felt overworked and underappreciated. Fairly or unfairly, some of them—especially Margot Kidder—blamed Kemeny for the film's problems.

Kemeny's difficulties were hardly over when the shoot was finished. He decided to forget about doing a theatre version for North America. The film would go straight to pay-TV—Home Box Office in the United States, Superchannel in Canada. But Slan and Dr. Allard, who were running Superchannel, insisted on the contractual stipulation that Kemeny had to deliver a separate theatrical-release version, from which they could recover some of the money they had invested in *Louisiana*. In their view, Kemeny and Héroux had wiped out Superchannel's financial hopes by putting the picture on HBO two years earlier than planned (so that Kemeny and Héroux could collect HBO's payment price earlier to cover some of their losses).

In order to collect on his letter of credit, Kemeny had to deliver the finished film to a bank in Edmonton. With the help of Superchannel's lawyer, Richard Borchiver, Slan sought an injunction to stop the bank from paying Kemeny and Héroux. With $1.5 million at stake, Kemeny and Héroux told friends they were facing bankruptcy. Eventually they got their money, turning up in person with their letter of credit at the Edmonton bank at 9:00 A.M. the day the money was payable. But five years later Kemeny still wasn't on speaking terms with Slan, even when they found themselves alone together on a Toronto hotel elevator.

Meanwhile Margot Kidder married De Broca in France, broke a leg falling off a camel in Morocco and moved back into her California house with her new husband. It didn't last. A few years later, she and her daughter would put California behind them and move to New York. And she would win the lottery again by playing Lois Lane again in *Superman IV*. Then she'd be going home to do a TV film, *Margot Kidder's Yellowknife*, for John McGreevy's TV series *Return Journey*.

Louisiana hardly caused a ripple with the Canadian public. It went straight to TV and was received with polite indifference.

But first there was the world premiere of the two-hour feature film—one of its rare public screenings, as it turned out—at the 1984 Montreal Film Festival. The reviews were, to put it mildly, not good. Kidder's date for the premiere was Pierre Trudeau, who had resigned as prime minister six months earlier. Throughout the showing, Trudeau kept nudging Kidder to indicate his bafflement. "Margot, in the last scene you had five children. Now you only have two." Or, "Margot, you were just in the American Civil War. Now you're in the French Revolution."

Kidder got more and more frantic. At the conclusion of the film, she buttonholed Kemeny and brayed at him, "John, who *cut* [edited] this film?"

A few months later, when Kidder ran into Kemeny at the Jewisons' annual party, he implored solemnly: "Can't we make peace now?" And she broke into her goofy Lois Lane grin.

After everything they'd both been through, how could she stay mad?

4

Joshua Goes to Cannes

On a balmy spring evening, in the full glare of the lights and with gawking crowds lining the sidewalks, Ted Kotcheff — a prodigal son in his mid-fifties who had returned to Canada in the hope of repeating the greatest triumph of his career — made that big walk up the steps of the Palais des Festivals in Cannes. The date was May 17, 1985 — which will surely go down as one of the most perplexing days in the history of Canadian cinema. The occasion was the world premiere of *Joshua Then and Now,* Kotcheff's much-awaited movie version of the Mordecai Richler novel.

Somehow it didn't seem odd that this landmark event occurred not in Canada but on the French Riviera, at the centre of the world's gaudiest film festival. The Cannes Festival is, above all, a circus of hype and hucksterism — an expensive two-week-long indoor/outdoor party. Stretching along the beach is the Croisette, a grand boulevard where handsome palm trees are interspersed with classy chrome-and-glass-encased advertisements for movies. The signs, far too elegant to be called billboards, look most impressive at night when they are backlit. It is in this unlikely spot that the Canadian film industry gathers annually to partake of its favorite fantasy — that the world is waiting to see what Canada can put on the screen.

At a cost of $11 million (about $2 million over budget), *Joshua* certainly qualified as a heavyweight competitor. As for public reaction to what was on the screen, the premiere at Cannes loomed as a kind of Judgment Day.

In the influential Paris newspaper *Le Monde* the headline over a review of *Joshua* said simply, *"Canadien Juif,"* and in a funny way, that summed up Canada's big day at Cannes. Joining Kotcheff at the Palais were two of the film's stars. The American actor James Woods, aka Joshua, had spent the week enjoying his role of movie-star-as-playboy-on-the-make at a nonstop carnival. Gabrielle Lazure, the icily beautiful daughter of a Quebec cabinet minister who'd been chosen to play Pauline, Joshua's *haute-shiksa* wife, was trying to remain composed after learning hours before the world premiere that in the editing of the film her voice had been surgically removed; Pauline's lines were delivered in the intonations of Toronto actress Susan Hogan (uncredited).

Also on the scene were Robert Lantos and Stephen Roth, the only Canadian producers ever to have two movies in the official program at Cannes the same year, along with Canada's minister of communications, Marcel Masse. Just about the only VIP who wasn't there was that celebrated *Canadien juif*, Mordecai Richler, who caused quite a stir among the Canadian contingent at Cannes by announcing in a CBC radio interview on the eve of *Joshua*'s premiere that he hadn't been invited.

Even in absentia, Mordecai Richler was the true star of the film. He was not just a celebrity author but Canada's favorite high-cult curmudgeon — a rumpled, gruff-sounding oracle who could always be counted on to ridicule Canada's provincial customs. The book that established Richler as a literary force was *The Apprenticeship of Duddy Kravitz*, published in 1959 when its author was still relatively young and unknown. The 1974 movie version had been one of the few triumphs in the history of Canadian cinema. It was also one of the few English-Canadian movies of its period to turn a profit.

Joshua Then and Now was, in a way, an attempt to repeat that triumph on a larger scale. So was the musical *Duddy,* which had crash-landed en route from Edmonton to Broadway only a couple of months before the filming of *Joshua* began. Like Hollywood, Broadway occupies a special place in the imagination of Canadians. On the one hand, it represents the epitome of crass American commercialism which Canadians like to look down on. On the other hand, the dream of making it on Broadway carries with it the ultimate seal of approval.

When Richler was first approached about turning *Duddy Kravitz* into a musical, he turned to his friend Sam Gesser, the Montreal impresario, for advice. Gesser wasn't primarily a producer, although he had some experience in that area, but he had the air of someone Richler could trust, so Richler sold Gesser the stage rights to *Duddy* for one dollar. That turned out to be the costliest one-dollar purchase of Gesser's life.

After trying for several years to put the elements together, Gesser finally launched the musical *Duddy* with the collaboration of the Citadel Theatre in Edmonton. The director was the king of Canadian musical theatre, Brian Macdonald, and the star was a dynamic American named Lonny Price. The show was supposed to tour Canada after its Edmonton run and then go to New York, but there was trouble even before it opened in Edmonton. It had many good things, including an electrifying performance by Price, but the songs by Jerry Leiber and Mike Stoller weren't strong, and the show simply wasn't ready. Gesser canceled the first few stops of the tour in favor of more preparation, and since Macdonald was busy elsewhere, he brought in Paddy Stone to take over as director. Sinking more and more of his own money into *Duddy,* Gesser hoped he'd be rescued by friends interested in bringing the show to New York, but on a grim Sunday in Ottawa, after a run at the National Arts Centre, Gesser pulled the plug. The show had an illness as terminal as Duddy's Uncle Benjy's.

In the summer of 1984, as he went directly from working on the stage version of *Duddy* to the screen version of *Joshua,* Richler must have wondered whether one was a bad omen for the other. And there was reason to be nervous. Right from its inception, *Joshua* had been more than just another Canadian movie. An awful lot seemed to be riding on it—perhaps too much. That was partly because everyone wanted a repeat of *Duddy Kravitz,* and partly because after the boom-and-bust years of Hollywood North, Canada needed a movie strong enough to carry the flag.

The making of *Joshua* was an exhausting, trying experience for the burly Kotcheff. More than a year earlier, when he let the word out in L.A. that he was going back to Canada to make the movie version of a Mordecai Richler novel, not everyone was impressed. One night at a cocktail reception, a studio executive turned to him and asked the loaded question others were too polite to ask: "Why are you going up to Canada to make that crappy little movie when you could stay down here making hits for us?"

The answer to that question would be a mouthful, summing up Kotcheff's career, if not his whole life. After growing up in Toronto's Cabbagetown, the son of a Bulgarian immigrant grocer, he had landed a job with CBC television, then gone abroad to make a name for himself. In 1957 when Kotcheff met Richler, both were young, expatriate Canadians knocking about Europe. People had been telling Kotcheff for years that he ought to meet Richler, and finally he did, at a wine garden in Tourette-Sur-Loup, in southern France.

They drank together all afternoon. Richler, who had cashed in an insurance policy and run off to Paris to hang out with Terry Southern and other American artists in exile, had just split from his first wife. Kotcheff was on his way to London where he wanted to get into TV. They decided to share a flat. Richler was working on a new novel at the time — *The Apprenticeship of Duddy Kravitz.*

Kotcheff became a fixture in British TV and the West End theatre. In TV his mentor was Sydney Newman, a fellow refugee from CBC Toronto who eventually became head of BBC drama. A legendary story about one of their not-infrequent arguments is told in *Play for Today,* a memoir by their mutual friend, Irene Shubik. Newman is supposed to have accused Kotcheff of ingratitude, claiming that he (Newman) had raised Kotcheff out of the gutter. To which Kotcheff retorted: "Wait a minute. You mean from the gutter to you is *up*?"

Both Kotcheff and Richler married, and their social set was delineated in *St. Urbain's Horseman,* whose hero, Jake Hersh, is part Kotcheff (an expatriate director) and partly Richler (a Jew from Montreal's St. Urbain Street living prosperously abroad but still in conflict with himself about his roots).

Richler and Kotcheff had worked together on the British film *Life at the Top,* and they wanted to put together a production based on Richler's *The Street.* But it proved easier to get the financing for a movie based on Richler's other book about St. Urbain Street. After several false starts (the money kept falling through — a typical Canadian affliction), Kotcheff finally shot *Duddy Kravitz* in 1973. He added a dimension — the movie is more generous in spirit than the book — and thereby gave the tale emotional power. The pacing has an electric charge; the marvelous cast of characters creates a certain time and place that linger long after the end.

Kotcheff went to L.A. immediately and became the most desirable of movieland creatures, the bankable director — although from a creative and critical point of view none of his Hollywood films could match *Duddy.* Five of his six Hollywood movies have been major box-office winners.

Fun with Dick and Jane (1977) was a crude satire with George Segal and Jane Fonda as a middle-class couple who turn to crime to keep up their conspicuous consumption, but it was a box-office winner. The returns were more modest, but still respectable, on the comedy-thriller *Who Is Killing the Great Chefs of Europe?*, which featured Segal and Jacqueline Bissett in the leading roles, but was saved by Robert Morley's deliciously funny supporting performance as the editor of a gourmet magazine who is eating himself to death. Kotcheff hit the box-office jackpot again with *North Dallas Forty*, a football epic produced by former Paramount boss Frank Yablans.

Commercially, though, the big one was *First Blood* (1982), with Sylvester Stallone as a Vietnam veteran who goes berserk in a small U.S. town. The picture took in a phenomenal $50 million and was one of the top-grossing films of the year. That put Kotcheff in an enviable position. He turned down the sequel to *First Blood—Rambo*, which turned out to be one of the biggest-grossing movies in history—but a studio would have to think twice before saying no to a project Kotcheff wanted to do.

And he followed up with *Uncommon Valor* (1983), an action movie about the psychological consequences of the Vietnam war from the losers' side. Gene Hackman starred as a retired colonel who returns to Vietnam on a mission (financed by an oil tycoon) to rescue U.S. prisoners of war still being held years after the end of the war. Though it didn't make as much money as *First Blood*, it was a better, more complex film. Indeed, Kotcheff's only Hollywood flop was *Slip Image*, an offbeat, lacklustre study of an ordinary kid who gets sucked into a religious cult.

In L.A., Kotcheff learned to be a master player in the intricate game of dealing. In Hollywood's crazy ambience, gambling for high stakes dominates both art and business. It is possible to spend years developing projects that never get made, yet be paid princely wages and be considered quite successful. A hot director quickly gets submerged in a tangle of agents, options and projects that have already been in someone else's hands or will fall into someone else's hands.

As Kotcheff once remarked, "By the time you get to make the film, you feel you've already made it four times. Putting the deal together saps your energy. Of course, you don't just sit around and wait for projects. I usually have several scripts in development. If you get to do one in four of the projects you develop, you're doing well."

Kotcheff could easily have sat in Hollywood accepting assignments to direct the kind of movies the studios seemed to want, but something kept drawing him back to dream projects in Canada—for which it's the ultimate challenge just to raise the money to get the pictures made. *Joshua Then and Now* probably couldn't have been made without the financial muscle that Kotcheff's name brought to the enterprise. For years he'd been itching to film another Richler novel, but attempts to raise money for *St. Urbain's Horseman* and *Cocksure* had fallen through.

It took Lantos and Roth more than four years to put together the deal on *Joshua* with three major investors —Telefilm Canada, CBC television and 20th Century Fox. The budget was set at just over $9 million, not unusual in Hollywood but whopping by Canadian standards. It was on the basis of Kotcheff's track record that Fox put up $2 million (U.S.) for distribution rights.

The executives at Fox weren't enthusiastic about the subject or the casting (James Woods as Joshua Shapiro, the French-Canadian Gabrielle Lazure as Pauline Hornby, and Alan Arkin as Joshua's lovably crooked father) but finally they told Kotcheff, "Well, you've had a couple of winners before, so okay."

As Lantos noted, "The element we had to offer a Hollywood studio was Kotcheff. These days, studios rarely get involved in a serious film about human relationships unless it has Warren Beatty or Dustin Hoffman in it. What Fox sees is the combination of Richler, Kotcheff and Montreal, and what they want is a bigger-budget, more commercial *Duddy Kravitz*."

Even at the best of times, *Joshua* would have been hard to finance. In 1980, when the book was published and immediately optioned by Lantos and Roth, the Canadian movie industry was starting to come apart. *Joshua* began to look like one of those doomed projects that get planned and talked about for years and then never get made. In the end, three key factors made it happen: the emergence of Telefilm Canada, which dispensed funds from the Broadcast Fund; the commitment of CBC and 20th Century Fox; and the dedication of Kotcheff.

Joshua was by far the most prestigious and expensive movie Lantos and Roth had ever produced, and the extraordinary cost of producing *Joshua* was a problem right from the start. The story has a huge cast of characters, episodes in scattered parts of the world, as well as flashbacks and flash-forwards. In order to tap Telefilm's Broadcast Fund and maximize the amount of money they could raise in Canada, Lantos and Roth decided to create a two-part TV series as well as a theatrical movie. The CBC stretched its investment to the limit in exchange for four hours of material to be shown over two nights.

The deal was enormously complex, and the script went through a staggering nineteen drafts. The delays seemed endless. Lantos and Roth raised the cash budget of $7.4 million through the combination of Telefilm, CBC and Fox money, along with a small amount from private investors. The remaining $1.8 million of the $9.2-million budget was pieced together through deferments from the producers and director as well as private investments.

Kotcheff's fee, $1 million (U.S.), was made up of half-cash and half-deferment. Richler earned $350,000 (U.S.). The producers' fees came to about $1 million, including deferrals. James Woods was paid $250,000 (U.S.) for playing the title role, and Alan Arkin got $150,000 (U.S.) for playing Joshua's father.

When a movie as expensive as *Joshua* is produced independently rather than with the unlimited bankroll of a major studio, the role of the completion guarantor becomes extremely important. In this case the guarantor was Douglas Leiterman of the Toronto firm Motion Picture Guarantors. Leiterman, like most film completion guarantors, is backed by Lloyds of London, which insures the insurer. According to Leiterman (the onetime executive producer of *This Hour Has Seven Days*), he had never, in eight years in the business, run into the kind of trouble that developed over *Joshua*.

There were indications of money trouble even before shooting began in August 1984. Leiterman knew *Joshua* was going to run over budget, but he hoped the producers would raise additional investment money, or that the overrun would be contained within an $800,000 contingency allowance. He was wrong. In late September, he discovered that the film had overshot its budget by an alarming fifty percent—which precipitated a crisis meeting on an October morning in the boardroom of CBC English TV network vice president Denis Harvey.

Leiterman, whose company was on the hook for the overrun, was threatening to take the movie away from the producers and get it finished as cheaply as possible. Everyone in the room knew that would lead to a nasty scandal.

Between them, Telefilm and CBC had already poured $4.6 million of public money into the film; at a time when cutbacks loomed everywhere, it wasn't going to be easy to justify further expenditures. Yet there was a feeling that *Joshua* wasn't just another film; too much was riding on it to allow it to be jeopardized.

The major players hoped to save the film by each putting in a little extra money, but by the time Kotcheff arrived in Toronto in November for editing, Leiterman had taken control and all the partners were conferring with their lawyers. One of the few things that united them was the hope that a hit would end their disputes and get them all off the hook. But they knew that in order to become profitable *Joshua* would have to gross more than $20 million at the box office.

The producers claimed they had an insurance policy that the insurer was refusing to make good on. The guarantor claimed he was being converted to an unwilling financier. After a lot of acrimonious dispute, all the Canadian partners had to make financial compromises—but 20th Century Fox, which under a new management had little at stake, held firm to the letter of its contract. In the end, it was Lloyds of London that stepped in with the major chunk of the money to rescue the picture. The man from Lloyds, at any rate, decided *Joshua Then and Now* was a masterpiece.

"The problem with the film industry in Canada is that people have a B-movie mentality," said a weary, besieged Kotcheff. "That's why so few good Canadian movies have been produced. I'm making an A-picture here."

Joshua should have been a glorious homecoming for Kotcheff, who remarked during the shoot, "I think I do my best work in Canada. When I'm back here, I know these people, how they look, how they behave, how they smell, everything about them. A director needs that."

Joshua's selection for the competition at Cannes was the occasion for much swelling of Canadian pride. "It's a masterpiece," crowed André Lamy, who had come to Cannes as executive director of Telefilm Canada, even though everyone knew Lamy's days at Telefilm were numbered. "We backed it, and we were right. I hope it will demonstrate to the rest of the world that we can produce a film of international stature with a subject that is one-hundred-percent Canadian."

There may have been a touch of self-serving wishful thinking in Lamy's assessment, but that was understandable. Telefilm had invested heavily in the film, and *Joshua* represented his last shot at vindication. It wasn't exactly a surprise when Lamy, an awkward holdover from the toppled Liberal regime in Ottawa, discreetly left Cannes before the big day. He had, after all, been fired by Marcel Masse, the minister of communications in Brian Mulroney's new Tory government. Masse's Cannes agenda included canvassing opinion in the Canadian film community and shopping for a successor to Lamy, preferably female. (Adrienne Clarkson, who was at Cannes as host of the Ontario government's annual film-world cocktail party, was high on his list but was not interested in the job.)

"As Canadians we have to be pleased and proud that this film was selected," Masse remarked during a lunch on the beach with Canadian journalists. "The fact that it's here is very important. It's like winning a big international sports event."

Yet the real point of the exercise was to nudge 20th Century Fox, which held world distribution rights, into giving the movie a first-class release. From Hollywood's point of view, a movie about a Montreal Jewish writer didn't have the scent of a box-office winner, but everyone understood that if Fox didn't get behind *Joshua* with a major marketing campaign, the film was doomed. Cannes could be used as a marketing tool. People were still talking about the way Francis Coppola, six years earlier, brought *Apocalypse Now* to Cannes and invited the press to advise him how to end it. The trick was to attract attention.

The night before its premiere, *Joshua* had been celebrated at a lavish champagne dinner for 140 people at

Roger Vergé's three-star Moulin de Mougins, one of the most revered restaurants in all France. The $15,000 tab—which was covered with a little help from Telefilm, Queen's Park and Quebec City—exceeded the cost of certain low-budget films.

After gobbling the last of Vergé's *petites pâtisseries*, dinner guests had gone directly from the restaurant to a special midnight showing of Canada's other entry in the official selection at Cannes, from the same producers. The picture was *Night Magic*, Lewis Furey's musical fantasy with Carole Laure as an angel and Nick Mancuso as a music-hall performer who falls in love with her. The mood of the champagne-quaffing Canadians suddenly turned flat. *Night Magic* turned out to be a very long, very whimsical, talking song, and it seemed to put the whole audience into a coma. Except in Quebec and France, where Laure and Furey have a huge following, the film was clearly unreleasable. The only saving grace was that some of the icky-adorable words were inaudible owing to the sound of feet making for the exits.

In the small hours of the morning, as people stumbled out of the Palais into the brisk night air, it had become obvious that Canada's dreams of international cinematic glory that year rested squarely on the uncertain shoulders of Joshua Shapiro. In the 1970s, Canadian films like *Les Ordres, Outrageous!* and *J.A. Martin, photographe* had created at least a small frisson at Cannes, but it had been years since the Canadian contingent at the festival had had any reason to express national pride. Thousands of movie-lovers from around the world had learned to be skeptical about Canadian productions. *Joshua Then and Now* was the movie that was supposed to change all that.

At a lunchtime press conference the next day, Kotcheff was in a cocky mood, insisting, in response to a hostile question, that he'd be pleased to have his film described as parochial and provincial.

That night at the Palais evening showing, the black-tie audience couldn't have been more delighted by the movie or more responsive to its exuberant humor. At the end of the screening, the film earned the week's warmest ovation. And at a post-gala party the mood was euphoric.

But the euphoria faded when, back in Canada, *Globe and Mail* film critic Jay Scott reported that the international press, who attended a morning screening, loathed *Joshua*, dismissing it as a TV series that didn't belong at Cannes. Lantos, an aggressive Hungarian with an explosive temper, was enraged. The producer thought he'd scored a triumph — until he started getting condolence calls from *Globe* readers. "Canada has a unique tendency to look for ways to self-destruct," he fumed.

No doubt there were critics who disliked *Joshua*, especially among the leftists of the Third World press who tend not to be amused by celebrations of bourgeois life, especially Jewish bourgeois life. Still, the reviews in France were mostly positive. Burbled *Le Figaro*: "*Joshua* has the effect of a welcome, sunny beach in a festival which makes a profession of gravity." On the other hand, *Libération*, voice of the Left, commented: "We have now reached the bottom of the barrel."

It was hardly a shock when, at the end of the festival, *Joshua* failed to win any prize, let alone the Palme d'Or.

At Cannes, where it was possible to step back and look at the movie whole, with an audience, a few points became clear. Alan Arkin stole the picture with a marvelously ribald performance as Joshua's father, the Bible-quoting crook, Reuben Shapiro. James Woods was riveting and intense as the Jewish rebel who conducts his own war with the Westmount establishment, although lacking in Jewish identity and the personal qualities that might give the audience a reason to care about him. Gabrielle Lazure as the WASP princess Joshua marries was a disaster, even with the voice of Susan Hogan. The flashback structure was highly problematic, and the ending—which would be re-edited before the film's North American release—was baffling.

The first hour of the film hurtles along with energy and color, focusing on the conflicting family backgrounds of Joshua Shapiro, Jewish literary frog, and Pauline Hornby, golden *shiksa* princess, and on their entertainingly rocky courtship. But once Joshua and Pauline are married and back in Montreal, the movie falters. Pieces of the story seem to be missing, and the film's sour view of WASPs would have had protesters marching the street if it had been directed at any other identifiable group. The second half of *Joshua* is curiously off-target, with villains who don't seem to be a recognizable part of the Canadian social landscape.

Odious comparisons were inevitable, and *Joshua* just wasn't in the same league as *Duddy Kravitz*. A number of things had gone very wrong. The constant atmosphere of financial crisis had taken its toll, sapping Kotcheff's energy, and in the end he was unable to camouflage problems inherent in the script and the casting.

Joshua Then and Now had its North American premiere on the opening night of Toronto's Festival of Festivals, and everyone was in a buoyant mood. It had been a week of celebrations. A few days earlier, Ted Kotcheff had married Laifun Chung in Toronto, where the families of both bride and groom reside. The wedding was a Bulgarian-Chinese coproduction, and the 200 guests observed both Macedonian folk-dancing and the ritual signing of an oriental silk scroll. Among those present were producers Robert Lantos and John Kemeny, whose two companies had recently announced their own marriage into the giant firm Alliance; Mordecai and Florence Richler; Ted Allan, who while trying to organize a movie about his mentor, Norman Bethune, had gone with Kotcheff to China, where the bride and groom met.

In the days between the wedding and the premiere, the mood of celebration continued. *Maclean's* magazine gave Joshua a cover story. In a speech at an industry lunch, Kotcheff paid tribute to the technical expertise of the Canadian film industry. The Toronto *Star* pronounced *Joshua* "a joy to behold." And in the pre-film speeches at the gala opening, Ontario's culture minister, Lily Munro, competed with Marcel Masse, the man from Ottawa who was emerging as a kind of savior of the arts, for the right to pay tribute to *Joshua*. (Unfortunately she seemed to think the title of the film was *Joshua Here and Now*.) And when the VIPs from the film itself were introduced to the audience, the one who drew the thunderous standing ovation, and seemed unprepared for it, was Mordecai Richler.

The film had been slightly improved since Cannes, with a re-edited ending that was less baffling than before. The glitzy opening-night crowd at the Toronto film festival loved the picture, and that was perhaps enough to assure *Joshua* a healthy run in Toronto. *Joshua* was also a modest hit in Montreal, Beverly Hills and Miami—all markets with large and prosperous Jewish communities. But in New York, the city with the largest and most sophisticated Jewish population in the world, the movie opened and closed almost simultaneously, perhaps as a result of singularly vicious reviews. And in most North American cities it never opened at all.

Among the various partners in the project, only CBC got what it bargained for. For 20th Century Fox, the loss of several million dollars was a not particularly overwhelming write-off, to be chalked up as a minor folly of the previous regime. In Hollywood it would be regarded as an unimportant footnote in Kotcheff's career. But for Lantos and Roth, whose company lost perhaps a million dollars, the bite was more painful.

Almost a year after the film's world premiere at Cannes, Lantos and Roth sipped champagne again, when *Joshua* won a Genie for best Canadian movie of the year. But by then the celebrating was offset by the grim realities of the balance sheet.

On the eve of the Cannes Festival, Lantos had remarked: "What happens in Cannes could be pivotal. On the one hand, I can't wait, and on the other hand, I dread it. For Stephen Roth and me, this could be the high point or the low point of our career."

What he hadn't anticipated was that it would turn out to be both at once.

5

Riding with Oscar

Denys Arcand had never been farther west than Salt Lake City, which he'd once passed through on a skiing trip, but in March 1987, he finally made it to Los Angeles, acting out the fantasy of thousands of starstruck kids — the newcomer as Oscar nominee. His surprise hit sex comedy *The Decline of the American Empire* had been nominated by the Academy of Motion Picture Arts and Sciences as best foreign film of 1986, making it inevitable that Arcand would experience the full Hollywood treatment. For a few magical weeks Quebec cinema had become Fantasyland's latest enchanted kingdom, and Denys Arcand its emperor.

Few casting directors would consider the cheerfully flippant iconoclast from Deschambault (a small town on the north shore of the St. Lawrence River halfway between Quebec City and Trois Rivières) well suited for the role. Oscar nominees, after all, are expected to be modern-day Candides, wide-eyed believers in the fairy tale. Denys Arcand, however, was the aging bad boy of Quebec cinema. Although in his late forties, he still seemed to be the cocky, sharp-witted troublemaker at the back of the class who tries to catch the teacher in an embarrassing contradiction. Arcand's small, black eyes darted around a room looking for signs of moral sham, and the lines that had started to appear only added to his quizzical, doubting air. Even his smile had a mocking edge to it. How could a man with Denys Arcand's personality, a man who had made a career out of exposing and ridiculing hypocrisy and pretense, keep a straight face at the world's most entertaining extravaganza of hypocrisy and pretense?

It was all very well to be the darling of the critics at the Cannes Film Festival, where *Decline*'s ascent had begun in May 1986, when it was shown in the prestigious Directors' Fortnight section of the festival, and won the International Critics Prize. It was all very well to be the toast of Toronto, where *Decline* had its North American premiere the following September on the opening night of the Festival of Festivals. It was all very well to be shown at the New York Film Festival and then become entrenched as an art-house hit at the fashionable East Side Plaza cinema (regarded by owner and operator Garth Drabinsky as a jewel in the crown of his anything-but-declining North American empire). And it was all very well to be honored by the New York Film Critics, who anointed *Decline* as best foreign film of the year (even though they did schedule the presentation ceremony at Sardi's opposite the Super Bowl telecast, thereby creating a glittering list of no-shows).

But being nominated for an Oscar was beyond the wildest dreams of even the unflappable, sardonic son of a Quebec riverboat pilot. Produced for a modest $1.6 million, *Decline* had already taken in about $20 million at the box office, including more than $3 million in Quebec and another $1 million in the rest of Canada. But an Oscar would not only add further lustre but might well add millions to the film's revenue.

For generations the Arcand males had been seamen, but Denys' father knew the day was coming when the work of river pilots would be done by radar, and he wanted his sons to become doctors or lawyers. That's why the family moved to Montreal. Denys' sister became a criminologist; his younger brother became an anthropologist; and Gabriel Arcand, who plays a mysterious outsider in *Decline,* became a fringe theatre actor and has appeared in almost every film his older brother directed.

It was as a student of history at the University of Montreal in the 1960s that Denys internalized the teachings of Maurice Seguin. "He believed economics were at the root of everything," Arcand recalled years later. "He told us that we [French Canadians] were numerous enough and strong enough to survive, but too few and too weak to thrive. We were therefore condemned to mediocrity. I am still haunted by his remarks."

At first Arcand's career contradicted his own pessimistic theories. In the early 1970s, Quebec cinema flowered briefly, and Denys Arcand was its triumphant enfant terrible. At the National Film Board he created something of a scandal with his exposé of exploitation in the cotton industry, *On Est au Coton.* It became a black-market hit after being banned by the NFB's commissioner of the day, Sydney Newman. After leaving the board, Arcand made two exposés of corruption, Quebec style—*Réjeanne Padovani* (1973) and *Gina* (1975)—which were received as the height of radical chic, separatist cinematic division. Then he more or less disappeared as a distinctive force, though he continued to work on such group projects as *Duplessis* (a French-languge TV series) and *Empire, Inc.* (an English-language TV series), both produced for CBC by Mark Blandford. And he directed *The Crime of Ovide Plouffe,* a doomed sequel to *Les Plouffe.*

But *The Decline of the American Empire* brought a sharp end to the decline of Denys Arcand. Before this movie's fabulous success, people asked whatever had become of Denys Arcand. The truthful answer was that he'd turned into a walking illustration of his own pessimistic thesis about the inevitable cultural failure of any society with a population as small as that of French Canada.

In the creative-arts community, almost all Quebeckers were radicals, and some, including the late Claude Jutra, danced in the streets of Montreal when the Parti Québécois came to power. That memorable night in 1976 should have ushered in a golden age for Quebec cinema, but René Lévesque's government was understandably more concerned with social and economic issues than with the arts. And the personal, political cinema that was the house specialty in Quebec was left by the wayside during Michael McCabe's reign in Hollywood North. By the late 1970s, successful movies were few and far between. Gilles Carle made a marvelous film, *Les Plouffe*, which was surprisingly deep and satisfying compared to the old TV series about the same family. And producer Roch Demers undertook an ambitious series of films for children, most notably the surprise hit *The Dog Who Stopped the War*. But for the most part Quebec cinema was in a deep slumber with only occasional stirrings.

Among those stranded by events was Jutra, the great writer-director whose 1971 masterpiece, *Mon Oncle Antoine*, was the runaway front-runner in the Canada's Ten Best poll conducted by Toronto's Festival of Festivals in 1985. *Mon Oncle Antoine* is not just a glowing, resonant movie; it is a movie that gave us a new way of seeing the history of French Canada. And Jutra's sprawling historical saga, *Kamouraska* (1973), based on the Anne Hébert novel, remains the most delicate costume epic ever made in this country. When opportunity dried up at home, Jutra began commuting to that "friendly foreign country," as he dubbed it, whose capital was Toronto. But when he made his first full-length feature in five years, *Surfacing* (1980), results were discouraging. The film was based on Margaret Atwood's unfilmable quest allegory. It had a bad script and lethal casting (American actors Joseph Bottoms and Kathleen Beller), and Jutra stepped in at the last minute, when it was too late to make changes, after another director (Eric Till) had walked away. Something positive came out of the experience, though: the producer of the film, Beryl Fox, promised that if Jutra would direct *Surfacing* she would raise money and produce the sex comedy he wanted to make.

That movie was *By Design* (1982)—the loopy story of two Vancouver lesbians (played by American Patty Duke Astin and Canadian newcomer Sara Botsford) who want to have a baby. *By Design* emerged from an original script by Joe Wiesenfeld, who shared screenplay credit with Jutra and David Eames, but the arresting combination of sly humor and buoyant generosity was identifiably Jutra's. The mark of his personality on the film was as clear as the insignia on some of the designer clothes worn by the characters, who are in the fashion business. (Unfortunately, the clothes in the movie are dreadful.)

In a stunning sequence of crosscutting, Saul Rubinek —the sex-obsessed photographer selected for stud service—thumbs through a pornographic magazine while trying to make love to a distracted Astin; she's brought to orgasm by telephone murmurings from Botsford, herself in bed elsewhere with a sensitive Swedish boy. Jutra's universe seems to be ruled by a quirky deity, perhaps a bit squirrelly and with a fondness for chaos, but still essentially benevolent.

By Design, produced in English, should have been the beginning of a fruitful comeback for Jutra, but the film provoked a great deal of hostility. It was bad-mouthed in advance by journalists and industry insiders who were still punishing Jutra and Fox for *Surfacing*, and who considered jokes about homosexuality a sign of bad taste. *By Design* failed commercially, and it never opened in New York, though it earned excellent reviews from Pauline Kael in *The New Yorker* and Michael Sragow in *Rolling*

Stone, among others. Yet, apart from his final film, the imperfectly realized *La Dame en couleurs, By Design* stands as Jutra's last hurrah. Suffering from Alzheimer's disease, Jutra vanished in November of 1986; his body was found on the shore of the St. Lawrence River the following April. Like the character named Claude he played in his autobiographical first feature *A tout prendre* (1963), Jutra engineered his own disappearance, choosing death by water over life in intolerable circumstances.

One gifted young director seemed to inherit the Jutra tradition of Gallic humanism combined with delicate comedy. Francis Mankiewicz made *Les Bons Débarras,* the one great movie produced in French in Quebec during the PQ years, in collaboration with Réjean Ducharme, an established novelist. Despite its downer title (which translates roughly as "Good Riddance") and its squalid setting in a small town in the Laurentians, this mother-daughter saga is anything but depressing. The audience is kept spellbound by two extraordinarily charismatic actresses — horse-faced, big-boned Marie Tifo as Marie, a backwoods Mother Courage, and bewitching, pubescent Charlotte Laurier as Manon, the illegitimate little princess manipulating her overextended mother.

The film tells the story of Manon's intense need to transcend — through a ferocious, devouring love for her mother — her grim destiny. Manon has a need for poetic intensity and a taste for gothic romance; she wants to steal her mother away from others who have emotional claims. Recoiling from a world that fails to answer her yearnings, this nymph becomes a sacred monster, creating her own interior world and pulling her mother into a cloistered *folie à deux.*

Francis Mankiewicz, whose cousins Herman and Joseph were legendary figures in Hollywood, came to Montreal with his parents as a refugee after World War II. *Les Bons Débarras* won a vanload full of Genies, but six years later Mankiewicz was scrambling for work in TV, unable to get financing for his feature-film projects, much like Denys Arcand prior to making *The Decline of the American Empire*. The bleak view of a Quebecker's destiny essayed by Mankiewicz and Ducharme in *Les Bons Débarras* ties in with the pessimistic views Denys Arcand picked up at university—and Mankiewicz himself became a walking illustration of the thesis.

Arcand almost became a history professor, and, indeed, *The Decline of the American Empire*—preoccupied with the jaded emptiness of middle-aged academics who pursue casual sex because they've lost interest in other goals—is in a sense Denys Arcand's way of coming to terms with the academic life he never followed through on. He continued to observe it from a safe peephole beyond the scholarly fringe.

Even for a movie as brilliantly made as Arcand's *Réjeanne Padovani*, the audience was very limited. The reason was obvious: the mainstream audience does not turn out for shocking exposés from the land of hopelessness. But when he made *Decline*, Arcand found a way to tap a subject of great popular interest yet remain true to his obsessions.

The idea was to make a movie as sardonic as Arcand's earlier political films but to substitute sexual exposé for political exposé. He would focus on the sex lives of people not very different from himself, the sophisticated French-Canadian academics of his own generation.

Arcand knew he had to do something dramatic to pull his career out of its rut. He knew that the National Film Board, which had money to invest in coproduction with private filmmakers, was not the place it had been when he defected with nose-thumbing bravado fifteen years earlier. He knew he couldn't make an expensive film, full of spectacle, so he decided to concentrate on what he could film well and inexpensively—people talking to one another, but talking brilliantly and revealingly. He knew that if he was going to put talking heads on the screen, and still expect people to pay money to see them, the talk had better be titillating.

Roger Frappier, a friend of Arcand's and, in the old days, a militant radical, had become a producer at the Film Board. He told Arcand, "You are worth more than what you've been doing lately. I have $30,000 for you. Go home and write something, and I'll find a way to produce it."

Arcand must have known, too, of the Film Board's surprise success with an unassuming, low-budget, English-language sex comedy, *90 Days* (1985). It was originally billed as a sequel to *The Masculine Mystique,* a ponderous essay about male befuddlement in the feminist era, and few were eager for a follow-up. But in *90 Days,* directed by NFB veteran Giles Walker, earnestness gave way to likably screwy comedy. The characters included a failed womanizer who is offered $10,000 for his sperm and an eccentric loner who flies in a mail-order bride from Korea, and the film had the throwaway charm of an updated Ernst Lubitsch trifle.

The jokey thesis of *Decline,* offered by one of the female characters during a radio interview, is that our intimate lives reflect the fact that we are living through a period of a declining empire—precisely the kind of era in which people pursue hedonistic goals. Arcand's attitude is so droll and offhand that at first we don't take this idea seriously. It seems to be merely his way of tossing off a facile explanation for the kind of behavior he's showing. But toward the end, the tone of the film darkens, and Arcand tries to get at the emotional consequences of shifting sexual morality.

Decline is a sexy house-party movie—a cross between Renoir's *Rules of the Game* and *The Big Chill,* with cuttings from Buñuel's *The Discreet Charm of the Bourgeoisie.* Yet, with its articulate, educated characters who talk a blue streak, it recalls most of all the films of Eric Rohmer (such as *My Night at Maud's*)—except that Rohmer's characters don't come on like *Penthouse* Forum correspondents.

Four men spend their day preparing a meal in a country chalet on Lake Memphremagog while their four women colleagues and companions work out on Nautilus machines at a sports complex. Throughout the proceedings, both the male chorus and the female chorus chant non-stop about their wild sexual experiences, as if trying to outdo one another. The group includes one male homosexual, one female masochist, one sadistic, nonintellectual outsider, and a few prodigiously heterosexual practitioners of infidelity.

Arcand has always had a muckraking sensibility, and in his political films he was much better at exposing the malaise than at proposing a cure. Arcand is at heart a pessimist who sees no solution to the problems he describes. In *Decline*, turning from politics to sexual politics, he showed with relentless glee the cracks in a society of restless sexual wandering.

Denys Arcand is strictly the bemused voyeur—and so is the audience. Above all, this is a movie for knowing adults; it even has literary and intellectual jokes. And in the cinematic wasteland of kiddie shows, here is a movie for everyone starved for sophisticated conversation.

There was no doubt that *Decline* was the most assured and polished Canadian movie of the year, and it got rave reviews from all three Toronto newspapers. As one of Arcand's earliest champions, I felt odd about giving only qualified praise to the movie that was finally earning the kind of success I felt Arcand deserved long before. Yet I couldn't help feeling there was a thinness that prevented *Decline* from being deeply satisfying.

Where he faltered, it seemed to me, was in trying to make the audience pay the price for the outrageous sexual attitudes with which they'd been entertained. Several of the characters are shattered in the denouement, when at the dinner they've been preparing all through the film, Dominique, the historian and author whose theories have made her a media darling, deliberately makes an indiscreet revelation. Arcand wants the audience to be shattered, too, or at least moved.

There's a control and subtle fluency in Arcand's work with a skillful acting ensemble: Remy Girard as a flabby, jolly adulterous professor; Dorothée Berryman as his naïve, adoring wife, Louise, who is destroyed when his philandering is exposed over dinner; Yves Jacques as the homosexual art historian who feels fully alive only when he's cruising; Louise Portal as an untenured divorcée who's also a masochist; Gabriel Arcand as her sadistic, fond-of-leather boyfriend; Dominique Michel as the head of the history department who has just published a new book and who chooses to humiliate Louise and Remy with her casual revelation at dinner; Pierre Curzi as a pedantic, divorced professor; and Geneviève Rioux as the beautiful young graduate student who works part-time at a massage parlor.

But these characters, with their constant jabbering about sex, are essentially cartoons, so it comes as a bit of a surprise when Arcand reveals that they have feelings. Arcand clearly enjoys exposing the foibles of smart people, and the audience enjoys it, too. But isn't he on dangerous ground when he starts offering moral overviews? Isn't he, indeed, turning himself into the very kind of pompous pop theorist that he was satirizing at the beginning of this movie?

Not, apparently, in the eyes of the public or members of the Canadian movie community. Only one week before the Oscar ceremony, Arcand was the runaway winner at the Genies. The film made almost a clean sweep of the awards, collecting eight statuettes—a feat matched by only two previous Quebec films: Claude Jutra's *Mon Oncle Antoine* in 1971 and Francis Mankiewicz's *Les Bons Débarras* in 1980.

With all the adulation for *Decline*, a Quebec film by an important new director, a thirty-two-year-old former news cameraman named Yves Simoneau, was virtually lost in the shuffle. *Pouvoir Intime*, a low-budget thriller, was an exercise in directorial style. Starting with an unremarkable tale of a robbery gone awry, Simoneau constructed a tense, subtle mood piece about psychological warfare, waiting games and the endless variety of claustrophobic, dead-end traps. *Pouvoir Intime* earned several Genie nominations, but on awards night it was strictly an also-ran.

Arcand won two Genies personally — for best director and best original screenplay. Two of the actors — Louise Portal and Gabriel Arcand — won in the best supporting acting categories. And *Decline* also was cited for best sound, sound editing and film editing as well as for best movie of the year. The picture even won the Golden Reel award for its record at the box office. According to René Malo, who produced the film in collaboration with the NFB's Roger Frappier, about 1.2 million Canadians had bought tickets to see the film.

"Who would have guessed that *The Decline of the American Empire* would result in the rise of Canadian cinema?" chortled Frappier.

Presenting the screenplay award to Arcand, a flustered Margot Kidder called him back to add something else: the $5,000 cheque (the Sydney Newman Award) that accompanies the Genie statuette in this category. Kidder joked that given his success, Arcand obviously didn't need the money. "I'll let you see my bank account," countered Arcand.

Though the bubbly flowed into the small hours at Sutton Place, the official Genie hotel, the Genies were somehow a shadow event. At the end of typical conversations about the Genies, there was always increased excitement about the Oscars, as if they represented the real world, not the let's-pretend world of Canadian culture. After all, weren't the Genies themselves a slavish imitation of the Oscars? Even in decline, the American cultural empire was the one for which Canadians, even fervent nationalists, reserved their awe.

And so it came to pass that Denys Arcand arrived in L.A. for one of the strangest experiences of his life. Garth Drabinsky, whose company, Cineplex Odeon, was handling *Decline* in the United States, had hired Renee Furst, an aggressive New York film publicist, to promote *Decline* during its Oscar bid. Telefilm Canada put up $50,000 toward the campaign with the stipulation that the loan would be forgiven if the film lost but would have to be repaid if it won the Oscar. Cynics claimed this was another case of the old Canadian syndrome, namely "If you win, you lose; if you lose, you win." But there was a simple economic logic operating here: a film that wins an Oscar can afford to pay back a loan.

Americans are hospitable to foreigners, and each nominee for best foreign film was assigned a host, a member of the Academy of Motion Picture Arts and Sciences. Arcand's host was veteran actor Lew Ayres, whose career dates all the way back to the 1930 classic, *All Quiet on the Western Front*, and who is perhaps best known for the title role in the *Dr. Kildare* movie series.

"They're very considerate," Arcand noted. "It's a change from Cannes, where a visiting director is treated like shit."

In Hollywood, a foreign guest is treated politely even by those who dislike his film. Some academy voters turned up at cocktail parties in Arcand's honor and chatted with him even though they were clearly offended by his film. One veteran director told him his portrayal of women was especially regrettable. "It is our duty as filmmakers to portray women as goddesses," the elderly gentleman lectured the upstart.

In order to vote for best foreign film, an academy member must have seen all five nominated films. Renee Furst's job was not only to promote the film but to make sure voters went to see it. It tends to be the older, retired members who have time to go to the screenings of all the nominated films. This means the voting tends to be done by the most conservative wing of an organization that tends to be conservative in general. Early on, Arcand realized that this regulation could work against his film, since younger audiences were more enthusiastic about it than older audiences.

But Hollywood was titillated by *Decline*—partly because Paramount Pictures had bought the rights to remake the film in English. A Hollywood script doctor —David Giler, whose credits included *The Money Pit*, *Aliens* and *Beverly Hills Cop II*—had been hired to write an Americanized version of the script. Giler had worked on the script of *Fun with Dick and Jane* with Mordecai Richler, whom Giler pronounced the funniest collaborator he'd ever had. Los Angeles *Times* critic Charles Champlin accused Giler in print of being an "art vandal" in the case of *Decline*, and Giler seemed to enjoy the accusation.

Denys Arcand hardly seemed to mind. "My film is already made," he told a newspaper reporter, "whatever happens with the remake, and it has been seen by more people than I ever thought would see it. If I can live with the new script, I'll probably direct it. If I can't, I'll just come back to Montreal and work on another French film."

That might have been a relief after the dizzying round of escapades and assignations in California. To the Polo Lounge for breakfast with Charles Champlin, who could be counted on to write something nice about Denys and his film in the all-powerful L.A. *Times*. To a cocktail party, organized and paid for by Cineplex Odeon, for voting members of the academy. To the Canadian consulate, every California Canuck's home-away-from-home, for more handshakes and pats on the back from distinguished cocktail sippers. The Canadian community in Hollywood was rallying round; Dan Petrie, one of the senior expatriate Canadians in L.A., and Arthur Hiller, whose commercial comedy *Outrageous Fortune* was currently cleaning up at box offices all over North America, made a point of stopping by to offer their congratulations.

When Arcand escaped to an antique car show one Sunday afternoon, someone grabbed him, saying, "Come with me. Mancuso is here and he wants to meet you." Arcand thought he meant Nick Mancuso, the Toronto actor who was making it in Hollywood. "Thanks very much," said Arcand. "I'm sure he's very interesting, but I would rather look at cars than talk to an actor."

"No, no, you fool, it's Frank Mancuso."

"Frank Mancuso? Who's he?"

Only the president of Paramount Pictures, the studio planning to make the English version of *Decline*, and a man one might spend months trying—unsuccessfully—to reach on the phone.

And sure enough, there he was, one of the most powerful men in Hollywood, wearing a T-shirt and a baseball cap, waiting to chat with the kid from Deschambault.

The day before the Oscar ceremony, Arcand was a no-show at a reception for Canadian nominees. He'd gone instead to Disneyland on an outing arranged annually for foreign-language nominees. "I had a great time," he burbled later. "We were escorted past the lineups, received by Disneyland dignitaries and given a lavish dinner. And I got to see the new film Coppola has done for Disneyland."

The Oscar ceremony is timed for the convenience of eastern TV audiences; L.A. is three hours behind New York. On the way from the hotel to the Music Center, where the presentation show is staged, the *Decline* group learned that the chauffeur of their limousine was named Oscar.

"I hope you're not the only Oscar we meet tonight," quipped Arcand. Nevertheless, he was betting $150 on *The Assault*, a Dutch film about dealing with the Nazi occupation.

The Oscars, Arcand decided, were all an illusion anyway. The funniest illusion was the one given the TV audience of an auditorium packed with nominated stars. Since many of them spent much of the evening in special lounges for nominees, returning to their seats only when the announcement was about to be made in their category, stand-ins in fancy dress were placed in their seats so the cameras wouldn't be panning rows of empty spaces.

For Arcand the bubble burst when Anthony Quinn opened the envelope on the evening of March 31 and read the names of the people who had made *The Assault*.

Back in the limo, the visitors from Montreal asked Oscar the driver to change his name.

And the next day Arcand jokingly told a reporter, "I should have brought a windbreaker with me. The climate in Hollywood gets very cold when you're an also-ran."

The carnival was over, and Denys Arcand was impatient to get on with his next movie, *Jesus of Montreal*, about a mostly out-of-work actor who survives by playing Jesus in local Catholic pageants. Launching and promoting *Decline* had taken almost a year out of Arcand's life. He was tired of being a huckster and a politician; he wanted to get back to being a filmmaker. It was exhausting to be constantly surrounded by people who were always pushing and promoting and thinking positively. It was time to go home — where people didn't stare at him as if he were an alien if he shrugged and cracked sardonic jokes. Back in Quebec, Arcand would be free to be pessimistic, with no pressure to have a nice day.

6

The World According to Garth

In office corridors, at restaurant tables and in airport waiting rooms, the single most oft-asked question in the Canadian movie industry must surely be, "What does Garth really want?" His full name is Garth Howard Drabinsky, but throughout the industry he is known to both friends and foes simply as Garth. The foes have become a lot quieter in the past few years as the man they love to hate has risen to higher plateaus of power. There's no shortage of people in the industry willing to tell tales about Drabinsky: about his phone calls from his private jet (with engine noises in the background); about his demand that a magazine arrange for Yousuf Karsh to take its cover photo of him; about his $35-million lawsuit against the Toronto *Star*. But when people tell tales about Drabinsky, they do it furtively.

The reason is simple. If you're in the film business, you probably can't afford to have Garth Drabinsky as an enemy. As the president of Cineplex Odeon, Drabinsky controls about 1,500 North American movie-theatre screens (two-thirds of them in the United States) in about 500 locations. (The exact figures change almost every week.) By 1986 the company had 12,500 employees and 100 million patrons, and did more than $400 million worth of business. Drabinsky's power base is no longer limited to Canada; a series of takeovers has made him a major force in the U.S. theatre market, and, indeed, he seems to be single-handedly reversing a long history of American domination of the Canadian film industry.

Drabinsky not only runs the second-largest and fastest-growing movie-theatre circuit in North America, he's also a major force in film distribution through Cineplex Odeon Films. He has started to collect honors, such as the Air Canada Award at the 1986 Genie ceremonies and a special citation at the 1987 World Film Festival in Montreal. And his backers include one of Canada's richest families, the Bronfmans, and one of the most powerful multinational corporations in the world — the Hollywood-based Music Corporation of America (MCA), which owns, among other things, Universal Studios.

"I've got more strength and authority in Hollywood than any Canadian," Drabinsky claims. "And when I scream at them down there, I expect people to listen, and to act." Certainly no one could accuse Drabinsky of failing to do his share of screaming. At times he carries on like an enraged upstart who's trying to get even. One night in September 1986 his legendary temper exploded at a meeting of the Toronto film festival's executive committee when Drabinsky's colleagues, ignoring his advice, voted to oust festival director Leonard Schein. Drabinsky let them know in no uncertain terms what he thought of the board members who had voted against Schein.

Success doesn't seem to have had a mellowing effect on Drabinsky. It hasn't taken the edge off the scrappy disposition of the showman with the booming voice and an ego to match. Something still rankles. He's still trying to show somebody something, and to teach painful lessons to anyone who fails to treat him with the respect he regards as his due.

Only a few years ago Drabinsky was on the ropes, all but bankrupt. Now, after the spectacular reversal of his fortunes and the phenomenal success he has made of his company, he seems as driven as ever.

It's easier to understand Drabinsky if you think of him as a Canadian version of the media tycoon played by that young prodigy, Orson Welles, in his brilliant 1941 movie *Citizen Kane*. The commanding voice, the bombastic rhetoric and the jowly face all fit the model. Welles, who was twenty-four when he cast himself as Charles Foster Kane, aka William Randolph Hearst, gave the impression of playing someone much older, and so does Drabinsky, who, though just under forty, comes on like a schoolboy trying to be Harry Cohn, the most feared of Hollywood tycoons, or Winston Churchill. Drabinsky is so fiercely competitive he likes to vanquish his rivals, not just outsmart them. And, like Kane, he's a self-dramatizing grandstander, conscious of creating his own myth, and given to thunderous pronouncements.

Instead of Kane's Xanadu (or Hearst's castle in San Simeon, California), Drabinsky has a mobile symbol of his power — a private plane, which allows him to swoop into the farthest corners of his domain and make surprise visits to theatre managers, often to bawl them out for a messy lobby or a disgusting bathroom. No one ever made the mistake of calling Drabinsky modest, understated or self-effacing. Drabinsky shrugs off the antagonism his style provokes: "Envy and jealousy always prevail in small-minded people, maybe more so in the Canadian context because of the relative insecurity of the country."

To Herman Mankiewicz, the veteran newspaperman and Hollywood writer who wrote the script of *Citizen Kane* for Welles, Hearst was a great subject for satire, partly because poking fun at him was so dangerous, given his capacity for wiping out enemies. And though no one has written a script about Drabinsky (yet), some of his wittier colleagues in the Canadian film industry see Drabinsky essentially the way Mankiewicz saw Hearst.

There's no mystery, however, about Garth Drabinsky's Rosebud. Whenever he makes a public appearance, making his way to the stage with a pronounced limp, it's clear what Drabinsky has been fighting all his life to overcome. He got polio at three and had a series of painful operations throughout his childhood — one every summer until he was twelve. The experience left him with a mixture of determination and rage. He compensated by becoming a champion school debater (his speeches are still written and delivered in the style of a student orator), a flamboyant showman and a crack entertainment lawyer. And by working obsessively, often eighteen hours a day, seven days a week. "Because I didn't have a normal childhood," he explained years later, "I compensated in creative and academic pursuits."

While still in law school, helping out in his father's air-conditioning business during his summer breaks, Drabinsky wrote the textbook *Motion Pictures and the Arts in Canada: The Business and the Law.* He became a high-flying lawyer-cum-entrepreneur, then a flamboyant movie producer in the Hollywood North era. The story of how Drabinsky became a sort of apprentice to N.A. (Nat) Taylor, one of the veterans of the theatre-operating business, has become part of Canada's show-biz lore. Drabinsky was a law student when he came to Taylor with an unlikely scheme, and Taylor put him in charge of his weekly film trade magazine. Taylor had sold his theatre circuit to Famous Players years earlier, but he still had a dream of multiplex theatres on a grand scale. Years earlier, Taylor split the Elgin theatre in Ottawa into two auditoriums, and started a revolutionary trend. Drabinsky had the youth and energy to translate Taylor's ideas into actuality, so Taylor and Drabinsky launched Cineplex together. They started with the Eaton Centre in Toronto, where they opened an eighteen-screen operation in 1979, and quickly spread across Canada and eventually into the United States.

During the late 1970s, Drabinsky was primarily known as a movie producer. (He was also briefly a theatrical producer: his biggest gamble, a $1.3-million Broadway musical entitled *A Broadway Musical*, opened and closed at the Lunt-Fontanne Theatre one night in 1978.) And in 1981 he was chairman of the board for On Stage '81, a never-to-be-repeated Toronto theatre festival that was a creative success but left a long list of creditors. (Drabinsky helped pay off some of those debts when he presented the epic silent film *Napoleon* as a benefit.)

Looking back on his period as a movie producer, Drabinsky told a journalist: "Some film investors had dreams of avarice. I couldn't deliver those dreams in the early days. But I gave 400 percent and put my own money in. I was the pioneer. How much experience was there to draw from?"

In collaboration with his Hollywood partner, Joel Michaels, Drabinsky produced six movies between 1976 and 1982: *The Disappearance, The Silent Partner, The Changeling, Tribute, The Amateur* and *Losing It*. Although he hasn't produced a movie since 1982, he has collected more Genie nominations than any other producer. *The Disappearance* disappeared without making it into theatres, resisting the efforts of miracle workers to re-edit it. *The Silent Partner,* directed by Daryl Duke, was a made-in-Toronto thriller about a bank holdup at the Eaton Centre during the Christmas shopping season, with Elliott Gould as a bank clerk drawn into the plot, and Christopher Plummer being maniacal in a Santa suit. And *Tribute* was a screen version of the stage play by Canadian expatriate Bernard Slade, with Jack Lemmon repeating his stage role as a New York press agent who makes gags out of anything, even the fact that he has terminal cancer.

Drabinsky's one real hit, and his big award-winner, was *The Changeling,* a relatively expensive haunted-house thriller starring George C. Scott. When it was released in the spring of 1980, the press releases didn't call the film a ghost story; they described it as "a horrifying parapsychological experience."

The *Changeling* might have been fun had it been done

with a light, playful touch, but Peter Medak—a Hungarian director who does most of his work in England—specializes in heavy labor, and the picture was leaden.

Drabinsky's movies were on the whole glossy and well produced, but they had the stamp of Hollywood North just when Hollywood North was sinking fast. This is one reason Drabinsky got more involved in Cineplex and put producing movies on the back burner. There were other reasons: Cineplex was in trouble, and Taylor wasn't getting any younger.

By the end of 1982, Drabinsky was at his lowest ebb since the debacle of *A Broadway Musical*. In its year-end annual statement, Cineplex reported losses of $15.5 million. High interest rates were cited as the culprit, but Cineplex had other problems as well. By early 1983 creditors were screaming, and Drabinsky had to make concessions. He vacated the glittering offices in the Eaton Centre in downtown Toronto. And he backed away from the much-touted restoration of the historic Elgin/Winter Garden Theatre in downtown Toronto. (As a result, Drabinsky found himself in litigation with the Ontario government, which had agreed to turn the Elgin over to him.)

All this led to much clicking of tongues and shaking of heads among those who had always found Drabinsky's bombastic, self-dramatizing style a bit much. They were looking forward to the fall of Garth Drabinsky and his empire.

Yet only eighteen months later, Drabinsky was triumphantly executing one of the most astonishing coups in Canadian show-business history, the takeover of the Canadian Odeon theatre chain. When the deal closed at the end of June 1984, Drabinsky took control of 297 screens. With the Cineplex network, that gave him a total of 446 screens at 185 locations. (Famous Players had 456 screens at 201 locations at that time.)

Drabinsky's takeover of Odeon was a classic case of the goldfish swallowing the whale. Playing a major role in the

Cineplex saga were Charles and Edgar Bronfman who (through Cemp Investments Ltd. of Montreal) had become major investors in the Cineplex Corporation in November 1983. It was the leverage provided by the Bronfmans that put Drabinsky in a position to buy Odeon. With the move of Astral Bellevue Pathé Inc. (a company in which Edward and Peter Bronfman share control with the Greenberg family) into the First Choice pay-TV operation, the Odeon deal amounted to the Bronfmanization of the entertainment industry.

The theory behind the Cineplex operation was that there was money to be made by playing specialty movies and Hollywood films that had already run their course at Famous Players or Odeon. Since each Cineplex theatre offered a number of small auditoriums, any given film could survive without drawing huge crowds. A film doing a lot of business could easily be moved from a smaller to a larger house within the same complex, and vice versa. Traditionally, the longer a film played, the lower proportion of the exhibitor's revenue had to be paid to the distributor. It seemed to follow that it would be more profitable for a theatre operator to play a film for a long time in a small theatre than to play it for a short time in a large house.

That was the theory, but it became apparent that in most places there wasn't even a small audience for the foreign and art films provided by Pan-Canadian, Drabinsky's distribution company (later renamed Cineplex Odeon Films). And the two major chains were making it hard for Cineplex to get more commercial pictures even on a "move-over" basis. There were weeks when Cineplex bookers desperately scanned the obits, hoping a star or a well-known director had died, so his old films could be thrown into a theatre for a retrospective tribute.

No wonder Drabinsky and the Cineplex Corporation teetered on the brink of financial catastrophe in early 1983. Even Drabinsky's mentor, Nat Taylor, thought the game was over. But before the end of the year, the company had made a dramatic recovery, with a reported net income of $760,963. Declining interest rates helped, but there were other significant factors. Once Pan-Canadian realized the value of its film library, it made substantial sales to pay-TV and broke into the video-cassette market. But the most dramatic turnaround came with the signing of what was soon known as The Undertaking.

For decades, the showing of Hollywood movies in Canada had been governed by a family compact made up of the two big chains (Famous and Odeon) and the Canadian branches of the big Hollywood movie companies. Almost automatically Famous Players (owned by Gulf & Western, the corporate giant that owned Paramount Pictures) got the first run of all films from Paramount, Warner Brothers and MGM/UA as well as two-thirds of the product from 20th Century Fox. Odeon was content with Columbia, Universal and one-third of Fox. Small chains and independents got leftovers.

The challenge to this system began with a nationalist impulse. In the mid-1970s Canadian filmmakers lobbied for a better crack at getting their films into the theatres, and the Combines Investigation Bureau in Ottawa became involved. It became apparent early on that under existing laws the two big chains had free rein. But since the distribution companies were legally obliged to operate competitively, there was a better chance of effecting change by going after them.

Drabinsky had his own reasons for getting involved. Cineplex was having a rough time making it with specialty films, but there was no way of grabbing first-run movies unless the company could break the stranglehold Famous and Odeon had on the market. Massive research was compiled by Drabinsky's staff. Then, in June 1983, on the eve of the Restrictive Trade Practice Commission hearings, at which executives of the distribution companies were to face a public grilling, there was a breakthrough.

Rather than face an embarrassing public trial (which they might well lose), six distribution companies (Paramount, Fox, Warner Brothers, MGM/UA, Universal and Columbia) agreed to change their practices.

This was nothing less than a revolution. Under the new system, the distribution companies would invite bids on each new movie. Famous, Odeon, Cineplex and other would-be exhibitors could offer terms. The chains had to submit their offers, which included such items as the number of theatres, the number of seats, the house expenses, the number of playing weeks the movie was guaranteed to play and what percentage of revenue would be turned over to the distributor. For a while, competition was intense, with whopping offers for blockbusters. The distributors, who had been forced into this arrangement, cleaned up. But the situation was destined to change once there were two major chains again instead of three.

For three decades Odeon theatres in Canada had been owned by a British firm, the Rank Organization. But by the late 1970s Rank was ready to dump Odeon. The parent company was undergoing a massive reorganization, and the Canadian chain, though profitable, was insignificant to the international empire. And it became more trouble than it was worth once the Canadian government began taking an aggressive stance on the subjects of investing in Canadian productions and giving screen time to Canadian movies. There were a number of suitors for the chain, but it was finally sold to a dark horse. Mike Zahorchak, a Czech immigrant who had settled in St. Catharines, Ontario, and built up a small family-run theatre chain, bought the Odeon circuit for $28 million, which was regarded by some as outrageously high at the time. Odeon's screens were added to those Zahorchak controlled, and his chain became substantially larger. But Zahorchak died suddenly in 1982, and after two years, during which Odeon was run by his wife and children, the company went up for sale again.

Some people speculated that the Zahorchaks might not

want to sell to Cineplex, and at first Drabinsky was nowhere to be seen in the wooing of Odeon. David Fingold, whose family had been involved in joint-venture theatre interests with Odeon for thirty years, negotiated the purchase. Only when agreement in principle had been reached did Fingold introduce Cineplex into the transaction. The Fingolds had agreed to sell their joint-venture interests in certain Ontario and Quebec Odeon sites to Cineplex in exchange for Cineplex shares.

After the Odeon deal, Drabinsky was riding high. He fired two-thirds of the head-office staff and demanded that the rest take pay cuts. And within a few months of the takeover, Cineplex reported a 1984 profit of $12 million.

And so it came to pass that Drabinsky, backed by the Bronfmans, was in position to challenge the biggest Canadian entertainment dynasty of them all—the U.S.-controlled Famous Players. Famous had been a thorn in Drabinsky's side ever since Cineplex was created. He had some scores to settle.

The day of retribution came in May 1986, when security officers with guard dogs descended at dawn on the Imperial Six theatre on Toronto's Yonge Street strip. The theatre, one of the most profitable in the Famous Players chain, had originally been a grand old movie palace and had been split into six auditoriums in 1973. But the legal ownership of the building was very complicated; there were, in fact, two separate owners and two leases. One lease had expired, and Famous was balking at the landlady's terms for renewal. At one point in the negotiations, a spokesman for Famous even sarcastically suggested the lawyer for the other side call Garth Drabinsky. Before long, Drabinsky had signed a lease. His half of the building included part but not all of certain auditoriums. Famous was still lessee of half the theatre, but after Drabinsky's carpenters were done, Famous could reach its auditoriums only through two fire exits.

"What Cineplex did was unconscionable, irresponsible

and unfair," complained George Destounis, who has since retired as president of Famous Players.

To which Drabinsky retorted: "Obviously it was very effective. There was a competitive edge involved and a certain amount of retaliation, but I found it repugnant that this American corporation was squeezing her [the landlady]."

The Imperial remained closed for more than a year. Famous lost interest in its half, largely because business improved markedly at its other downtown cinemas at the Sheraton Centre. But Drabinsky announced plans to reopen his part of the building before the end of 1987.

Meanwhile, a funny thing happened to The Undertaking. By 1987 each of the major distributors was exclusively supplying one of the two big theatre chains, and bidding was a dead issue.

Drabinsky continued expanding his empire by building new theatres in Canada and taking over failing chains in the United States. Before his near-bankruptcy he had launched Cineplex in L.A. with the Beverly Center, atop a Beverly Hills shopping plaza.

One of Drabinsky's most openly critical L.A. competitors when the Beverly Center opened was Henry Plitt, the operator of the fourth-largest theatre circuit in the United States. According to Plitt, L.A. moviegoers were too sophisticated for the small screens at the Beverly Center, which had more auditoriums than any other theatre in the area. "They're not going to be competitive with other theatres," said Plitt. "With them it's like watching movies in your living room." But before long, the Beverly Center complex was taking in more revenue per seat than any other theatre in L.A., Plitt theatres included.

Nevertheless, when the Cineplex Corporation teetered on the brink of collapse, Drabinsky's creditors forced him to sell his half of the L.A. theatre to his U.S. partner, Detroit developer Alfred Taubman, who already owned the other half of it. However, Drabinsky had salvaged the right to buy it back, at a handsome price, and in 1983 he was able to do so.

Then in the summer of 1984, while he was still tying up the Odeon deal, Drabinsky heard that someone was quietly negotiating to buy the Plitt circuit. He acted very quickly, offered more than the other bidder, and came away with a deal that gave him 574 screens in twenty-two states for a price of $65 million (U.S.).

Suddenly Drabinsky was a major player in the United States. In January 1986, he brought in his highest-profile partner, the giant MCA. In MCA chairman Lew Wasserman and president Sidney Sheinberg, he had attracted two of Hollywood's sharpest businessmen. At first, MCA came in for a thirty-three percent interest in Cineplex (price: $75 million [U.S.]); four months later MCA increased its holdings to fifty percent for an additional $76 million.

The extent of MCA's hold on Cineplex became a serious concern. Yet the infusion of MCA cash allowed Drabinsky to gobble up even more theatres. He bought the RKO Century Warner Theaters of New York for $179 million (U.S.), the Neighborhood Theaters of Richmond, Virginia, for $21 million, and the Sterling circuit in Washington state for $45.5 million.

But Drabinsky wasn't merely buying up old theatres; he was creating new space-age movie palaces, refurbishing old theatres and acquiring a reputation as a sage. His visionary concepts for "heightening" the moviegoing experience offered salvation to an industry staggered by devastating competition from North America's favorite electronic toy. The VCR machine was threatening to put moviegoing into the past tense, like train travel.

What were Drabinsky's remedies? Spending money, big money, to redo old movie houses in high style. Building new theatres with state-of-the-art projection systems and sound systems. Plush carpets, marble floors and original art in the lobbies. Pastries and cappuccino, and real butter on the popcorn. (One touch that's sheer Garth Drabinsky:

paper bags for the popcorn, which can be crumpled when empty. They take up less space than hard round tubs — saving the company one million dollars a year.)

"There are parts of the United States where the theatres are in significant disrepair," Drabinsky preached. "We are determined to heighten the moviegoing experience to a level unheard of since the advent of TV. . . . Everything starts from the premise: you have to understand your theatres. I can understand volume of space and what you can do with it a lot better than most of my competitors. That allows me to do things like build theatres in locations nobody else would accept."

"There just aren't enough Drabinskys around," said *Fortune* magazine. But Alan Friedberg, a competitor who runs a smaller U.S. chain of theatres, wasn't a convert. "The notion that he's some latter-day messiah is misguided, self-serving and obnoxious," he remarked.

Ignoring such doubters, Drabinsky continued to spread his gospel and build ever grander temples for gatherings of the faithful. His congregation consisted of born-again moviegoers, lured back from their living rooms with improved amenities. There's no question that Drabinsky has made going to the movies a much more pleasurable experience. It should have been obvious all along that one reason people were staying home more was that they didn't particularly enjoy going to grotty, smelly dives with garbage on the floor and gum stuck to rickety old seats. It should have been obvious, but until Drabinsky came along, nobody was doing much about it. Others doubted it would pay off. Drabinsky demonstrated with one house in L.A. that a renovation could raise the weekly box-office revenue from $7,000 to $60,000. Among Drabinsky's treasures now is the Granville in Vancouver, a seven-screen Art Deco showcase where restored old splendor coexists with new construction.

In December 1985, Drabinsky opened his most impressive Toronto complex, the eight-screen Canada Square cinemas at Yonge and Eglinton, built over a bus garage. In his own immodest words, this was his "latest monument to the leisure of the eighties," what with space-age projectors, contoured seats, sculpted candy counters and, in two of the auditoriums, a Lucas THX sound system. At the opening, which was accompanied by champagne and Cajun food, Drabinsky unveiled *Move-Ease,* artist Gordon Rayner's startling thirty-five-foot mural in the lobby.

Ontario Premier David Peterson was otherwise engaged, so he sent a Liberal MPP, Tony Ruprecht, who kept referring to the man who needs no introduction as "Mr. Strabinsky." A Tory MPP had trouble sorting out his Plitts from his pits, but quipped that if Drabinsky's expansion into the U.S. continued, Ronald Reagan would soon be worrying about Canadian cultural imperialism.

To which a knowing observer might retort that if Reagan took on Drabinsky, he'd need a full nuclear arsenal. Hardly a week passes without a startling revelation from Cineplex headquarters. Item: In 1986 Drabinsky collected a salary of $946,672, in addition to $3.3 million in stock options. The company's 1986 profits were $31.6 million, up 153 percent over 1985. Item: Merrill Lynch predicts that by 1988 Cineplex revenues will exceed $659 million. Item: On June 30, 1986, Drabinsky opened the world's largest movie complex, an eighteen-screen extravaganza in Universal City, on the lot of Universal Studios. Item: Drabinsky has announced plans to spend $40 million over two years to refurbish fifty-six screens in New York, where he has already transformed a seedy Times Square barn into the glittering Cineplex Odeon Warner theatre, and reclaimed the tiny Carnegie Cinema from the vermin that sometimes outnumbered the customers in the bad old days. Item: In August 1987 Drabinsky announced plans for a huge complex including several cinemas on the site of the Lothian Mews and the adjacent University Theatre, once a Famous Players flagship, in midtown Toronto.

Anyone who doubts that Drabinsky has clout in the U.S. market should consider the case of *The Glass Menager-*

ie. Drabinsky paid $2.3 million (U.S.) for worldwide distribution rights of a new version of the Tennessee Williams play, starring Joanne Woodward and directed by Paul Newman, her husband; he then recovered the entire amount by selling video rights to MCA. Becoming visible as the godfather of such a prestigious release, and doing so without financial risk, was a shrewd manoeuvre. Drabinsky got maximum publicity for the film by getting the Newmans to appear at a press conference at the Cannes Film Festival, even though they hate such media circuses.

Newman playfully told reporters, "Garth is testifying in the Iran-Contra scandal tomorrow. Watch what happens to Cineplex stock then. You know that $8 million in a Swiss bank account? Garth's got it."

Swiss bank account or no, some scoff that, no matter how big Drabinsky's empire grows, running theatres is just being a glorified popcorn salesman. They believe his creative drive was thwarted when he had to stop producing movies, and that he yearns to return to production. Drabinsky once demurred, "There is nothing very exciting about line producing a motion picture. There's no ego gratification in that process. Now I don't have to sit on a set and watch people eat doughnuts or wait impatiently while a director has a fight with an actor."

But he has also boasted: "If I announced tomorrow I was going back into films, it would have a tremendous impact. I'm in a position to bring this industry to a new level of maturity."

That could be so much Drabinsky bombast. Or it could be the truth. Probably producing movies wouldn't be enough for him now. He'd have to run a studio. He'd have to be our Irving Thalberg, the model for F. Scott Fitzgerald's *Last Tycoon*. Canada doesn't have a major studio, but who knows? Drabinsky could create one.

Couldn't he? Garth-watchers have learned not to say there's something he can't do. But would his own studio be the elusive answer to the lingering question, "What does Garth really want?"

PART II
MIXING MEDIA

7

Heroes for the Small Screen

Can reruns of *Dallas* and *Three's Company* do what the War of 1812 failed to do—destroy Canada's will for national survival and deliver us into the hands of the Americans? That's only a slight simplification of the view of nationalists who argue that English Canada is being colonized by cable television. The Canadian Broadcasting Corporation has always had the mandate of holding the country together, of reflecting the scattered regions to one another, but CBC television, tarnished by commercials and imported American entertainment series, has never enjoyed the same respect as its higher-minded sibling rival, CBC radio. In information programming—news, current affairs and documentary films—Canadian TV has had its share of triumphs and has managed to differentiate itself from American TV. But creating Canadian drama with its own style and personality has proved more problematic. For decades TV producers, executives and bureaucrats have agonized over the need to develop a distinctively Canadian popular drama, especially on TV, but that goal has proved elusive—especially when it comes to creating popular, plausible heroes.

The Canadian psyche seems better suited to information programming than to drama, partly because of the documentary traditions established in this country by

John Grierson, founder of the National Film Board. The essence of drama is conflict, and Canadians—historically and by temperament—tend to avoid conflict. Moreover, there has never been the same willingness to commit money and resources to TV drama as there was to information.

Take the case of *The Journal*. Behind CBC's decision to launch the program in 1982 lay the notion that if it could create one prime-time hour that revealed the country to itself, the network could justify its continued existence and public support. So CBC's flagship newscast, *The National*, was moved up one hour, from 11:00 P.M. to 10:00 P.M., to be followed by an all-new, thirty-eight-minute, five-nights-a-week magazine program.

In a way, this was an attempt to revive CBC's great days of current affairs programming. In the 1950s, when Canadian viewers had fewer choices on the dial, CBC had a huge audience. Current affairs programs were the public network's greatest achievement between 1952, when the network went on the air, and 1966, when the abrasive *This Hour Has Seven Days* (a precursor of *60 Minutes*) was killed off by CBC management.

The payoff on CBC's gamble on *The Journal* was startling. The program was a huge hit, winning well over twenty percent of the viewers in a highly fragmented, competitive market. During the course of any week, one-third of all English-speaking adult Canadians watch the program at least once. Going head-to-head with popular entertainment shows, the package doubled CBC's audience in the crucial ten-to-eleven P.M. time slot, creating a formidable journalistic institution and giving CBC a strong new identity and sense of purpose just when it was most desperately needed.

Mark Starowicz, *The Journal*'s brusque, hard-driving executive producer, talked jokingly of his mission to "stop the Americans at the border." And the success of his program was the first hopeful sign in more than a decade that CBC had a fighting chance to resist American domination of its airwaves.

But when it came to drama, there was no development as revolutionary (or as costly) as *The Journal*. At best, there were only small successes in a generally barren landscape. Everybody likes to look back fondly on the golden age of TV drama, but how the public reacted at the time was another matter. In the 1950s, following a typical highbrow drama on the CBC's *Festival* series, outraged complainers would jam the network's switchboards; in many parts of the country, they didn't have the option of switching to another channel.

The golden age was long gone by the time the CBC recruited John Hirsch to take over its TV drama department in 1974, and so was most of the audience. Indeed, drama had reached such a low ebb that Hirsch—an internationally respected stage director who had arrived in Winnipeg after World War II as a teenaged refugee speaking no English—was regarded as a miracle doctor. But after a few months in the job, Hirsch complained in interviews: "We are dealing with antiquated equipment, studios that leak and money that is not enough to do a good series of Mickey Mouse cartoons. Out of this we are supposed to create a national drama? It's ridiculous."

Everyone was exhausted by the arguing by the time Hirsch left in 1978, but he had managed to cook up Canada's only really successful half-hour situation comedy series—*King of Kensington*.

The odds against such a success were enormous, because English Canada had little tradition of popular culture. Decades earlier it seemed to have been settled that Canadians accepted the responsibility of creating some sort of official culture, sanctioned by schoolteachers and churned out by state institutions like the CBC and the NFB; but for their popular entertainment, Canadians lived psychologically across the border, listening to Jack Benny and Fred Allen on the radio, and adopting the fantasy world of Hollywood as their own. The list of Canadian TV shows that had become popular was very short: *Hockey Night in Canada, Wayne and Shuster, The Plouffe Family* and *Front Page Challenge*.

Some people felt the CBC should stick to serious drama and continue to import mass entertainment from Hollywood, where they knew how to do it. Hirsch knew that situation comedy came out of burlesque and vaudeville—traditions Canada didn't have—and that successful American sitcoms tended to be made by machines such as the Norman Lear machine or the Mary Tyler Moore machine. Hirsch invited his old friend Perry Rosemond—a former Winnipegger who had become extremely successful producing TV variety shows in Hollywood—to create such a machine for CBC. Rosemond was more interested in creating a specific series.

When Hirsch and Rosemond got together, however, inevitably the talk turned to stories about Winnipeg's North End. *King of Kensington* grew out of their mutual love for what Rosemond remembered as "an ethnic zoo with horse sense, humor and profundity." What made it great, in his mind, was the sense of brilliant insight coming from unexpected places; the guys at the card tables upstairs over the bakery were a lot smarter about politics than people in government.

Hirsch and Rosemond were afraid that if the show was set in Winnipeg, someone would insist on producing it in Winnipeg, and they felt it would work better coming out of Toronto.

Rosemond wanted a show that wasn't like American shows; a show Canadians could watch "because it was ours." American comedy often depended on hostility, but this didn't seem to be part of the Canadian character. They wanted a good-hearted hero—and came up with Larry King—who was always helping people. And it was essential to emphasize the mixture of ethnic identities rather than to invent an American-style melting pot. At first the concept revolved around a club; the family was secondary. Later the balance shifted, and Larry King's wife and mother became more important than the club. Larry King himself was a liberal, although there's not much doubt that in North Winnipeg he would have been a Marxist. The Jewishness of the show wasn't disguised—former Winnipegger Helene Winston played Larry's mother—but the hero also had a pert gentile wife—Fiona Reid.

Al Waxman, an old friend of Rosemond, was an actor who had just about settled on a career as a director when the role of Larry King came along. He had the right common-man, big-hearted slob kind of looks for the part, and he was very persuasive as a big klutzy guy with the emotions of a child, whose face registers every perception with the emphasis of a cartoon. Waxman touched a popular nerve; his Larry King was the character you remembered from your old neighborhood, and the show seemed to take place in some collective memory-fantasy district rather than any actual neighborhood. That's why *King of Kensington* became so popular, running for five years until Waxman decided to quit in 1980. It was a sign of CBC's inertia that there was only a halfhearted attempt to develop another series for Waxman, and Waxman wound up in L.A. playing Lieutenant Bert Samuels, boss of TV's favorite female detectives, in the long-running hit CBS series *Cagney and Lacey.*

After bureaucrat John Kennedy replaced Hirsch, the CBC seemed to give up on drama. Oh, we still had *The Beachcombers,* a long-running series that could pass for American anywhere in the world, and earned the CBC brownie points for continuing to produce a network program in Vancouver. *For the Record* stumbled on, long past the point of usefulness, like a onetime fiery radical who had turned into a wheezing old bore, latching on to victims at cocktail parties to expound on the ills of society. Research showed that the CBC audience—slightly older, better-educated and more rural than the general TV audience—wanted more shows suitable for family viewing. But there was little sense that CBC drama was on the road to somewhere, and there was hardly a trace of the talented actors, directors and writers who from time to time were creating sparks in Canadian movies and theatre.

One lively exception was *Empire, Inc.*, a six-part miniseries that aired in the spring of 1983. *Empire* was produced and conceived by Mark Blandford, a bilingual ex-newspaperman from CBC's Montreal studios who had his own unit and had also masterminded the *Duplessis* series for CBC's French network. The stylish trashiness of *Empire* came as a delicious surprise. Who would ever have dreamed that CBC's TV drama department, that staid bastion of bland decorum, boring good taste and noble intentions, had the juice in it to turn out a slick, pulpy series that could beat the American networks at their own favorite game?

Empire was a luridly entertaining potboiler, put together with lip-smacking glee. A sensationally energetic performance by veteran actor Kenneth Welsh gave Sir James Munroe, WASP titan of the Montreal establishment, the irresistible drive of an older, goyish Duddy Kravitz. And his entertaining wickedness set the tone for the whole show.

Empire broke the spell and saved the audience, for a brief period, from deadly high-mindedness, the chronic disease plaguing CBC. Yet afterward we had to settle back into the cozy mediocrities of *Home Fires* and *I Married the Klondike*.

One of the few bright spots of the mid-1980s was the surprise success of *Seeing Things*, an offbeat series with Louis Del Grande—a manic American who'd lived in Toronto for years and had previously been a writer and an actor in the theatre as well as a producer and writer on *King of Kensington*—as clairvoyant newspaper reporter Louie Ciccone. His method of solving mysteries was simple: he had visions. The show was seen in more than thirty countries, including Spain, Cyprus and Ecuador. The *Village Voice* praised it as "the closest TV has gotten to Woody Allen in his salad days." The Cubans, who see themselves as being mechanically inept, loved Louis for being even more klutzy than they were. And El Al, the Israeli airline, bought one episode only—the one featuring a rabbi. After six years and forty-three one-hour episodes, *Seeing Things* finally signed off for good in April 1987.

Other attempts to create a regular series with both Canadian content and genuine popularity have been less successful. *He Shoots, He Scores,* a French-network series about hockey players dubbed into English and retitled, had a patchwork quality. *Street Legal,* about a group of hip Toronto lawyers, sounded promising, but its only real function was to make its American counterpart, *L.A. Law,* look good.

In December 1986, CBC showed a made-for-TV movie, *9B,* with so much energy and buoyancy that it should have been parlayed into a series. Robert Wisden, an unknown actor from Edmonton, brought great style to the role of Bob Dawson, a bewildered British immigrant teacher coping with a high-school class full of mouthy troublemakers in the wilds of northern British Columbia. Based on a true story by Vancouver journalist Don Hunter, the film, produced and directed by James Swan from a script by Graeme Woods, had an outback charm.

Wisden's performance invited comparison with Jon Voight's memorable work in the neglected 1974 movie *Conrack.* Wisden played Dawson as a reckless man who needs to make a connection with his students in order to feel alive. (The film fudges on the subject of its hero's sex life, which one senses might not be as tame as the pieties of CBC family drama require.) Wisden's spark made it clear to the audience how one teacher can make a huge difference in the lives of certain kids. Dawson has trouble getting through to the kids until he tries writing a play for them to perform in competition. But the qualities that make the play appealing to the kids get Dawson into trouble with the educational establishment. In another country, *9B* would have been developed into a series; this being Canada, nothing happened.

Oddly enough, while CBC's TV-drama producers had trouble creating popular characters with a Canadian I.D., such figures did occasionally emerge in documentary films about real subjects. One of the most captivating was Harry Rasky's profile of Teresa Stratas, the poor little Greek girl who rose from the slums of Toronto to sing triumphantly on the stage of the Metropolitan Opera. Her father had traveled from a remote village in Crete to Toronto wearing his dead brother's boots; her mother saved money by making the children's clothes from flour sacks. This would have been great material for a trashy miniseries like *Queenie*, based on Michael Korda's thinly fictionalized account of his aunt, Merle Oberon. But somehow in Canada a fictionalized TV series about Teresa Stratas didn't quite seem right; a documentary film was so much more . . . Canadian.

Stratas is almost as famous for her tempestuous personality, her fierce will, her need for solitude and her penchant for last-minute cancellations as she is for her electrifying talent, but Rasky, a relentless pursuer of the great and famous, doesn't take no for an answer. This, after all, was the man who took a taxi to Marc Chagall's home in the south of France and arrived unannounced to film a major documentary feature about Chagall's life and art. When that didn't work, Rasky got the mayor of Jerusalem to pressure Mme Chagall, and the result was the film *The Colors of Love*.

When Stratas declined on grounds of modesty and privacy, Rasky got her to read his book, *Nobody Swings on Sunday*, in which she learned that he was an immigrant boy who used to deliver freshly killed chickens to his parents' customers. Once she started talking about their shared experience, he told her this wouldn't really be a film about her, it would be a film about immigrants.

Stratasphere, which was first shown on CBC early in 1983, is only incidentally about immigrants. What holds it together is the mesmerizing personality of Stratas. In the film's best sequence, she thrusts the score of Alban Berg's opera, *Lulu,* at the audience and describes, in winningly mock-solemn terms, her battles with it. "I've raped the score, I've loved it, I've killed it, we've had our ultimate battle, and it's all in my head now."

The New Yorker may have been exaggerating slightly when it described her Toronto childhood as Dickensian, but she was born over a Chinese laundry, and she got to see her first opera when a drunk customer who ate a meal at her parents' restaurant left opera tickets in lieu of money.

Rasky often wins international awards, but his choice of subjects — Michelangelo, Westminster Abbey, Anne Frank, Arthur Miller — suggests he's hell-bent on achieving greatness by association. Yet, despite one's misgivings, *Stratasphere* was captivating. When Stratas walks across the plaza at Lincoln Center where Anne Bancroft and Shirley MacLaine tore each other's hair out in *The Turning Point,* it's a reminder that this film is more dramatically persuasive than any Hollywood melodrama could be. The comedy offsets the pathos of the world's reigning opera star who still worries that the world might discover she's bluffing.

The only serious rival to Stratas for the title of most compelling real-life subject of a CBC documentary is Marilyn St. Pierre, a convicted forger who spent most of her life in jail. In John Kastner's film *Prison Mother, Prison Daughter,* Marilyn exudes the elusive, magnetic quality that pulls an audience in. She's a pudgy, spirited fighter who, with her short-cropped, reddish-brown hair and her big, earnest eyes and her croaking Tallulah Bankhead voice, has the charisma of an old Hollywood heroine. She wins the audience over by making us feel she's not holding anything back, that she's risking everything she's got. Marilyn has such a desperate edge she seems naked and vulnerable, and she's so spectacularly effective at dramatizing her own anguish she comes close to parody.

Kastner has won three Emmy awards, but he has never made a film as upsetting as this—the fourth and last of his prison films. The prison daughter of the title is Darlene Baldwin, a young dental assistant who has drawn an absurdly harsh sentence (seven years) for "conspiracy to import" a few pounds of hash oil. Her devastated family can't accept what has happened; to them, she's an innocent who never smoked, drank or even got a parking ticket. But Kastner's original intention of tracking Darlene in jail was curtailed by a guard who decided she would draw too much heat from other inmates if she were followed around by a film crew. Kastner used some of Darlene's story in fictionalized form in the drama *Turning to Stone*, written by Judith Thompson and directed by Eric Till, but it didn't have nearly as much impact as the story of Marilyn St. Pierre, as told in the documentary.

As the film opens, Marilyn has been sent off to jail just after giving birth to her fourth child. The baby is in the care of her common-law husband, an unemployed welder named Al Trudell, and Marilyn is so desperate to be reunited with her son that when Al says he's ready to give the child up to the Children's Aid Society, she attempts suicide. When she goes before the parole board, the deck is stacked against her: at age twenty-nine she has a record of a hundred petty offenses, and the officials have heard her excuses and promises before.

Because there is no halfway house in Windsor, the parole board releases Marilyn into Al's custody. Al turns out to be unstable, alcoholic, abusive. But when Marilyn and the baby move out, she violates the terms of parole; and her parole officer, who comes across as relentlessly unempathic, seems blinded to the facts about Al and keeps blaming Marilyn. When the Children's Aid Society takes the baby, and a court has the boy put up for adoption, Marilyn, having lost everything she cared about, reverts to her old self-destructive ways.

What is most shocking about the film is that viewers can't help siding with Marilyn, even when she lies.

Not only did Marilyn lose her parole; she was later convicted of another petty crime and sentenced again. Marilyn was a model prisoner on the verge of gaining her freedom in September 1985, when she came to the set of *Turning to Stone* to seek out Kastner. He couldn't see her that day but arranged to visit her in jail the following week. But by then she had bolted. Officially, Marilyn left on a shopping pass and failed to come back.

She was on the lam until January 11, 1987, the night *Prison Mother, Prison Daughter* was shown on CBC television. That night she crossed the border from Detroit to Windsor to watch the film with her family — and was picked up by police. Before long she was in the Vanier Centre, with a jail term of several months to serve. But by this time she had also become the unlikeliest star in the history of CBC television. Maybe when she finally gets out of jail, CBC could dream up a weekly series for Marilyn. She has so much more vitality and personality than most of the wholesome, virtuous characters offered up to the Canadian TV audience.

The same could not be said for the version of Terry Fox's life concocted for TV. The one-legged kid who ran more than five thousand kilometres and raised $24 million for cancer research was without question a member of that most endangered species, Canadian heroes; his death made him a legend. His story might have become the subject of an intriguing film, perhaps a documentary about the media circus touched off by Fox's Marathon of Hope (not even his death could end it), but instead it was turned into *The Terry Fox Story*, a 1983 made-for-TV movie which, after a brief theatrical release, found a large and receptive audience on Home Box Office, the giant U.S. pay/cable channel.

Ralph Thomas, the director of this film, had created the *For the Record* series for CBC drama. His first movie after leaving CBC, *Ticket to Heaven*, had a docudrama format, but the explosive subject released something exciting in Thomas. On the other hand, *The Terry Fox Story* was like a bigger, more expensive *For the Record*, with that same air of deadening rectitude. In the title role, Eric Fryer is likable and willing, but he's no actor, and it's obvious his main qualification is that he's a one-legged athlete (eliminating the need for a double or trick photography).

The filmmakers must have been so determined to make Fox into the most saintly all-Canadian boy who ever lived that they weren't going to risk offending anybody. According to a book about Fox by Toronto *Star* reporter Leslie Scrivener, when Terry got the bad news from a doctor — that the pain in his knee was caused by a malignant tumor, that his leg would be amputated, that his chances of surviving were only slightly better than fifty-fifty — he said, "Oh, fuck, I'm not ready to leave this world." At that moment, in Scrivener's account, Rolly Fox, Terry's father, went into shock. It wasn't the terrible news that startled him; it was Terry's language.

This might be the beginning of an interesting family drama, but in the film, Thomas and the script back away from it. The Terry on the screen says angrily to the doctor, "What the hell am I supposed to do without my leg?" And Terry's father natters, "Don't swear, Terry."

Terry Fox couldn't have better served the purposes of the Toronto *Star* if its editors had invented him. His story, with its daily guarantee of fresh incidents and locales, was an ideal circulation booster. Here was the ultimate human-interest story, combining such elements as youthful ideals, a doomed hero, a freakish athletic contest and spectacular misfortune.

The decision of the country's largest-circulation newspaper to assign a reporter to follow Fox was a turning point which the movie alludes to without examining its implications. Thanks to the *Star*, his reception in Toronto was a spectacle that would have made Cecil B. DeMille blush.

Fox may not have realized it at first, but the *Star*'s interest in him canceled his right to a private life. In her book, Scrivener recalls how Terry tried out on her the idea of having a girl join his party to alleviate his loneliness. Maybe he understood that she had him in the position the Hearst press had Hollywood in during the era when an actor's career could be destroyed if his personal life didn't meet the moral standards of Louella Parsons.

The *Star* couldn't have its front-page saint tainted by the hint of sex. Scrivener, by her own account, advised Terry it wouldn't be a good idea. In the film, Terry is so clean-cut that when he gets involved with a woman, she is not only a therapist but a born-again Christian. And he tells her the marathon comes first; he can't be distracted by any involvement with her.

When it comes to the creation of dramatic Canadian heroes, no case is more bizarre or troubling than the one raised by *Charlie Grant's War*, a made-for-TV movie shown on CBC in January 1985. If the movie had been labeled fiction, it could be considered a huge success. But the filmmakers gave viewers the distinct impression that they were dealing with documented facts — which is where the messy questions crept in.

Charlie Grant, sometimes called the Canadian Raoul Wallenberg, was a Scottish Presbyterian from Toronto who became a successful businessman in the 1930s and wound up in Hitler's camps — which he survived. Returning to Canada after the war, Grant became a familiar figure who took up the cause of bringing refugee orphans to this country, and delivered a series of speeches and radio broadcasts denouncing racial prejudice.

Charlie Grant's War starts with the premise that Grant

risked his life getting hundreds of Jews out of Austria on fake passports. In the wake of *None Is Too Many*, the book by Irving Abella and Harold Troper concerning Canada's refusal to provide a haven for more than a handful of the doomed Jews caught in Hitler's net, it's understandable why Canadians would want desperately to believe in the myth of the righteous gentile. But the facts about the real Charlie Grant remain an enigma.

As a young man Grant had an urge to see the world. He wound up working for a diamond-brokerage firm owned by a Jew, Paul Trefius, and spent his time traveling around the capitals of Europe, buying and selling precious gems. When Trefius died, he left the business to his star salesman. Grant was a bit of a bon vivant, and at the peak of the Depression he was living high — staying at the finest hotels on both sides of the Atlantic, eating at the best restaurants, having affairs with beautiful women, hobnobbing with aristocrats and celebrities.

Anna Sandor's script was always problematic but Martin Lavut, who directed *Charlie Grant's War*, camouflaged its weaknesses and did a masterful job of creating subtext. And in the title role, R.H. Thomson managed to make Grant into a character rather than a mouthpiece for noble ideals. His performance is one of the high points of his impressive career. Thomson never makes the mistake of overplaying. He tones down scenes that could have been phony, and he keeps building small human details and levels of ambiguity within the character.

Thomson is less imposing than the real Charlie Grant, who weighed more than 200 pounds in his prime (though he weighed only 100 pounds by the end of his ordeal), but he's good at projecting quiet inner strength. Thomson's Charlie isn't a zealot or a crusader, and he isn't bucking for sainthood; he's a daring adventurer who learns fast.

Thomson gets small details right. He knows how to handle diamonds. There are hints of a rogue and a con-man-hustler in his characterization. This offsets the excessive saintliness and martyrdom built into the script, which takes Grant through a seven-year nightmare of jails, concentration camps and prisoner-of-war camps. According to the film, Charlie helps Jews get phony passports, and the Nazis get even by having him arrested on trumped-up currency charges.

For those who'd read *None Is Too Many*, one of the more intriguing aspects of the film was its treatment of what was going on in Canada. The film invents meetings between Charlie's mother (Marigold Charlesworth) and the two people who were most responsible for keeping Jews out of Canada — the notorious Frederick Charles Blair, director of the Immigration Branch, and Prime Minister William Lyon Mackenzie King. The latter is played by that exuberant actor Larry Reynolds, who had such a good time impersonating King in the stage play *Rexy* a few years earlier. This time the P.M. is a sweet little man sipping tea with Mrs. Grant while telling her that she should be proud of having such an idealistic son, though he regards the idea of letting a lot of Jews into Canada as politically impossible. At the end of the film, Charlie returns to Canada a hero — and refuses to shake the hand of a politician who did nothing to help.

The film stirred up a controversy that raged for months. According to Irving Abella, material from *None Is Too Many* was grafted to Charlie Grant's story without credit. In reality, Grant had no dealings with King or Blair, and the episode about his mother's visit to Ottawa was pure fiction. And there was an ironic twist: Abella and Troper had considered using Grant's story in their book, but after combing archives in London, Paris, Geneva, Vienna and Jerusalem, they failed to find any corroborating evidence to prove Grant obtained any phony passports or saved the lives of any Jews. In order for Grant to find a place of honor among other certified "righteous gentiles" at Yad

Vashem, the Jerusalem memorial to Holocaust victims, some survivors who were saved by Grant would have had to step forward and provide testimonials.

As TV drama, *Charlie Grant's War* was strong stuff. But Sandor and producer Bill Gough (her husband) got caught in the risky business of mixing fiction and documentary. So much of their film was fictionalized that sorting out the facts from the dramatic inventions became a perilous business. And their Charlie Grant—acting out Lester Pearson's old dream of Canada's destiny as the world's conscience and guardian angel—became the most elusive and puzzling figure in the country's odd new parlor game of concocting heroes to meet the needs of its collective psyche.

8

The Americans Are Coming, The Americans Are Coming

Jack Valenti is a short, wiry, bustling man with the Texas drawl and the Great Society zeal of Lyndon Baines Johnson (his former boss) and the cool Boston mannerisms of John F. Kennedy. For a few years he had been special assistant to the president of the United States, and he retained excellent connections in Washington. But his job for more than two decades has been president of the Motion Picture Association of America in which capacity he looks after the interests of the Hollywood establishment. In his mid-sixties he had become accustomed to doing the talking and to being listened to, and he spouted a mixture of Great American Way homilies and Bartlett's wisdom of the ages. His rhetorical guns were aimed squarely at Ottawa and at those dangerous Canadian nationalists who thought they could skim off some of the one billion dollars Canadians spend annually at the movies — cream that Hollywood had traditionally taken out of Canada without putting back so much as a glass of two-percent.

Historically, every time Canadians had tried to break Hollywood's stranglehold on the Canadian box office, pressure was brought to bear, and the Canadians backed off. And the Hollywood studios had gone blithely on, behaving as if Canada were part of their domestic territory.

In the fall of 1985 Marcel Masse, then minister of communications, received a report from a task force he had commissioned. The task force recommended strengthening Canadian distributors. In February 1987, Flora MacDonald, Masse's successor as communications minister, made a startling announcement. She was going to introduce legislation to establish a licensing system (already approved by the federal cabinet) for distribution of movies. The new system would limit foreign companies —such as Columbia Pictures, Universal, Warner Brothers and Paramount—to distribute in Canada only movies that they had produced, financed, or for which they held worldwide distribution rights. Other movies, produced and financed independently, would have to be handled by a Canadian distribution company. That would mean certain blockbuster movies, such as *Crocodile Dundee, Platoon* and *Gandhi,* would no longer be handled in Canada by their U.S. distributor. Instead, they would be handled by Canadian distribution companies, which would be expected to invest a good chunk of the profits in Canadian movies. If these rules had applied in 1986, forty-nine films handled by U.S. companies would have been distributed by Canadian companies with profits of about $2.4 million.

MacDonald's announcement got a standing ovation from an audience of Canadian film-industry insiders, but she was unable to introduce legislation within a few weeks, as she promised. Two months later she found herself facing a showdown with Valenti, who had forced a meeting by getting President Reagan to raise the issue with Prime Minister Mulroney during an official visit to Ottawa.

Valenti may not have realized it, but by trying to twist Ottawa's arm to protect his clients, the Hollywood studios, he was turning himself into the stereotype so dear to the hearts of Canadian cultural nationalists — the vulgar, pushy American who behaves as if he has every right to boss Canadians around. Indeed, the intrusive American has become one of the few unifying themes in Canadian culture, especially films.

Ticket to Heaven, the rousing 1981 movie directed by Ralph Thomas, is a parable in the form of a thriller, and it encapsulates the ultimate Canadian ambivalence about Americans. Only a few months earlier the hero-victim of the movie, David (played by Nick Mancuso), had been a healthy young man living a good life in Toronto with his girlfriend. Now, after a few months in northern California with a God-happy cult, he has undergone an amazing transformation. His stare is vacant, his clothes spartan, and he spends his time, dismayingly, selling flowers to passersby and telling them the lie that the money goes to a drug rehabilitation program. *Ticket to Heaven,* in other words, is about a Canadian who takes up residence in the United States and immediately gets turned into a zombie. The happy ending occurs when David is rescued by Canadian friends — spearheaded by Saul Rubinek as a high-strung stand-up comic — and brought home after being reverse-brainwashed by a deprogrammer (R.H. Thomson).

Ticket to Heaven was loosely based on Josh Freed's book *Moon Webs,* which started as a series of articles for the Montreal *Star,* about Freed's friend Benji, who was sucked into a group run by the Unification Church while visiting California. Renouncing everything from sex to alcohol, working twenty-two hours a day and using brainwashing techniques perfected in the Korean war, the Moonies, as they became known, claimed as many as three million converts. And though Thomas came to it from *For the Record,* the movie escaped the stigma of that series, with its earnest approach to social problems. Maybe that's because it was ignited by the heat of a terrific subject: religious cults and their horrifying knack of turning mixed-up middle-class kids into slogan-chanting fanatics.

One could argue that it's entirely incidental that David is from Canada and the cult is in the United States. In fact, a couple of years after completing this movie, the husband-and-wife team of producer Vivienne Leebosh and director Ralph Thomas left Toronto and moved to Los Angeles, without being either brainwashed or kidnapped. Still, the pop myth of the innocent Canadian who becomes a zombie under the spell of dangerous American extremists expresses the paranoia that Canadians have always felt living next to a not-always-so-friendly giant. They look normal, they sound friendly, and there's something engaging about them — but Watch Out.

The fable of the seductive and disruptive American intruder who roars across the border to dazzle, charm and intimidate his northern neighbors gets played out in original Canadian screen tales such as *My American Cousin*, a charming, female, coming-of-age memoir written and directed by Sandy Wilson, and *Canada's Sweetheart: the Saga of Hal C. Banks*, a muckraking case study — part documentary and part drama — directed and narrated by the sardonic and insightful Donald Brittain.

My American Cousin is a low-budget feature made mainly for CBC television that became a surprise hit in movie theatres when it was released in 1985. The audience was captivated by the comedy inherent in Canadian ambivalence toward Americans. The film is set in the Okanagan Valley in 1959. To Sandy, the twelve-year-old heroine, when her cousin Butch, a cool, uninhibited sixteen-year-old hunk, zaps in from California in a splashy red Cadillac convertible "borrowed" from his mother, it's as if Tab Hunter had walked off the screen and into the lives of Sandy and her friends.

Sandy, wonderfully played by Alberta schoolgirl Margaret Langrick, is bursting to break away from the well-ordered dullness of life in Penticton, where rock and roll is played only on Saturdays, and life proceeds carefully and without abandon under the watchful eyes of her parents.

"Nothing ever happens," Sandy confides to her diary. We are back in the age of innocence, before cable TV. And so when her cool cousin arrives at her door he seems like an answer to her prayer. He's strutting proof that there are better things to do than stay in your room listening to civilized recordings of light classics such as "Some Enchanted Evening."

Butch, smoothly and entertainingly played by John Wildman, is a spiffy, ducktailed dreamboat in tight jeans —just what Sandy has been waiting for. He's the agent of her deliverance from dull respectability. The movie reaches a giggly plateau when Butch takes Sandy and her friends on a joyride, winds up on the lam from a police car and takes a dip in the lake. The pubescent flirtatiousness is engaging, and the excitement over such forbidden pleasures as speeding and listening to "Sh-Boom (Life Could Be a Dream)" is infectious.

Taking off from an incident she remembers (her real cousin died behind the wheel of his flashy car a few years later), Wilson managed to do something Canadian moviemakers rarely do: she was true to her own experience. And the producer, Peter O'Brian, was willing to do what Canadian producers rarely do: he relied on his instincts and took a chance on fresh talent.

Richard Leiterman's cinematography turned the pastel-pastoral prettiness of the locations into a perfect comic foil for the yearnings of kids who fail to appreciate it because they're impatient to experience the road to hell. And the movie's good humor put the audience in such a benign mood that even if *My American Cousin* failed to delve deeply enough into the psyche of the society and the characters it depicted, people were willing to settle for the pleasures it did offer.

In its own low-key, winning way, *My American Cousin* captures the way Canadians feel at once inferior to Americans and superior to them. Canadians feel so dull and square by comparison; yet Americans are, after all, so vulgar and disruptive. Cousin Butch represents the forbidden pleasures that Sandy and her friends, with their protected Canadian upbringing, have been cut off from. That's why they swoon over him, and those in the audience who remember this period may also swoon.

But Butch's parents, who arrive to take their rebel son back to the other side of the border, are cartoons of American vulgarity. The tone isn't mean-spirited—we don't really dislike them—but we feel better knowing the whole family is returning to the United States.

Canada's Sweetheart—a TV film coproduced by the National Film Board and shown on CBC television in the fall of 1985—explores a less charming side of the American intrusion in Canada. Like *My American Cousin*, this, too, is a period piece about American-Canadian relations a quarter-century ago, and also concerns a boisterous American who is fond of Cadillacs.

Here again an American intruder is welcomed to Canada for what turns out to be an upsetting visit (lasting in this case for thirteen years). Here again there's a sense of relief when the rowdy visitor returns to the U.S.A. That's where the similarities end. *Canada's Sweetheart* isn't reassuring, because the visitor, the late Hal. C. Banks, was clearly an appalling thug. It's as if the Lee J. Cobb villain from the movie *On the Waterfront* had taken over Canada.

Hal Banks was a known criminal who had already served four years in San Quentin and had been charged with kicking a man to death in San Diego before he was given carte blanche to clean the Communists out of Canada's shipping trade. How he reigned over Canadian waterways for thirteen years as head of the Seafarers' International Union (SIU)—thanks to the enthusiastic support of respectable Canadian politicians, other union leaders and businessmen—makes for a dismaying, fascinating, complicated story.

Don Brittain tells it with masterly authority, mixing drama with documentary footage more smoothly than anybody else. The film is held together by quiet, deadpan outrage and irony—a specialty of Brittain's, who is the off-screen narrator as well as the writer-director.

The instigator of the project was Richard Neilsen, a producer, writer and journalist who once worked for a railway union embattled with Banks, and who helped gather the evidence for the Norris Commission, whose findings toppled Banks. In the first half of *Canada's Sweetheart,* Brittain uses black-and-white for the documentary interview sequences, which gives them the air of a hard-boiled Hollywood film noir of the late 1940s. Then he switches back to color when the Norris Commission (appointed by the Diefenbaker government) breaks the case open.

The casting of baby-faced hulk Maury Chaykin as Hal Banks gave the film a chilling, compelling power. Chaykin is a bit reminiscent of Broderick Crawford, especially in his *Born Yesterday* role. And there's a hint of the performance Robert De Niro gave as Jake La Motta in *Raging Bull.* But Chaykin—an American whose mother came from Winnipeg—is also an original. And in this role he was spellbinding. (Chaykin has worked extensively in Canada and gained landed-immigrant status—like Banks.)

Chaykin's Banks had the moves and nuances of a goon, but there was a touch of buffonish comedy in his thick, curled lips and his defiant stare. And he had perfect timing, moving his hulking frame with alarming precision.

Chaykin found a core of charm and playfulness in Banks, but he never overdid it. There was an element of unpredictability that created an exciting sense of mayhem. This was not a character you'd ever want to cross.

Brittain jokingly described Chaykin as "so scary I'm afraid to be in the same room with him." The transformation was so complete that while you watch the film there are moments when you forget Chaykin isn't the real Hal C. Banks.

The story of "Brother" Hal Banks, as he was known to his fellow SIU thugs, says something about Canada in the 1950s and 1960s that is not very pleasant; and the period is not so distanced as to be without the power to shock. *Canada's Sweetheart* raises a lot of messy, nasty questions. Perhaps the most disturbing sequence in the film is an interview with Jack Pickersgill, a member of the St. Laurent cabinet, who speaks carefully about the help the Liberals gave Banks to cut through red tape.

When Banks came to Canada in 1949, it was because the St. Laurent government was determined to break the Communist-controlled Canadian Seamen's Union, which was threatening worldwide disruptions to block Marshall Plan aid. So Banks was allowed to do his dirty deeds: blacklisting, intimidating, bribing, blackmailing and attempting to arrange to have dissenters bumped off or beaten to a pulp.

But why, exactly, was Banks allowed to preside as head of the SIU for more than a decade after the Communist threat was over? Why did a cabinet minister smooth the way for an ex-con to gain landed-immigrant status in Canada? Why did it take so long before his activities were censured? Why, when he jumped bail to escape going to prison, was his extradition quashed on orders from Dean Rusk?

The story of Hal Banks was, among other things, a black comedy out of Dostoyevski. Banks arranged sexual escapades for his influential friends at his Montreal apartment (which featured a two-way mirror), then threatened to embarrass them with photographs if they didn't go along with him. He was not only kept in power but actually given the sort of honors reserved for the most distinguished members of the elite: he led delegations to Geneva, and gave a speech to the Law Society of McGill University.

He loved the attention when *Maclean's* called him "bombastic and charismatic." He boasted in a letter to a girlfriend in the United States: "Nothing is impossible. I might even be elected prime minister." In a memorable tantrum scene, he complained, "What's the matter with your fucking country? You invite me up here to do your dirty work and clear out the Commies. Then you crap all over me."

Banks saw himself like the title character in *My American Cousin*, and like that rebellious teenager, he returned to California, operating a water-taxi business in San Francisco until his death at age seventy-six in September 1985, just a month before the TV airing of the film. He was gone but not forgotten. Maybe he didn't get to be prime minister, but thanks to Donald Brittain he did get to be a national TV icon — the American cousin Canadians wished they could disown. It would be nice to be able to pretend he remained in this country beating up people for thirteen years for some reason other than the obvious one — that Canadians were willing to put up with it.

If there were a contemporary equivalent of Hal Banks, he'd probably be more interested in the film business than the waterfront. Ever since Hollywood producers discovered they could make their films more cheaply in Canada and with great technical support, Canada has become Hollywood's latest and biggest back lot. Usually Canadians are only too glad to work with visiting Americans. But occasionally there's an incident that casts the Canadian support staff in the role of innocent victims and the visiting American hotshot in the role of carpetbagging troublemaker.

Like cousin Butch in *My American Cousin*, Billy Jack —aka Tom Laughlin, the man who created the Billy Jack character and played him in several American movies —was a self-dramatizing visitor from south of the border who made life more dramatic for a while and then vanished in a puff of smoke.

The saga began with a memorable press conference in Los Angeles in the fall of 1985. Announcing the start of production of *The Return of Billy Jack*, to be filmed mostly around Toronto, Laughlin made his statement from a lectern built over thirteen large Lucite cylinders, each bursting with one million dollars in cash (or so he said) and protected by armed, uniformed guards.

Billy Jack, the character, is a romantic who wants to protect the weak, punish the bad guys and go out in a blaze of glory. But he has this pacifist girlfriend named Jean (played by Laughlin's wife, Delores Taylor), who looks like Eva Marie Saint and preaches like Joan Baez, and is big on the power of love and nonviolent resistance. *Billy Jack* became a show-biz legend in 1971, when Laughlin took control of the movie away from Warner Brothers, which had given it a halfhearted release, and turned it into a huge hit. This was in the heyday of the counterculture, and *Billy Jack* was a psychodrama about a freedom school full of dispossessed misfits fighting bigotry. The ads explained: "You've got due process, Mother's Day, supermarkets, air-conditioning, the FBI, medicare, AT&T, a two-car garage, Congress, country clubs, state troopers, the Constitution, color TV and democracy. They've got Billy Jack."

But *The Trial of Billy Jack* (1974) lacked the freshness of the original, and *Billy Jack Goes to Washington* (1977) didn't even get a national release. Still, Laughlin pressed on, taking on the Hollywood establishment the way Billy Jack took on the bad guys. With *The Return of Billy Jack*, he had a new cause—the crusade for lost children, who, he claimed, were being snatched off the streets of the United States at the rate of 500,000 a year.

Shooting began in New York in December and moved to Toronto just before New Year's 1986. In mid-January, Laughlin invited the press to watch a scene being shot at a warehouse used to store floats and creatures from the annual Santa Claus Parade. In a relaxed mood, Laughlin spoke about his battle with Warner Brothers, his mission to save children and the wonders of Toronto as a place to make movies. Indeed, he seemed to be making Toronto-boosting his latest crusade.

But on January 30, Laughlin suspended production after being hit on the head with breakaway glass. (That's a glass made for movie stunts; it's supposed to look as if it's breaking without actually breaking.) The official explanation was that production was being delayed while he recovered from a concussion. Laughlin and Taylor flew to L.A. Anxious inquirers were told they'd be coming back to resume production and would hold a press conference. But the project was rumored to be in financial trouble. Paycheques were bouncing, and some members of the crew gradually realized as the February mornings got colder and emptier that their work on the production was over (though no one had actually told them so). After a couple of weeks, most crew members got tired of waiting and took other work—many of them on the Mary Steenburgen film *Dead of Winter.*

On February 19, Donald Martin and Virginia Kelly, the two Toronto publicists who had been working on the film since Laughlin arrived in Canada, sent out the most startling press release of the shoot: "Effective immediately, Mr. Martin and Ms. Kelly wish to dissociate themselves from the production of *The Return of Billy Jack*. In a letter to Mr. Laughlin, Mr. Martin cites as their reasons the following: nonpayment (to date) of outstanding fees and reimbursement of expenses, amounting to several thousands of dollars; and failure to respond adequately to a request for further information concerning the resumption of production."

A few weeks later, news came from Hollywood that Laughlin had recovered. According to rumors, he had solved his financial problems by selling the movie to Paramount Pictures. Production was ready to resume. He would fly to Toronto and give a press conference explaining all.

Days went by and Laughlin didn't turn up. Finally Delores Taylor came to town with a six-figure bundle of money to pay off outstanding debts. Donald Martin, the embattled publicist, called her to ask whether there was a cheque for him. Definitely not, Taylor told him. Laughlin was very angry about Martin's public defection, which had been covered in the *Hollywood Reporter.* Taylor told Martin he would be hearing from Laughlin's lawyer. It was then Martin realized that not only was he not going to get his $8,000 but Laughlin was actually going to sue him.

The next week William Wellman, Jr., supervising producer of another Laughlin film, was in Toronto wrapping up loose ends. Noting that *The Return of Billy Jack* would resume production in Arizona rather than Toronto, Wellman blamed the crew for Laughlin's decision to shut down the Toronto operation. The way Wellman saw it, the crew abandoned Laughlin while he was convalescing. It was all because of a misunderstanding; money sent by wire had gone astray.

Put that way, it sounded almost as if Laughlin had been driven out of town by ungrateful beneficiaries of his largess—people who should have had faith in their leader but didn't. Perhaps his next movie could be *Billy Jack's Revenge Against Toronto*. Think of the ad campaign: "You've got Casa Loma, the CN Tower, the Courtyard Café and the 75-cent dollar. They've got Billy Jack."

And, let us not forget, they've also got Jack Valenti, the man who discovered that the biggest difference between being a flack for the White House and being a flack for the Hollywood studios was that Hollywood paid a lot more. When Flora MacDonald heard that Reagan had proposed to Mulroney that the question of restricting Hollywood's operations in Canada simply be folded into the free-trade talks, she was furious. She had already made her pledge to the industry in public, and if she backed down now she would look ridiculous. The compromise was that she would agree to a meeting with Valenti, at which he got to express his point of view.

On the appointed afternoon, Valenti came to MacDonald's Ottawa office along with his Canadian representative, Millard Roth. After an hour-long meeting, during which Valenti argued his case with indignant force and MacDonald refused to give way, Valenti stormed out and gave an odd press conference at the elevator near her office. Speaking to reporters who had been tipped off about when and where to wait for him, Valenti offered a show-biz variation on the old domino theory of Communism in Asia.

"If we allow this measure to come into law," Valenti told the reporters, "this will have a contagion effect around the world. This could very well ruin our global film trade. That's why we're so upset about it. We already know that practically every country in Western Europe and Latin America is looking at this proposal. This measure doesn't have anything to do with creativity. It doesn't have anything to do with film production. Essentially, it's a measure that is going to allow about six individuals in Canada who own distribution companies to make a lot of money."

What Valenti was discussing, clearly, was nothing less than the decline of the Hollywood empire — something he seemed to feel the entire world ought to be doing its damnedest to prevent. Where was Hal Banks when you really needed him?

9

Second City, Second Country

John Candy does a devastating parody of the sleazy Hollywood producer. Slipping into character, he turns into Paul Lafarge of Blue Ribbon Productions, placing a call to a rising comic actor from Canada: "John, I don't know if you've heard of us or not. It doesn't really matter. We've done a lot of industrial shorts. I almost got into *Star Wars* there. I had that, uh, Lucas, uh, I know him very well. Anyway, I don't want to bore you with any of those details. I've got a great script here written just for you, and I think it's going to be a heck of a blockbuster. I saw you in *Stripes*—just great work there. Have you seen *Porky's*? This is kind of a *Stripes, Porky's, Animal House* kind of thing with just a touch of skin in it. I think it's gonna be funny. It just needs. . . . Do you rewrite? Do you like to rewrite? 'Cause we'd like to use your input as a writer as well in this. By gosh, if we shoot it in Canada, with the point system they have up there. . . . You could direct it too if you wanted to . . .'

The kicker to the joke is that, as their forays to Hollywood become longer, Candy and his former cohorts from SCTV—a weekly comedy series produced in Canada from 1977 to 1983—are increasingly at the mercy of people like Paul Lafarge. SCTV was regarded by many critics as one of the greatest sustained achievements in the history of North American television, on a par with *Your Show of*

Shows in its salad days. And the beauty of it was that Candy and his gang of zany friends, as they sometimes called themselves self-mockingly, didn't have to suffer the fools and hustlers of Hollywood. They just went to work and let their imaginations soar.

But that was then and this is now. Canada is no longer an anchor for the talented members of the troupe. And in a way their presence in Canada always seemed incidental. Except for the fluke case of the McKenzie Brothers sketches, SCTV's subject was only occasionally and casually Canadian — as it was in their spoofs of alternate theatre, of *Goin' Down the Road*, of Brian Linehan and of *The Journal*. Most of the time their target was the popular culture that's dominant in North America — commercial television made in U.S.A.

Maybe if they had called it the Second Country instead of the Second City, people would have understood what it was doing in Canada. The name was originally a humorous reference to the condescending way New York regards Chicago, and the local reference stuck even after the satirical, improvisational, revue comedy movement, which started around the University of Chicago in the late 1950s, spread to other places. In the beginning, the hip comedy of Second City was an escape from the America of General Eisenhower and the *Ed Sullivan Show*. It was influenced by sources ranging from Italian street theatre to Lenny Bruce. Among the pioneers were Mike Nichols, Elaine May, Shelley Berman, Alan Arkin and Barbara Harris. Pretty soon they had relatives all over the map: Paul Mazursky, Joan Rivers, Robert Klein, Valerie Harper. Sometimes it seems as if everybody who has done anything in contemporary comedy — whether in movies, TV or theatre — has been connected in one way or another with Second City.

The Toronto group began in 1973 as a separatist wing of the Chicago company under the management of Bernard

Sahlins. One night in Chicago, Sahlins asked the cast to whip up a special show because in the audience would be a famous critic from Canada, Nathan Cohen. Partly because of Cohen's enthusiasm, Sahlins decided to open a Toronto branch. "We knew it wasn't New York or L.A.," Joe Flaherty recalled years later, "but Bernie was sure it was the town of the future."

Like one of those fur-trading explorers sent to the New World from Europe, Flaherty was sent to Toronto to develop the new company. He was amazed at the local talent waiting to be discovered. Toronto at the time was a city ready to blossom. It had been transformed by postwar immigration, plus a building boom and a spree of government spending on the arts. In the wake of the Vietnam war, it also became a lively city-in-exile for American war dissenters, within a day's drive of New York, Chicago, Washington and Boston. And it had plenty of talent; among those who turned up at the first audition were Gilda Radner, John Candy and Jayne Eastwood.

The first summer on Adelaide Street was a disaster; there was no publicity, no air-conditioning and no liquor license. The Toronto operation was already in trouble a few months later when Andrew Alexander, a young show-biz entrepreneur from Toronto, went to Chicago to do a promotional job for a dinner theatre and heard about the problem from Chicago's Second City people.

In 1974, Alexander was a budding impresario in search of a project, and this was it. His track record — selling ads for a suburban weekly newspaper, publishing a ski magazine and producing the final, dreadful edition of the annual Canadian revue, *Spring Thaw* (after buying the rights to the name from Mavor Moore) — was less than dazzling. The Toronto Second City may have seemed like another loser waiting to deliver the final blow to a star-struck masochist, but Alexander fooled a lot of people by turning it into a thriving empire which annually grosses several million dollars. Within a few years he controlled a Toronto cabaret show, the Old Firehall restaurant where it was staged and a weekly TV program syndicated to stations in major U.S. cities.

But in 1974 he was broke, and he bought the rights to Second City for one dollar from Bernard Sahlins. Then he moved the show around the corner from Adelaide to the Firehall, a floundering restaurant he took over with $7,000 of other people's money. Among the performers he inherited were Candy, Radner, Flaherty and Eugene Levy.

Candy was a baby-faced twenty-two-year-old when he joined the troupe. Born in Newmarket and brought up mostly in the East York area of Toronto, he studied theatre arts at a Catholic boys' school, took a journalism course for a year and wound up touring from park to park in a children's tent show.

Levy made his film-directing debut while attending McMaster University in Hamilton during the late 1960s. The tycoon of the McMaster Film Board was Ivan Reitman, and after they'd both left school, Levy worked as coffee boy for $60 a week on Reitman's film *Foxy Lady* (1971) and graduated to leading man in Reitman's *Cannibal Girls* (1972) before joining the cast of *Godspell*, which also included two other future SCTV regulars.

Another refugee from McMaster was Dave Thomas, who edited the school paper, *The Silhouette*, and spent four months in the cast of *Godspell* before he decided to quit and become an advertising copywriter. He was doing very well but got bored and joined the group at the Firehall when he was twenty-six.

Andrea Martin, an Armenian, grew up in Portland, Maine, and studied mime in France before landing in Toronto in 1970. Before getting into Second City she played the girl next door in *Foxy Lady* and performed along with Levy and Thomas in *Godspell*.

Catherine O'Hara grew up Irish and Catholic in a large

family in the Islington area of Toronto. She had been working as a salesperson at Fabricland when she landed a part in a show at the Global Village, a small Toronto theatre. But she got fed up with method acting and broke into Second City's touring company while working in the coat-check room at the Old Firehall.

The TV show was launched in 1976. By that time Alexander had already lost two of his regulars, Gilda Radner and Dan Aykroyd, to NBC's *Saturday Night Live* (created by another Toronto writer-performer, Lorne Michaels). It wasn't easy holding on to performers. The Second City stage shows were a magnet for fresh young talent, but with its low budgets, young audiences and improvisational techniques, Second City was an institution writer-performers were happy to graduate from. The TV show gave Alexander a way to hang on to some of the talent he was developing. Almost the entire cast of the TV show had graduated from the Firehall, and the performers were happy to have the chance to reach bigger audiences and make more money. In one form or another, the show lasted eight years, moving like a gypsy commune from one temporary home to another. And it has been in syndication reruns since production stopped in 1984.

The genius of the TV show was that it didn't do the obvious and transfer skits from the cabaret; instead, it created a new landscape, a self-contained world that became a parody and a commentary on the whole video environment. Within this warped fantasy environment, SCTV was a little station serving the town of Melonville. Joe Flaherty played Guy Caballero, the genial owner of the station. And for the first season, the station manager was played by Harold Ramis, who then left for Hollywood, where he became a hot screenwriter and later a writer-director. SCTV delivered samples of various lunacies flourishing all over the TV schedule in punchy, fragmented flashes, the way they'd be seen by a TV addict who just happened to be sitting in front of the set jumping from one channel to another.

Structurally the show was laid out with brilliant intricacy. The audience was bombarded by a whole range of promos, previews, commercials, commentaries—which all seemed to be interrupting and playing off one another. The sense of a continuous TV schedule was achieved by the repetition of certain features and characters—not just the newscasts and commercials and movie parodies, but such regulars as Joe Flaherty's Sammy Maudlin (the self-congratulatory game-show host), Andrea Martin's Edith Prickley, with her leopard outfits and chortling sales pitch, Eugene Levy's Bobby Bittman (the world's most obnoxious stand-up comic), Catherine O'Hara as Hollywood gossip columnist "Rhoda" Barrett and airhead starlet Lola Heatherton, John Candy as roving restaurant critic Johnny Larue and the squeaky-voiced sidekick to the host of Fantasy Island, Dave Thomas as Art ("Women Say the Darndest Things") Linkletter.

SCTV started as a half-hour series on the Global network, with syndication to a small group of U.S. stations. Production moved to Edmonton in 1979 when Dr. Charles Allard became an investor. While in Edmonton it underwent a metamorphosis and emerged as a ninety-minute program on NBC. During its Edmonton period, the show underwent various traumatic developments. Many of the regulars came and went, and newcomers, including Robin Duke, Tony Rosato and Rick Moranis (recruited by Dave Thomas), were brought in. The most important late addition to the cast was Martin Short, whose brilliant lampoon of celebrity interviewer Brian Linehan (Short's character was named Brock Linehan) was enjoyed even by American viewers who had never seen the original Linehan. In the funniest of these sketches, Brock gives singer Linda Hopkins his double-whammy gaze and launches into an insanely long, complicated, aren't-you-wowed-by-my-research question, which has something to do with Daryl Zanuck and a 1930s movie. She looks at him as if he's out of his mind, and it turns out that Brock's researcher got Linda Hopkins muddled up with Miriam Hopkins.

On NBC the show had a terrible time slot—from 12:30 A.M. to 2:00 A.M. Saturday morning—but still managed to draw about five million U.S. viewers regularly. Everyone agreed the show deserved a bigger audience, but NBC couldn't justify the cost of the show given its time slot, and Alexander couldn't strike an agreement with NBC executives on a new time slot. SCTV was caught in an NBC power struggle. Alexander wanted it to alternate with *Saturday Night Live*, Saturdays at 11:30 P.M., but SNL was considered one of NBC's own, and SCTV was regarded as a dangerous outside rival. After this impasse, Alexander opted to put the show on the Cinemax cable system for its final season, where its potential audience was even smaller.

While SCTV was on NBC, there was a shorter one-hour version on some CBC stations, starting an hour earlier. The McKenzie Brothers—Dave Thomas and Rick Moranis as a pair of True North bumpkins—were born because the CBC needed two minutes of extra Canadian content. Mocking the notion that the show wasn't Canadian enough, Thomas and Moranis created Bob and Doug—parka-wearing, beer-guzzling nerds with an imaginary talk show, *Great White North*, on which they would discuss such pressing issues as the shortage of parking spaces at doughnut shops. Their ultimate put-down, "Take off, eh?" became a national craze. Ironically, their send-up of Canadian thickheadedness became phenomenally popular with U.S. viewers.

From the start, Thomas and Moranis hit it off, and their partnership provoked a rift with others in the group. Moranis was the new boy and the upstart, the only member of the team who hadn't come out of the Firehall. Joe Flaherty, the official godfather of the group, became upset because Moranis was writing so much of the script, and there was a tremendous competitiveness about which performers got the best material and time spots in a given episode.

Moranis and Thomas discovered that two could work faster than seven, and developed a McKenzie Brothers sideline. Their record album turned into a surprise hit, selling about 800,000 copies, including 500,000 in the United States. That was followed by a film offer. Alexander was upset because he was frozen out of these ventures. When Thomas and Moranis quit SCTV, they left a trail of bitterness. At one point Flaherty went so far as to say that if they came back to the show, he'd leave.

Strange Brew, the $5-million McKenzie Brothers movie, wasn't officially a Canadian production. It was financed by MGM. Thomas and Moranis followed the advice of Hollywood executive producer Jack Grossberg, who told them they'd be better off to direct it themselves than to trust someone else. The movie turned out to be no more than an amiable TV sketch blown out of proportion, with a story line about an evil genius (Max Von Sydow) who tries to take over the world by spiking the beer at a brewery. The film had an eager-to-please air, but anyone hoping for brilliant wit and sophisticated adult satire was bound to be disappointed. Thomas and Moranis were like the Two Stooges, and they didn't have the force of personality to hold the big screen.

Inevitably the gang broke up along the road to Hollywood. The elusive dream was always to make a big SCTV movie, with juicy parts for everyone, but this wasn't easy to achieve. In 1983 the notion got as far as a sort of SCTV convention in Los Angeles, with several members brainstorming. But nothing came of it. Almost everybody from the show was pursuing an individual movie career.

One of the first SCTV arrivals in Hollywood was Harold

Ramis, who defected after the first season of the TV show. In Ivan Reitman's *Stripes*—the story of two dunderheads who enlist in the U.S. Army out of carelessness and apathy, then accidentally turn into national heroes—Ramis was one of the script writers as well as Bill Murray's on-screen sidekick. Ramis was a link between Reitman and the SCTV group, and *Stripes* featured three other SCTV performers. John Candy played a soldier known appropriately as Ox; Dave Thomas showed up as the ringmaster of a porn mud-wrestling attraction; and Joe Flaherty did a cameo role as a thickheaded Russian guard outsmarted by the heroes. But they were all overshadowed by Ramis, who gave Bill Murray the kind of balance that Bing Crosby gave Bob Hope in the *Road* comedies. With glasses that seem too old for his baby face and a good-boy demeanor played off against the hidden craziness in his personality, Ramis was a bit like Harold Lloyd, the silent comedian. What he projected were slyness and knowingness behind a facade of reserve and good manners. And Ramis managed to bring several SCTV performers together in his 1986 film *Club Paradise*, which was most notable for Andrea Martin's movie debut.

Almost every one of Ramis's former colleagues on SCTV eventually succumbed to the seductive lure of Hollywood. Once there, they had to play by Hollywood's rules, which usually meant giving up control of their own material, which the group had taken for granted while they were doing their TV show. Perhaps the most frustrating experience for several members of the gang was an ill-fated comedy that eventually was released (in the fall of 1983) under the title *Going Berserk*, whereupon it sank like a stone.

It started with a script called *Drums Over Malta* written by several SCTV people. Any resemblance between that and the movie actually released was strictly coincidental. The title *Going Berserk* was an accurate description of the experience of those who worked on it. Candy, Levy and

Flaherty were brought to Universal by Montreal producer Pierre David. With fellow SCTV writers Paul Flaherty (Joe's brother) and Paul Belucci, they wrote a spoof roughly patterned after Alfred Hitchcock's *North by Northwest*.

The bosses at Universal acted enthusiastic about the script but dragged their feet about proceeding with it, partly because Gene Wilder had made a similar movie, *Hanky Panky*. The next thing they knew, David Steinberg had been assigned to direct the project, and outside writers had been hired to do a second draft, which, as it turned out, retained almost nothing of their material.

In twenty years Steinberg had traveled from the scrambled ethnic mosaic of Winnipeg's North End (where they still call him Duddy) to the cerebral new frontier of the University of Chicago campus to the sunbaked show-biz promised land of southern California. During that time he had moved through a fairly hilarious array of non-sequitur careers: fast-talking street hustler; dedicated young rabbinical student; literary devotee sitting at the feet of Philip Roth around the time Roth was writing *Goodbye, Columbus;* satirist at Second City, Chicago, picking up pointers from Elaine May, Barbara Harris and Alan Arkin; stand-up comic in the big-money territory; a TV talk-show regular who became a favored substitute for Johnny Carson on *The Tonight Show*. And now he had completed an apprenticeship in his latest career: Hollywood movie director.

Steinberg had come to Hollywood as an iconoclastic outsider, a sarcastic social commentator with a cutting edge. His nervy Moses sermon, considered sacrilegious by Middle America, helped bounce the Smothers Brothers off CBS. He learned that being called "intelligent" by Hollywood executives wasn't necessarily a compliment; it was an explanation of why they weren't going to hire you.

Steinberg met Burt Reynolds on the talk-show circuit in the early 1970s, and they became buddies. They also became business partners in a film production company.

And Reynolds made it possible for Steinberg to direct a studio movie when he agreed to star in *Paternity*, a comedy about a cocky, rich playboy who craves a son but not a wife—and sets out to find a woman with whom he can make a business deal to bear his child.

Steinberg spoke of the film in terms of Preston Sturges, the great satiric writer-director of the 1940s, but *Paternity* wasn't a movie destined to make anyone forget Sturges. Trying for Cary Grant subtlety, Reynolds seemed paralyzed in his role. In his eagerness for mass approval, Steinberg kept snuggling up to the audience. Was it really possible that a man who made his reputation as a ferocious social satirist was trying to get by with an adorably wise black maid, a precocious little boy and heartwarming dialogue like "I want to be there when he discovers gravity"? After this movie, the big question about Steinberg was whether he could beat the *Paternity* rap.

Steinberg was no stranger to the cast of SCTV. In the mid-1970s, several of them had been regulars on Steinberg's short-lived weekly comedy series on CTV. It was on that show that Martin Short created the character Johnny del Bravo, a nervy, ego-tripping, pop vocalist. John Candy played Spider, the bandleader. And Flaherty had also been a regular on the show.

One night in 1979, Steinberg had a kind of public family party with several SCTV regulars on the CBC's ill-fated late-night talk show, then called *Canada After Dark*. Appearing as guest host, Steinberg welcomed Catherine O'Hara, Martin Short and Dave Thomas to the show. And Candy frequently stayed at Steinberg's house during his California sojourns.

Yet Steinberg wasn't completely trusted or admired within the SCTV family. He was suspect—like a rich uncle who had moved to the United States and made it big, but at a price that the family was always whispering about.

What got Andrew Alexander into a flap about *Going Berserk* were press references to the film as "an SCTV movie." He thought he had the whole thing straightened out after he ran into Steinberg at NBC in Burbank and asked him not to encourage such misconceptions. Alexander got the impression that Steinberg agreed completely, but a couple of weeks later Alexander turned on his TV set and found Steinberg hosting *The Tonight Show.* When asked what he'd been doing lately, Steinberg said that he'd just finished "a movie with SCTV."

Steinberg wanted to use other SCTV performers besides the three who appeared in the movie, but several turned him down. Levy wanted to get out of the project but was advised not to break his contract. Steinberg kept promising there would be changes but Flaherty, for one, became more and more disenchanted as shooting progressed. "David is very smart, and he loves the *idea* of being a director," said Flaherty. "He keeps talking about the shot and the location. We kept saying, 'Yeah, but what about the content?'"

It was an especially painful experience for Candy, who had the largest role. Afterward, Candy described it as a learning experience, because he learned what not to do when making a movie.

Of the group, Candy had by far the most experience and the most success in movies. He has appeared in about two dozen movies, including Steven Spielberg's megaflop, *1941,* and *The Blues Brothers,* in which he costarred with his good friend, the late John Belushi. Candy's one big hit was *Splash,* a 1984 comic fable about a boy and a mermaid. Produced by Touchstone, a division of Disney, it wasn't strictly for children.

When director Ron Howard sent Candy the script for *Splash,* Candy wanted the role of the lunatic villain. Eventually he was persuaded to play Freddie, the brother of the New York fruit peddler (Tom Hanks) who has fallen for a mermaid (Daryl Hannah), and the role of the nutty bad guy went to Candy's colleague Eugene Levy.

The role of Freddie didn't exactly jump off the page,

and in the hands of a more conventional actor, it might have been just another straight-man role. But Candy turned Freddie into a wisecracking, high-living cartoon. In his best scenes he chain-smokes and plays racquetball at the same time.

Candy got sensational reviews, but according to Candy, he just did what came naturally. "It wasn't Willy Loman or King Lear," he explained. "People said, 'Wow, you can really act.' Hell, I was just doing what I've done for years on SCTV."

On the wings of *Splash*, Candy was ready for stardom, but when he did get a whole movie built around him — the hot-weather comedy *Summer Rental*, with Candy as the father of an ordinary American family renting a cottage where everything goes wrong — the results were too feeble to advance his career.

Catherine O'Hara's Hollywood adventures were even more painful than Candy's. When she left the TV show in 1982, hoping to break into movies, her fans were so dismayed they took to grabbing her on the street and yelling at her. For a long stretch she had very little to show for all the time she spent sitting in hotel rooms in L.A. waiting for meetings with high-powered agents and reading for parts she didn't get. Then she did get a couple of roles in prestigious movies. In *After Hours*, directed by Martin Scorsese, O'Hara was the wacky driver of an ice-cream truck who pursued Griffin Dunne through the streets of nighttime Manhattan. In *Heartburn*, directed by Mike Nichols, she was a Washington columnist and gossipy good friend of Meryl Streep. Her work was fine, but both these films were disappointments from major directors, and there simply wasn't enough of O'Hara in either of them to make an impact.

On SCTV O'Hara had been a brilliant mimic of famous movie actresses, doing takeoffs on, among others, Katharine Hepburn, Jane Fonda and Meryl Streep, but becoming a movie actress herself was proving troublesome. She had been accurately called "the funniest woman on television," and her fans wanted her to become the funniest woman in the movies, too. But on the big screen she wasn't memorable the way she often was on TV, doing inspired bits like her impression of an idiotic actress playing Joan of Arc on *Witness to Yesterday* without knowing anything at all about Joan of Arc. As a minor participant in projects controlled by people whose sensibilities were remote from her own, O'Hara emerged as just another competent supporting actress.

Andrea Martin had better luck. She made a strong impression in a series of appearances on the CBS sitcom *Kate and Allie*. And in her first movie, *Club Paradise*, directed by Harold Ramis from a script he wrote with Brian Doyle-Murray and others, Martin came very close to doing a big-screen equivalent of her best SCTV work, such as the classic movie parody she did with Levy, *An Officer and a Gentile*. In *Club Paradise*, she plays the hell-bent-on-having-a-good-time wife of a sleepy-looking plastic surgeon (Steven Kampmann); she is determined to make the best of the sleazy package holiday in the Caribbean. A planeload of cheap vacationers who have been sucked in by mendacious travel brochures soon discover that the club's social director (Robin Williams) and his girlfriend (Twiggy) are swindlers.

Among the other SCTV veterans in the movie is Joe Flaherty, as a pilot who kisses the ground after a bumpy landing. Eugene Levy and Rick Moranis play a pair of infantile, sleazy businessmen, both named Barry, obsessed with "scoring" but scared of women. Andrea Martin carries the movie, throwing herself into each new catastrophe with gleeful abandon. But *Club Paradise* was not especially well received, either by the critics or the public; maybe its casual, thrown-together irreverence wasn't particularly fashionable at that moment. If there had been a whole series of movies made in the same style, with the same performers, they might have taken hold in the way the Marx Brothers movies did, but given the tepid response to *Club Paradise*, that didn't seem likely.

And so once again the SCTV performers went their own separate ways, each pursuing the big Hollywood score in his or her own way. By the summer of 1987, John Candy had another major movie in release—the feeble Mel Brooks spoof *Spaceballs*—and was working on two John Hughes movies (even though Hughes specializes in teenage movies, and it's too late for Candy to play teenagers). Rick Moranis had a success with *Little Shop of Horrors* and was also in *Spaceballs*. Catherine O'Hara was spending a lot of time saying no. And Martin Short was playing a lovable nerd in the hit fantasy *Innerspace* after *Three Amigos*, in which he costarred with Steve Martin and Chevy Chase, of which *Vanity Fair* film critic Stephen Schiff remarked: "*Three Amigos*—but only two laughs." Eugene Levy was keeping his family in the idyllic Rosedale section of Toronto and writing a script with a big juicy role for himself. Apart from O'Hara, who was still clinging to Toronto as a kind of refuge, he was the only SCTV alumnus living in Canada full-time. Meanwhile Candy, Short and Martin were living most of the year in L.A., though they all continued to maintain homes in Toronto. Even Andrew Alexander had moved to L.A., where he set up a new Second City club.

Shooting for a big success, Hollywood style, the SCTV gang let go of the wonky satiric empire they had created almost by accident for a few splendidly flaky years in the True White North. Their fans yearned for a reunion the way Beatles fans waited for the lads from Liverpool to get back together again. But those smart kids from SCTV weren't going to be kids forever. They still hung out together frequently and still regarded one another as family, but life had become more complicated. And most of them seemed all too ready to give up the special advantages that working in Canada had given them: a useful distance from the American popular culture they were satirizing, and creative freedom to express their brilliantly original point of view. Maybe if they'd stayed together and made small, inexpensive movies in Canada, they could have created a big-screen universe even more wonderful than the small-screen universe they had inhabited for a while, casting their gleeful shadows on the walls of the TV wasteland.

10

Mickey Mouse Meets Anne of Green Gables

Politics may make strange bedfellows, as editorial writers are fond of reminding us, but politics is an innocent business compared to the movies. Even by the standards of show business, the alliance of Telefilm Canada and Walt Disney Productions in a number of film productions must be regarded as passing weird. After all, the heirs of Walt and his brother Roy, while still warring with each other over the spoils of the Magic Kingdom, are dedicated to promoting the ideals of Middle America, while Telefilm is supposed to be encouraging the development of an indigenous Canadian film culture and providing a shield against the overwhelming shadow of the Hollywood giant.

Just exactly what an indigenous Canadian film culture might consist of isn't clear, apart from waving wheatfields, especially when one is speaking of films in the English language. But presumably it has something to do with an alternative style — with the freedom to be North American without being quite so fiercely and aggressively, well, American. Shouldn't it be clear to an avowed cultural nationalist like Peter Pearson, Telefilm's chief executive officer, that Disney represents the ultimate enemy of everything Canadians hold dear? If Canadian sovereignty means anything at all, doesn't it at least ensure that

Mickey Mouse and Donald Duck have to stay on their side of the border?

Cultural politics are not quite that simple on the world's longest undefended border. Disney has increased its hold on Canada for decades without much opposition. Indeed, even when Disney's long-running TV show became such a commercial liability that it was dropped by one and then another of the major U.S. TV networks, it remained one of the most consistently popular shows in CBC's schedule.

For years Disney had been trying to extend its insidious power over the minds of the True North. In 1984 it had the audacity to make a major movie out of Farley Mowat's classic saga of the Canadian North, *Never Cry Wolf*, and fill it with various vulgar Americanisms. Disney is also determined to extend its cable-TV operation into Canada; and it's probably inevitable that when the CRTC grants a license for a children's or family pay-TV outlet, whoever gets it will go into partnership with Disney and fill a good part of the schedule with Disney products. In the arena of film distribution, Disney had to operate quietly and unofficially while the Ottawa bureaucrats decided whether Disney was to be allowed to set up an operation like those of, say, Warner Brothers Canada and Columbia of Canada.

The most intriguing side of Disney's adventures in Canada, however, is its continuing involvement as a partner in Canadian film productions. Disney and Telefilm were the two major investors in the movie *One Magic Christmas* (1985). And Disney has invested in several key Canadian TV series—*Danger Bay, Raccoons, The Edison Twins*—shown on CBC in this country and on the Disney cable channel in the United States. Watching these programs, one realized that the Canadian mandate and the Disney mandate were not incompatible. In scores of movies like *The Love Bug* and at Disneyland itself, the Disney factory conjured dreams of an innocent America, with fresh faces and clean clothes and without ghettoes or major social problems. This mythical place is a land of sunshine, uncrowded spaces, clean air, smiling faces, happy times and good manners. And that comes close to summing up what English Canada at its best represents to the rest of the world if not to itself: America without the power and the problems, America the way it used to be before it lost its innocence.

Still, it's a bit of a shock to think of *Anne of Green Gables*, that most cherished and purely Canadian literary institution, as a Disney vehicle. The fact is, however, that it was Disney — in partnership with Telefilm again — that came to the rescue when Kevin Sullivan, the Toronto *wunderkind* who had made a triumphant four-hour TV film of *Anne of Green Gables*, set out to make a sequel. Astonishingly, the CBC, which had scored one of the greatest triumphs in its history with the film of *Anne of Green Gables*, wasn't willing to put up enough money to exercise control over the sequel. It was the combination of Disney and the Public Broadcasting System that made the $4.5-million sequel feasible.

Anne of Green Gables on the screen was full of surprises. Who would have guessed that Kevin Sullivan, who produced, adapted and directed *Anne*, could turn a safe Canadian family classic into a film saga as long as *Gone With the Wind*, and just about as irresistible? Or that Megan Follows in the title role would give the kind of legendary performance that launches international careers?

Of course, Lucy Maud Montgomery's story had a long history of surprising people, including its author. "Don't stick up your ears now imagining that the great Canadian novel has been written at last," she advised a penpal in 1909. "It is merely a juvenile story, ostensibly for girls. I did not dream it would be the success it was. I thought girls in their teens might like it, but that was the only audience I hoped to reach."

Such was the public clamoring that Montgomery could hardly escape from the creature she once referred to as "that detestable Anne." She had to write six books about the redheaded orphan from Prince Edward Island.

When *Anne* had its premiere on CBC television on two consecutive nights in December 1985, it drew one of the biggest audiences in the country's history — over five million viewers. Not surprisingly, it went on to sweep the first Gemini awards for excellence in TV. And in December 1987, CBC will show the five-hour sequel.

Anne of Green Gables and the sequel — which was seen first by Disney cable-TV subscribers in the United States and will be seen early in 1988 on PBS in the United States — are jointly the shining symbol of a startling turnaround in the Canadian film industry.

The success of the two *Anne* films is one of the most encouraging developments in the continuing saga of how the Canadian movie industry has turned into the Canadian television industry. This is partly the story of Peter Pearson, a nationalist filmmaker of the 1970s turned government bureaucrat of the 1980s, who, as the head of Telefilm Canada has become the only Canadian with the kind of power associated with the boss of a Hollywood studio. And it is partly an interesting lesson in how to make it in the shadow of the Hollywood dream machine — by collaborating with the Americans to the point of taking their money and breaking into their market, while at the same time more or less keeping control of the projects.

By 1981 it was clear that the bubble had burst for Canada's movie industry. Investors had been scared off by wild abuses and scandalously bad movies, and Hollywood North had self-destructed. It wasn't immediately clear what the federal government, which had more or less created the movie industry through an act of Parliament in 1968, planned to do about its crash. Then in 1983 the Trudeau government came along with a magic act. The Canadian Film Development Corporation turned into

Telefilm Canada, millions of dollars were made available through a new Broadcast Fund and the new rules were set out. To tap the fund a project had to have a prelicensing agreement from a Canadian broadcaster who agreed to air it in prime time. Presto: the dying Canadian movie industry was now the born-again Canadian TV-film industry.

This transformation provided a miraculous second chance for the film industry. Feature films as well as TV films could be financed through this system as long as they were licensed for television. Of course, to make them more attractive to broadcasters, a number of productions turned into hybrids. *Louisiana, The Blood of Others* and *Joshua Then and Now* were all shot both as feature films and longer TV versions. (That awkward arrangement lasted until 1986, when the Conservatives, spearheaded by Marcel Masse, then the minister of communications, gave the industry another incentive—the $33-million-a-year feature-film fund.)

The first head of the Broadcast Fund, and later executive director of Telefilm, was Peter Pearson, who had been teaching film at Queen's University after a frustrating career trying to make his own films. In 1969, two films made by Pearson for the National Film Board won eleven Canadian Film Awards, but he couldn't get work. He had managed to make one reasonably successful feature, *Paperback Hero* (1973), but he had spent several frustrating years trying to raise the money for his dream project, an adaptation of the Sinclair Ross novel *As For Me and My House*, which kept falling through.

When he came to Telefilm to run the Broadcast Fund, he decided to put his bad experiences behind him. Sensing that the filmmakers of his own generation were exhausted from the fight just to survive, he determined to find a group of younger, unknown people who hadn't been through these bitter experiences, and who would have the energy to make indigenous Canadian films for TV—films that would work on the country's own terms rather than imitate American movies and American TV shows. To a remarkable extent, Pearson succeeded. Along came a whole pack of young unknowns who brought forth such ventures as *The Kids of Degrassi Street* and *Sons and Daughters*—TV series that usually had American coproduction money and American distribution deals, but still managed to seem distinctly Canadian in style and content.

Yet the most surprising success of all was *Night Heat*, a cop show produced in Toronto that did its best to fudge its Canadian identity. Set in No-Name City, *Night Heat* seemed in some ways a return to the bad old days of Hollywood North. But it managed to be a classic example of how to take advantage of the system in the new era.

The show was the brainchild of a former New York cop by the name of Sonny Grosso, who had capped his career with the biggest heroin bust of all time. The story of that case was dramatized in *The French Connection*, with Roy Scheider playing Grosso. After that, Grosso went on to Hollywood as consultant of *The Godfather* and story editor of two other cop series.

Grosso wanted to create his own cop series. He and his partner approached CBS with the idea for a series called *Street Cop*, specifically aimed at the late-night audience. At first the plan was to do cinema-verité documentaries of actual police cases, but it was decided there wasn't enough dramatic value in the concept. CBS was interested in a late-night cop show but wasn't willing to put up big bucks.

That's when Grosso approached Arthur Weinthal, of CTV, the privately owned Canadian network, which was under pressure to increase its Canadian content. CTV was looking for a good series that could be produced in Canada. A group of private investors stepped forward; then producers Robert Lantos and Stephen Roth got involved. Lantos and Roth, who had produced a number of movies, headed the company RSL, which would soon merge with a company run by John Kemeny and Denis Héroux to form a new giant, Alliance Entertainment Corporation. They were trying to get a foothold in TV, but since they were both overextended with their film projects, including *Joshua Then and Now,* they turned *Night Heat* over to their apprentice, Andras Hamori, an immigrant hustler recently arrived from Hungary, who had been helping out on such RSL movies as *Heavenly Bodies* and *Bedroom Eyes.*

Knowing virtually nothing about how to produce a weekly action series, Hamori sensed that this was a chance he couldn't turn down. He'd have to bluff his way through. Lantos and Roth would be supervising producers, with Grosso and his partner, Larry Jacobson, as executive producers. But Hamori was the real producer, the guy who had to get the job done week after week. Shaking in his shoes, Hamori found himself driving to the Lakeshore Psychiatric Hospital (an old mental asylum, part of which the Ontario government sometimes makes available as a facility for producing films), wondering just when someone would call his bluff.

The producers had wangled a commitment to six episodes from CBS, which was looking for an inexpensive way to come up with a late-night series to be shown opposite NBC's *Tonight Show,* with Johnny Carson, which was so far ahead of the competition that catching up was considered impossible. To produce a new series in L.A. or New York would have cost about one million dollars per episode. *Night Heat* was produced for roughly half that, of which CBS put up only about one-third. For the U.S. network, *Night Heat* was a genuine bargain. It was also a great deal for CTV, which scheduled it in prime time.

Night Heat's costs were pared in a number of ways: using 16 mm instead of 35 mm; going for a gritty look that bypasses expensive sets and costumes; and shooting at night when there were few of the usual impediments to slow things down. The show didn't have the look of a fashion magazine, as *Miami Vice* did; its heroes wore cheap jeans rather than flashy, double-breasted suits, worked in a grungy, messy squad room and ordered in pizza a lot. They worked that other nine-to-five shift, the one that ends when the sun comes up.

The all-Canadian cast included Scott Hylands as the veteran Detective Kevin O'Brien, who has seen it all and is slightly disillusioned, and Jeff Wincott as his eager young partner, Frank Giambone. The twist is a character named Tom Kirkwood, played by Allan Royal, a newspaper columnist on the crime beat. (The name of his column, naturally, is "Night Heat.") Kirkwood delivers the opening narration, and his newspaper column closes the show every week. He's apt to say things like: "Most stories I cover because I have to. Once in a while something comes in that I'd cross the city on all fours to write about."

Night Heat lets the audience think Toronto could be Chicago or Philadelphia. There are no shots of the CN Tower, and when paper money is flashed, it's some hybrid funny-money that doesn't look exactly like American or Canadian currency. Toronto's notorious cleanliness did cause some problems. *Night Heat* crews routinely had to sprinkle garbage on a street before shooting, and one night they returned from a meal break to find that overzealous street cleaners had removed all their carefully arranged trash.

To the surprise of almost everyone involved, *Night Heat* became a huge success, pulling higher ratings than other CBS late-night offerings and beating *The Tonight Show* regularly in certain key markets. It was never an emblem of Canadian culture, but it did give certain Canadian actors, writers and directors a big break. Hamori graduated from the show and went on to produce movies for Alliance, including *Nowhere to Hide* (1987), with Amy Madigan.

Why should Telefilm support ventures like *Night Heat*, which is frankly aimed at the American commercial market? Because although Telefilm was spending Canadian taxpayers' money, the CBS sale minimized the risk involved. Moreover, CBS was helping create a Canadian TV industry, providing an entrance to the American market and giving a group of Canadians a chance to work on a show that would have exposure in major U.S. markets.

For the same reason, Telefilm backed *Covert Action*, a made-for-TV movie produced with an eye to a possible series, and *Adderly*, a late-night spy show for CBS, shown in Canada on the Global network. *Adderly* is produced partly by Robert Cooper Productions. Cooper, who once starred in the CBC's *Ombudsman*, produced a number of movies, including *Running* and *The Terry Fox Story*. Moving to Los Angeles, he had established links with the U.S. giant pay-cable operation Home Box Office. And early in 1987, he joined Lantos, Roth, Kemeny and Héroux in Alliance, making it by far the biggest film company in Canada. By this time Alliance was producing both movies such as *The Gate*—a snappy exploitation thriller that grossed more than $6 million in its first weekend of business in North American theatres in May 1987—and major TV shows such as *The Sword of Gideon* (based on the George Jonas best-seller *Vengeance*), shown on CTV and HBO in the fall of 1986, and the forthcoming weekly series *Mount Royal*. Alliance even had its own film distribution company.

In the summer of 1985, Pearson moved up from head of Telefilm's Broadcast Fund, taking over as Telefilm's executive director from André Lamy, who was regarded by the new Conservative government as a Liberal appointment. There were persistent rumors about other people with Tory connections, but in the end the job went to Pearson. His appointment was welcomed by the industry as a sign of good faith, not because he wasn't a card-carrying Tory but because Pearson was, above all, a man who knew how films were made and was an established cultural nationalist. And he was largely responsible for the success of the Broadcast Fund, which was providing a happy epilogue to the sad story of the Canadian film industry.

For those skeptics who asked why the public should go on subsidizing the film industry at all, there were a number of persuasive answers. First, there was the cultural imperative. Without special measures, Canada's home screens and theatre screens alike would be totally dominated by Hollywood. Then there was the economic argument: for every dollar spent, the government could get back three times that much in money spent in Canada. And the industry could point to a number of commercial and artistic successes.

For a while the boom was fueled by public money, either from Telefilm ($67 million in 1986) or CBC. At first private money was in short supply, because investors who had been burned were slow to recognize that Hollywood North was no more. But in 1986 Canadian private investors poured $150 million into film production, and the proportion of private money in Telefilm projects rose during a four-year period from three percent to twenty percent.

For the new era, there was a new breed of producer, a cautious, sober pragmatist who minimized risks. Take the Atlantis group, the producing team that won an Oscar for a half-hour TV drama based on an Alice Munro short story. Michael MacMillan, who formed the company along with fellow college friends Seaton McLean and Janice Platt, seems more like a young bank executive or guidance teacher than a movie producer. In fact, he's the financial wizard behind a company that in 1986 completely sold out offerings totaling more than $25 million. The company's carefully budgeted projects include the TV miniseries *Brothers by Choice*, the anthology series *Ray Bradbury Theatre*, a movie version of Margaret Laurence's novel *The Diviners* and a commercial U.S. TV series *Airwolf*. Atlantis also has the ultimate status symbol, its very own production studio in Toronto.

One of the few producers who dares to criticize Telefilm openly is Jon Slan, who won his movie-producing spurs in the mid-1970s. By the time he produced *Threshold* (1981), which got good reviews but died at the box office, the movie industry was pretty much a corpse, and Slan had moved on to run the Ontario wing of Superchannel, a new pay-TV network. Slan's outfit was the only profitable pay-TV operation in the country; his partner, Dr. Charles Allard, was losing money at Alberta Superchannel and was eager to make a deal with First Choice, the national licensee. Slan stepped aside, for a handsome payoff, and in 1985 got back into the film business. His first major project was a series of one-hour TV thrillers based on Raymond Chandler's private eye, Philip Marlowe, shown on Home Box Office. The budget was $9 million, raised through a public offering, of which $5.4 million was covered through pre-sales. Subsequent sales of more than $2 million promised to turn the series into a winner. Slan's next project is a new *Alfred Hitchcock Presents* series for Universal, the Hollywood studio.

A former college English professor, Slan acts more like a hustler than a scholar. He doesn't spend a lot of time talking about Canadian identity. His goals are commercial, and his sights are on the world market. The biggest challenge, he says, is to find good material.

Slan seems to have little trouble rounding up backers. He has made little use of Telefilm subsidy—if a project makes economic sense, Telefilm isn't needed—and he regards Telefilm as bureaucratic and inefficient. In his view the production boom was fueled not by any cultural imperative or by the policies of Telefilm but simply by the 70-cent dollar, which gave Americans the cost advantages for shooting in Canada. Like most Canadian producers, Slan—who has recently taken up full-time residence in L.A. with his family—was only too happy to do business with American production partners.

Clearly the Canadian film industry was on a roll. Private investment was booming again. The emphasis was on TV, but feature films also showed signs of revival. With the help of the 70-cent dollar, the value of film production in 1986 exceeded $300 million. A big chunk of that was Americans producing American films in Canada, but there were also a number of Canadian productions that had American partners. That was fine with Pearson, as long as the American partners were prepared to accept Telefilm's rules for Telefilm-backed projects. And so it came to pass that Peter Pearson, who had spent much of his life fighting for Canadian content, found himself going steady with Mickey Mouse. And what of it? With Kevin Sullivan in charge, there was no real danger that *Anne of Green Gables: The Sequel* would be Disneyfied.

Colleen Dewhurst, the magnificently craggy-faced, smoky-voiced actress who plays that stern Victorian spinster Marilla in both *Anne of Green Gables* and the sequel, has spent most of her career in the United States, but she was born Canadian and grew up in Montreal. *Anne of Green Gables* was the first book she remembers her mother reading to her, and those memories came back to her in 1972 when she bought a great country house in Prince Edward Island, which became an idyllic retreat for Dewhurst and her sons. Dewhurst said yes right away when she was asked to play Marilla, even though she didn't really know who Kevin Sullivan was, and it seemed to take him forever to put all the pieces together and get his project off the ground.

Sullivan got his start in 1979 by producing, writing and directing an adaptation of a Hans Christian Andersen fable, *The Fir Tree*, and then produced *The Wild Pony*, a family film made for pay-TV. But *Anne* was the big one, and the story of how Sullivan got to make it is a lesson in the importance of being stubborn.

In 1981, when Sullivan first checked with Farrar, Straus and Giroux, the New York publishers, about the rights to *Anne*, he was told they had been merged with those of the musical play, and that they belonged to Don Harron and Norman Campbell. Harron and Campbell wrote the show that has been running at the Charlottetown Festival since 1967. Sullivan was surprised to discover that no royalties were being paid to the author's estate.

In 1983, when Sullivan heard that the rights to the novel were going into the public domain, he checked again and realized that the legal department of the publishing company was confused. Sullivan decided there was only one way to sort it out. He had to become the world expert on the *Anne of Green Gables* copyright. He spent months studying copyright law. Meanwhile the CBC was besieged by producers who'd heard *Anne* was entering the public domain.

In 1907 Lucy Maud Montgomery had contracted all rights to *Anne of Green Gables* to the L.C. Page Co. for ten percent of the wholesale price of the book over and above the first thousand copies. Then in 1919 she signed over all the rights to five of the six Anne books for $17,500 (which was what she thought would be her lifetime earnings from the books). When Farrar, Straus took over L.C. Page thirty years later, the firm got those rights.

That seems clear enough, but new copyright laws (of which Montgomery was unaware) came into effect in 1924, and in that year *Anne* reverted to the author's estate. This was news to the independent producers who believed *Anne* was in the public domain, and it was news to Harron and Campbell, who felt sure they had the rights and fully intended to film their gold-mine stage musical.

Hollywood had been on to Anne Shirley for a long time. First there was a 1919 silent movie starring Mary Miles Minter (Mary Pickford's chief rival), which had Montgomery fuming in her diary about the outrage of having an American flag flying over Anne's school. That film has been lost. Then there was a 1934 talkie known chiefly for the fact that the child star, Dawn O'Day, actually changed her name to Anne Shirley and later appeared in a sequel, *Anne of the Windy Poplars* (1940).

In 1956, Norman Campbell and Don Harron collaborated on a live, ninety-minute TV musical for the CBC starring John Drainie, Toby Tarnow (as Anne) and Margot Christie, and it was produced again two years later. Mavor Moore remembered it in 1964 when he was producing the opening variety show for Charlottetown's Confederation Centre of the Arts, which was to be performed in the presence of the Queen. Diane Stapley's singing of the title song from the TV show went over so well that Moore commissioned a full-scale stage version for the next summer. Campbell wrote the music, Harron wrote the book and they collaborated on the lyrics. There was additional material by Mavor Moore and Elaine Campbell (Norman Campbell's wife).

The production, directed and choreographed by Alan Lund, was an instant hit and has been playing to full houses every summer since. This popularity has led to several national tours, productions in London, New York and Tokyo and two record albums. For twenty years they'd been talking about doing a movie. And that presented a roadblock for Kevin Sullivan.

"Two Canadian producers vie for *Anne of Green Gables*," announced a headline in the Toronto *Star*. According to Sullivan the publicity scared off potential buyers from TV networks who didn't want to get caught in a dispute. To sort out this problem it was left to Michael Levine, the hyperactive Toronto entertainment lawyer.

Levine looked at the case and, realizing how complicated it was, came up with a classic everybody-wins, "I-don't-think-we-have-a-problem-here" solution. Essentially his idea was to let everybody stay out of everybody else's way. Let Sullivan make his movie for TV as long as he stayed out of the theatrical market. Let Harron and Campbell protect their right to do a movie version of their musical, as long as they allowed Sullivan to make his TV film. That way, the estate was happy, CBC was happy and everyone saved years of frustrating court battles. Three years later, Harron and Campbell were no closer to doing their *Anne* movie, and informed onlookers were betting they never would.

Kevin Sullivan now had the inside track with the estate, whose principal concern was that any movie be genuinely Canadian. He raised two-thirds of the money through Telefilm and CBC, and scraped together the other million-plus through a complicated coalition involving the German TV system, CityTv and PBS (which showed a slightly different version in weekly installments two months after CBC aired its version).

Sullivan auditioned 3,000 girls for the title role. Katharine Hepburn suggested that her grandniece, Schuyler Grant, could play the part, and Hepburn could play a supporting role. Sullivan tested Grant and thought she was the miracle he needed, but Telefilm and the CBC held out for a Canadian, so he cast Schuyler as Anne's friend, Diana Barry. (Although CBC was demanding control of such crucial details, it wasn't willing to put up as much money as Sullivan had originally been promised, and there was a great deal of dramatic scrambling to make up the shortfall.)

Sullivan always wanted Dewhurst to play Marilla, the spinster who, along with her brother Matthew, decides to send for a boy from the orphanage to help with the work — and by mistake gets a girl. For the role of Matthew he landed Richard Farnsworth, the silver-haired former Hollywood stuntman who had made such a great impact in another Canadian film, *The Grey Fox*.

The big question about Megan Follows was whether she was too old. Anne is eleven when she comes to Green Gables and sixteen at the end of the book. In the film she's thirteen at the beginning and sixteen (Follows' actual age at the time of shooting) at the end. The daughter of two Canadian stage actors, Ted Follows and Dawn Greenhalgh, the young actress turned out to be such a pro that one never questioned her age.

There's nothing drippy or precious about Megan Follows as Anne. She has the air of romantic eagerness bordering on craziness that gives the character, and the material, a sharp enough edge to ward off cuteness. Anne is a hungry-for-attention charmer; she's also a hilariously excessive self-dramatizer, and she has an exhausting affliction: she can't stop talking. That makes her the perfect foil for Farnsworth, whose specialty is hardly talking at all.

Dewhurst, a sturdy earth mother, may be more than Lucy Maud Montgomery ever had in mind, but she's a marvelous match for the impetuous, hot-tempered Anne, and there's nothing cloying about the bond that develops between them. Their relationship is a series of sparring matches. Chalk up one for Marilla when Anne is forced to apologize to the bossy Mrs. Rachel Lynde (played by that fine actress, Patricia Hamilton); score one for the orphan girl in the case of the missing brooch.

There are many delicious acting turns, such as Charmion King's Aunt Josephine and, in an astonishing debut, Jonathan Crombie as Gilbert, the boy over whose head Anne breaks a slate. A couple of German actors (hired because of the German coproduction financing) seem out of place, but the cast, including Marilyn Lightstone, Jayne Eastwood, Jackie Burroughs and Rosemary Radcliffe, is mostly formidable.

Dewhurst is the anchor. She has rarely come across as strongly in movies as she does in her best stage performances (such as Josie in Eugene O'Neill's *A Moon for the Misbegotten*), but here she's magnificent. It's the chemistry between Dewhurst and Follows that provides an emotional payoff and makes Anne something considerably more than another safe, inoffensive piece of family entertainment.

Kevin Sullivan was deluged with demands for a follow-up, but for a long time he resisted doing a sequel, just because sequels tend to be, well, sequels. It was the eagerness of Colleen Dewhurst to do another *Anne* film that helped change his mind. To get the story he wanted, he had to put together bits of three different *Anne* books by Lucy Maud Montgomery.

In the sequel Anne leaves Green Gables for a teaching job and gets embroiled in a series of crises at her school. One of the plummiest roles is that of a grande dame presiding over the family of one of her students, and Sullivan's first choice for the role was the distinguished British actress Dame Wendy Hiller, who accepted. Dame Wendy gave the performance that Sullivan dreamed she would, but not without difficulty. The character was wheelchair-ridden, and it was problematic for the actress, who was just recovering from a hip operation, to get in and out of the wheelchair. One day she pulled the hip out of its socket and had to be taken to a hospital emergency room.

The other performance that makes an unforgettable impression in the sequel is Toronto stage actress Rosemary Dunsmore as the prickly school principal who makes Anne's life as difficult as possible. And Megan Follows makes a totally persuasive transition into adulthood. Against all odds Kevin Sullivan has deepened and expanded the saga, giving it emotional complexity and avoiding the curse of sequels. He's created so much glory that there's plenty of room for Telefilm, CBC and Walt Disney — perhaps the oddest ménage à trois in this country's cultural history — all to bask in Anne's glory.

11

Stage Fright

Martha Henry was neglected for years. It wasn't until *The Wars* (1982) and *Dancing in the Dark* (1987) that Henry finally became a leading lady in films, and by then she was well into her forties. Oh, she had been respected by Shakespeare aficionados at the Stratford Festival since 1962, when she made a stunning debut as Miranda in *The Tempest*. She'd spent a couple of years in England, where she appeared in a West End thriller and a BBC TV series. But partly because of her own self-effacing personality and partly because of the well-known Canadian habit of taking our own actors for granted while making a great fuss over visiting celebrities, she tended to be overlooked at Stratford even when she was giving such great performances as her Isabella in the Robin Phillips production of *Measure for Measure* and her Olga in John Hirsch's production of *Three Sisters* (both cornerstones of the 1976 season). And Henry had to wait years for a breakthrough in movies.

Martha Henry wasn't alone in this regard. Except for her 1966 appearance in Don Owen's *Notes for a Film about Donna and Gail,* the spectacularly talented Jackie Burroughs was badly used or else completely neglected by moviemakers—until her breakthrough performance in *The Grey Fox* (1982). Until then, a talent long treasured by Canadian theatregoers was relatively unknown to moviegoers. Burroughs was the bohemian rebel of Canadian theatre, and she appeared in several forgettable films in the 1970s. By the time *The Grey Fox* was made, it was already too late for her to play the parts she should have had when the industry was young. In *The Wars,* which was shot before *The Grey Fox* but released later, Robin Phillips cast her in a cameo as an old family retainer. And after *The Grey Fox,* Burroughs appeared in, among other films, *Judgement in Stone, Anne of Green Gables* and *John and the Missus.* In 1987 she went to Mexico to make a low-budget movie as part of a small collective; she was involved in producing and editing it as well as playing the central role.

In *The Grey Fox,* the first glimpse director Phillip Borsos gives the audience of Burroughs is as startling as Rita Hayworth's famous hairdo-first entrance in *Gilda.* Memorably done up as a Victorian lady, with a high-necked dress and a huge blue hat that appears to have a life of its own, like some monumental bird's nest, Burroughs bristles and simmers away under the finery, the auburn hair beneath the hat like a smoldering volcano about to erupt.

Kate, the character Burroughs plays, is an unmarried renegade—a fierce rebel who earns her living as a photographer long before working women or professional photographers were accepted conventions. She describes her work as "recording injustice with a camera."

Spiritually Kate seems to be a relative of both the Louise Bryant character played by Diane Keaton in *Reds* and Violet Decarmin, the gregarious, battered hooker Burroughs played on stage in Calgary in John Murrell's play *Farther West,* which starred Martha Henry as the doomed pioneer madam May Buchanan.

There's nothing understated or repressed about Burroughs; that's what makes her a perfect counterpoint for Bill Miner, the gentleman bandit played by American actor Richard Farnsworth. Miner, who has just arrived in Kamloops, encounters Kate in a newspaper office, where she is fuming at the editor about an editorial on the treatment of women in factories. When the editor refuses to print her letter on behalf of a national women's trade union, she tells him off — "You have the mentality of a grocery clerk" — and sweeps out. The scene is vintage Burroughs.

Why didn't the movie breakthrough of Martha Henry, Jackie Burroughs and other Canadian actors happen sooner? Because Canadian movie producers were mostly blind to the embarrassment of riches they had before them in the form of performing talent ready to be revealed to the rest of the world. Those who rarely bothered going to the theatre often said they couldn't cast their films in Canada. What they really meant was they felt more secure using American or British actors whom they knew of from movies made elsewhere. And when a Canadian actor was needed to meet the requirements for public subsidy, there was always a strong preference for Canadians who had long ago moved elsewhere: Donald Sutherland, Margot Kidder, Christopher Plummer and Geneviève Bujold.

The neglect of Canadian acting talent — surely one of the country's greatest creative resources — was one of the tragic absurdities of the Hollywood North era. Partly it was a symptom of the greed and shortsightedness of producers who didn't realize that if they developed stars of their own they would be helping to build a real film industry instead of just blowing bubbles. And partly it was a consequence of a peculiar cultural gulf: Canadian theatre had developed mostly from British traditions, while Canadian movies and TV followed American models.

Professional theatre did not truly flourish in this country until the mid-1950s, when a number of developments occurred more or less at once. First there was the founding of the Stratford Festival, which announced to the world that first-rate classical theatre could be produced in the middle of nowhere. Then there was the creation of the Canada Council, which signified the commitment of the Canadian government to develop the arts in this country.

Finally, the Manitoba Theatre Centre, which John Hirsch and Tom Hendry established in Winnipeg, provided the model for what became a string of regional professional theatres across the country. Yet, when people talked about Toronto theatre in the 1960s, they generally thought of touring Broadway shows. But in the early 1970s there began an explosion of creative activity. Suddenly there were audiences for original plays by Canadian playwrights, and a number of lively fringe theatres were born during a feverish period of cultural nationalism and government spending on the arts.

Canada started making feature films in significant numbers around 1968; but a decade later virtually no Canadian actor had become a movie star. And though Canadians were used to hearing laments about talented performers who had defected to Hollywood or London or New York, Martha Henry quietly reversed the process after moving to Canada from Michigan.

Henry was not the name she grew up with. She took the family name of her first husband, an actor who dropped the name and billed himself as Donnelly Rhodes. Before that she was Martha Buhs (pronounced *bus*), a painfully shy girl who lived most of the time with grandparents after the divorce of her parents, a gambling businessman and a nightclub musician. She worked at Toronto's Crest Theatre in its early years, then became one of the first, and most distinguished, graduates of the National Theatre School before landing at Stratford. She was a fixture at the festival until 1980, when she was one of the ill-fated quartet fired by the board only weeks after taking over the artistic directorship following the abrupt departure of Robin Phillips. The firing touched off the most painful controversy in Canadian theatre history, and since then Henry has declined all offers to act at Stratford. But she has continued to have a strong association with Phillips: she was a member of his ill-fated Grand Theatre Company in London, Ontario, and appeared in two Phillips productions in Toronto and one in Calgary.

It was Phillips who guided her through her first big movie role in *The Wars,* based on the Timothy Findley novel, which was filmed in the summer of 1981 but not released until the fall of 1983. It was one of the curiosities of Canada's movie history that so few of the country's major literary works had found their way to the screen. Yet the movie version of *The Wars* came out at the same time as a screen version of Gabrielle Roy's *The Tin Flute,* which had the dubious distinction of making *The Wars* seem by comparison better than it really was.

The Tin Flute is a saga of a downtrodden French-Canadian family living on the edge of poverty through the Depression and World War II. It has heavy doses of masochism and sentimentality, but there was no excuse for turning it into the crude, ludicrous soap opera that emerged under the direction of Claude Fournier. The picture was a veritable festival of clichés and stereotypes down to the poor, happy French-Canadian family escaping for a day from urban misery to the simpler joys of frolicking in the country during the maple-syrup season.

The Wars, though clearly no masterpiece, did manage to be civilized, polished and respectable. You had the secure feeling that Phillips had control of the material and knew what he was doing. And he had the courage to cast the gifted actors he had worked with on the stage at Stratford and in London without being bullied out of it by film financiers who might have preferred Americans with names recognizable outside Canada.

Martha Henry looked good in Edwardian hats, though after *The Wars* and the CBC TV series *Empire, Inc.,* movie audiences might have had the impression she was capable of playing only cold, controlling, upper-set WASP matrons, a shame, given the impressive range of her stage work. In *The Wars,* Henry seemed to be suffering almost as much as Marilyn Lightstone, as the much-oppressed matriarch of *The Tin Flute,* but in the former case the audience was encouraged to feel she deserved to suffer. After all, she was a rich, repressed woman with a limp husband (fellow

Stratford veteran William Hutt), and she was always trying to control people. There was a dying child involved in the story, as there was in *The Tin Flute,* and the child's death was associated with symbolism almost as heavy-handed as that damned tin flute—the rabbits of the dead child that had to be killed in some grotesque ritual.

The story of *The Wars* concerns the apprenticeship of the dead girl's brother, who goes off to war against her wishes. "I can't keep anyone alive," murmurs Martha Henry, "not anymore." The lavish garden parties seem to be thrown for the sole purpose of providing ironic counterpoint, and the conversation is terribly measured and literary.

Robert Ross, played by Brent Carver, another actor who'd worked with Phillips at Stratford and London, learns a little about life and observes the horrors of war. There's the usual set piece about the sensitive boy going to the brothel with his fellow soldiers, plus a romantic interlude in which he has a torrid affair in a frightfully British manor of a creepiness familiar to veterans of Joseph Losey films. The bizarre climax involves his decision to release horses from a burning barn in contravention of his officer's orders, and somehow the audience is meant to feel his death is caused by the coldness, bitterness and general hatefulness of his family. Robert has to free the horses to make up for those rabbits, and he has to defy military orders to get back at his parents.

As a film *The Wars* was a bit pat; the limitations were probably inherent in Findley's 1977 novel, which had some great sequences and an impressively sustained ironic distance but little in the way of emotional depth or original ideas. Phillips managed to catch the tone of the book, to frame the action effectively and to give it the resonance of being filtered through time and memory. The supporting cast included many Stratford and Toronto stage actors—Alan Scarfe, Barbara Budd, Domini Blythe, Clare Coulter—and the handsome art direction was by Daphne Dare, another regular Phillips collaborator.

Martha Henry won her first Genie Award for *The Wars*, but she wasn't at her best in it. It wasn't until *Dancing in the Dark*, three years later, that Henry showed moviegoers the qualities that had made her the first lady of the stage. Henry's performance, which brought her a second Genie Award, gave new meaning to the phrase "kitchen-sink drama." As Edna Cormick, the quintessential enslaved Ontario housewife, Henry cleans and scrubs and polishes and vacuums with the diligence of those anonymous women in the detergent commercials on TV.

In common with *Loyalties* and *The Decline of the American Empire*, two other Canadian movies released in the fall of 1986, *Dancing in the Dark* peered probingly into the dark corners of Canadian repression and sexual discontent. Canada's long winters, these three movies seemed to suggest, had produced a set of complex neuroses every bit as eccentric as the Swedish variety chronicled for the world in relentless detail by Ingmar Bergman.

Unlike the ladies extolling the virtues of oven-scouring pads or toilet-bowl cleansers on TV, the heroine of *Dancing in the Dark* is unable to attain salvation through cleanliness. Edna never blisses out on the discovery of a powerful new soap, or makes the audience feel that getting deep stains out is as rewarding as discovering her G-spot.

Who'd know if there was lint under the counter or a smudge on the fridge? Edna would know. So all day long she has to keep toilets and mirrors gleaming. This, you see, is Edna's perceived role in life. Looking after the house is what she does for Harry, the man to whom she has devoted herself totally for twenty years. Harry, as played by Neil Munro, stays at the office late a lot, and he doesn't offer Edna a whole lot of gratification, except for birthday dinners at a fancy restaurant. It's evidently too late to bother conceiving the child she always wanted.

Watching *Dancing in the Dark* with its awkward novelistic structure (Edna tells much of her story in voice-over flashbacks) and its obsessive drudgery, you begin to wonder if R.W. Fassbinder, the prolific German director, didn't die but merely turned into a Canadian. There's something perversely funny about Edna and her fetish, but the humorless tone suggests that neither director-screenwriter Leon Marr (making his feature debut) nor novelist Joan Barfoot was in on the joke. I couldn't help thinking how sublimely silly an SCTV version would be.

Yet Martha Henry delves so deeply and compellingly into the bleak horror of Edna's life that it is impossible not to succumb to her spell. One can overlook the predictable plot twists: the fact that Edna is evidently now in a mental home recalling how she got there, recording everything in a blue notebook; or the fact that when she discovers Harry's infidelity she pulls out a perfectly clean knife and . . .

It's a measure of Martha Henry's hypnotic, haunting performance that obsessive Edna gets to you even if you're aware of the clichés operating here. She holds the screen by divine right, like Liv Ullmann in one of her better Bergman downers. Even that perfect Martha Henry diction, which in other vehicles has seemed too schoolteacherly correct, is absolutely right for Edna. *Dancing in the Dark* might not be fun to sit through, but afterward you can't shake it off. Martha Henry's Edna seeps into your pores.

Canadian playwrights have generally fared even worse on the screen than Canadian actors. Among those who might have expected to make a mark in films, but haven't, are John Murrell, David French, George F. Walker, Michel Tremblay, Sharon Pollock, Erika Ritter and Larry Fineberg. How many times have memorable evenings of Canadian theatre been turned into dead, well-meaning TV events? The CBC has been the main culprit, but there was a dismal pay-TV version of Mavis Gallant's *What Is To Be Done,* taped before an audience, with canned laughter added later. The effect of bad screen adaptations is to preclude the material from connecting with a much larger audience than it would get on the stage. The larger public, taking a look at one of these flat TV versions, probably gets the false impression that Canadian plays aren't worth paying attention to.

Luckily, when it came to putting his extraordinary musical play *Rock and Roll* on the small screen, John Gray was determined to avoid the usual pitfalls. So was Les Harris, the producer of the TV version, whose track record included *Escape from Iran*, a made-for-TV movie with Gordon Pinsent as Ken Taylor, the Canadian ambassador who helped American hostages flee. And so Gray's witty, deeply felt musical about a small-town rock band (first staged in 1981) was transformed into a startlingly original and imaginative video experience, which was shown on CBC television in the spring of 1985 as *The King of Friday Night*. For once, a brilliant piece of theatre was given a new treatment and turned into a brilliant piece of TV, and the mass audience had a chance to share the sense of discovery that excited live audiences the first time around.

The show has an autobiographical basis, though there are some fine distinctions between *The King of Friday Night* and the life and times of John Gray. The band in the show is called the Monarchs and plays in the town of Mushaboom, Nova Scotia. Gray played with a group called the Lincolns, based in Truro, sixty miles northeast of Halifax. There was a certain unsavory aspect to this band, named after a car, which Gray is clearly fond of. Making $80 or $90 a week, the boys would spend it on fast cars and liquor, and race down the back roads at 110 miles per hour, roaring like animals.

The Lincolns played for eight years at community and legion hall dances, and toured towns in the region: Sackville, Moncton, New Glasgow, Amherst. According to Gray, one of the biggest advantages of being in a band was that you didn't have to ask girls to dance. With its rough-edged hooligan energy, the band provided a jubilant release from the sombre virtue prevalent in these communities. In 1978 the Lincolns got together for a two-night reunion, and 3,000 people turned out to cheer them.

That event inspired Gray to start writing a musical play —and a similar reunion (held in Mushaboom in 1981) is the focal point of the show.

John Gray's views have changed since his days as a rock musician. There's more than a trace of self-disgust when he analyzes what he was doing then: "We were playing hits from Chicago and Philadelphia, basking in second-hand glamor and borrowed charisma." Gray's satiric view of his younger self is apparent in *The King of Friday Night*, but he gave youthful hooliganism its due; the boisterous charm of those wayward boys, infatuated with American pop culture and feeling an urgent need to bust loose, made the show irresistible.

When Gray did get away from Truro (he moved to Vancouver and became a writer), a funny thing happened. He turned into a Canadian nationalist, repelled by American culture. It was Gray's interest in Canadian heroes that got him writing theatrical songs and plays such as *18 Wheels* and *Billy Bishop Goes to War,* which he and Eric Peterson performed all over the world. They wound up spending a year in the United States, and it wasn't a happy time.

Gray's sense of alienation from American culture intensified his need to maintain a distinctive Canadian alternative, and that led him to his latest project—fiddler Don Messer, who died in 1973, and his popular weekly TV show, *Don Messer's Jubilee*. Gray saw Messer as a hero victimized by bad guys at CBC headquarters who canceled Messer's show because they were too keen on following American fashions.

"Don Messer played tunes that implied traditional values Canadians wanted to keep," Gray remarked. "He transcribed tunes with the zeal of an archeologist preserving the memory of a lost civilization."

The way Gray saw it, "Don Messer was cast out for being too much like us." In the era of the Beatles, it was too embarrassing for CBC executives in Nehru jackets and love beads to see a bumpkin like Messer draw huge audiences.

The key to the success of *The King of Friday Night* was the decision not to do it as a filmed play. With the help of British director Andrew Gosling's team of electronic wizards, Gray stripped down the show and reassembled the parts into a fantastic video game.

We're introduced to a group of thirty-eight-year-olds with stage fright. They are members of the band who've come home years later for a public reunion. And they look back on the heyday of the Monarchs as their lost golden age. They're full of the ambivalent longing of adults looking back at a joyride that didn't take them anywhere. The ghost of Screamin' John, a local eccentric (played by Eric Peterson) who self-destructed behind the wheel of his car, keeps coming back to remind them of the dangers of living too fast, too soon.

Flashback: It's Friday night at the community arena of a Maritime town in the early 1960s. Several hundred kids have paid to get in, and they're impatient for the action to begin. Outside, a pink Ford convertible screeches to a halt, and out pour the local heroes.

The astonishing Frank MacKay, who sang with Gray and the Lincolns, plays Parker, the fat boy who becomes the Monarchs' lead singer. It's Parker's talent that transforms the band from scruffy curiosity to electrifying success. Before Parker turns up, the band is a motley crew, its sound is just awful. MacKay has lost a lot of weight in the intervening years, but he still has the moves of a fat boy—a Falstaff of small-town rock. For the big reunion, he flies in from Toronto, where he has an agent who wants to make him into "the Wayne Newton of the North."

There are elements of sadness and bitterness built into *The King of Friday Night*. Gray keeps things light and plays even failed hopes for gently nostalgic comedy, but there is a sense of rage below the cheerful surface. Parker is the only member of the band with extraordinary talent. The others must face the depressing fact that singing with the

Monarchs was the only interesting thing that ever happened to them.

For Gray, going back to Truro, where much of the TV version was shot, was an overwhelming event, not only because the very legion hall where the band once sang became the prime location for the filming, but also because Gray stayed with his parents while in town and slept in the same bed he'd had at the time. Among the old black-and-white snapshots flashed on the screen during one of the collage sequences is John Gray's picture from an old high-school yearbook.

The King of Friday Night may have seemed like a video natural, but moving it from stage to screen was no easy matter. Gray turned down an offer from Home Box Office, which wanted the play as a vehicle for Tom Jones. He also turned down Warner Brothers, which wanted to buy stage and screen rights. A genuine maverick, Gray has been resisting Hollywood temptations for years, preferring to live with his family in a middle-class Vancouver neighborhood in what he calls "the house that Billy Bishop bought."

Les Harris, an independent producer, got some help from Telefilm and made a deal with CBC, which wanted to add a laugh track (Gray vetoed it) and tone down the raunchy lyrics (Gray compromised). The technique that made the show visually inventive was multilayered chromakey; Andrew Gosling, Gray's British codirector, is a master of the form. Shots of the actors were scrambled with various photographs, backgrounds, posters, illustrations and painted scenes to create a highly stylized, at times surreal, look. The technique was perfectly appropriate to the fabled, faraway quality that Gray's musical memory tour suggests. In *The King of Friday Night*, he reclaimed his own past, without sentimentalizing it, and made the audience share his feelings about it and his sense of what made it important. That's a rare achievement on television — or anywhere.

In the fall of 1987, two Canadian stars emerged in modest, homemade Toronto movies. Sheila McCarthy, long known to theatre audiences as a winning funny girl for her performances in such shows as *Really Rosie, The Little Shop of Horrors* and Stratford's *The School for Scandal*, made her inevitable screen breakthrough in *I've Heard the Mermaids Singing*; and Craig Russell, who had starred ten years earlier in *Outrageous!*, returned after one of the longest intermissions in history to do it again in *Too Outrageous!*

A star was born in 1977 when at age twenty-nine Craig Russell played a Toronto hairdresser turned female impersonator—a character based on his own life story, more or less—in the surprise hit film *Outrageous!*. And for a while Russell soared on the wings of the film's success. But like some of the ladies he plays in his act, Russell had trouble handling success.

Russell had grown up unhappy in Scarborough, Ontario (Scar-beria, he likes to call it, stretching out the syllables in torment), dropped out of Cedarbrae Secondary School in a rage ("I found out why they called it secondary") and, while working as a typist for an insurance company, started the Mae West fan club. In 1967, when Russell phoned Mae to announce he was having a nervous breakdown, she invited him to come to Hollywood, move in with her and work as her secretary. He stayed seven months, long enough to be remembered: she left him $3,500 in her will. Back in Toronto, Russell started doing his female-impersonator act at gay bars while working as a hairdresser. His friend Margaret Gibson, recently released from a psychiatric ward, wrote a short story loosely based on her friendship with Russell. When the story was turned into a film, Russell was asked to play the character Gibson had modeled on him.

Outrageous!, a sentimental Cinderella fable directed by Richard Benner (a landed immigrant from New York) and produced by Bill Marshall for $167,000, marked the moment at which the gay world's satirical parody of show-biz lore finally achieved the breakthrough with the mass audience it had been leading up to for years.

But everybody didn't live happily ever after. Benner found himself back in New York driving a taxi. In 1981 Russell starred in one doomed stage musical—*Hogtown*, a curiosity set in Toronto, circa 1885. Tom Hendry wrote the book and lyrics; Paul Hoffert wrote the music. Brian Macdonald was the director, Peter Peroff was the producer and Russell played Belle Howard, a big-hearted madam who leads the fight against turning the city into a place "fit for a Christian and hell for everybody else."

Hogtown was a temporary change from Russell's club show. Most of the time he found himself trapped in an act he was getting tired of, playing Judy Garland, Mae West, Carol Channing, Bette Midler, Marlene Dietrich and other legendary ladies. And when Russell was down, he turned himself into a parody of Sunset Boulevard. As a compulsively bad boy, Russell was like Lenny Bruce in drag. And the act became a rancid expression of his hostility.

That's what happened one night at the Queen Elizabeth Theatre in Vancouver in the fall of 1981. Russell was trying to send a message to agents and managers he thought were cheating him, and he made the mistake of doing it on stage, by not delivering the show people expected. The audience stormed out, Russell was fired and the rest of his tour was canceled.

"They said, 'You're finished, try another country,'" Russell recalls. "For some reason it made the front pages of the newspapers. I was called indecent, disgusting and unprofessional. It was so blown out of proportion, I got the hint."

Russell spent the next five years in Europe, mostly Germany, with frequent changes of address. He thought he might have to stay away for ten years, but he came back after five—when the long-talked-about sequel to *Outrageous!* finally became a reality, with Roy Krost as producer. But Russell's reunion with Richard Benner, who was writing and directing *Too Outrageous!*, hit a snag shortly after Russell's arrival in Toronto. Russell's two dogs, Nancy and Baby, were still in Europe, and he was feeling unhappy and disoriented. When Craig Russell is unhappy, he misbehaves—which explains why he arrived for the first day of shooting with a visible cut above his eye.

Benner and Krost wanted to replace him, but Hollis McLaren—who had come out of retirement to reprise her role as Liza, the Margaret Gibson character—told them without Russell there could be no sequel. Telefilm and the Ontario Film Development Corporation also balked at the idea of replacing Russell with an American.

Once shooting started, and Russell's dogs arrived in town, everything went more or less smoothly. And in *Too Outrageous!* Craig Russell is definitely "on." There's a manic gleam in his eye, a buoyancy to everything he does when he gets a chance to play his famous ladies—Eartha Kitt, Barbra Streisand, Peggy Lee, Judy Garland, Bette Davis and Tina Turner. The film (which cost just under $3 million) is much more polished-looking than the original, but the formula is essentially the same. *Too Outrageous!* is full of pithy little nuggets of wisdom-to-live-by, and it's structured as a fairly maudlin victim fantasy. Liza and Robin both have lovers who betray them; there's a note of doom for the AIDS age; and the let's-stop-the-masquerade ending doesn't really work.

But when Craig Russell puts on his Tina Turner wig and stomps around with mock-insolent zest, we're liberated from Benner's squishy little pieties. Russell's act is a kind of tribute—a fond, witty commentary. He doesn't merely mime, and what he does goes way beyond "female impersonating." It's inspired and original in the same way as the work of the late Charles Ludlam and his Ridiculous Theatrical Company. Russell has the ability to become the character he's playing, and his satire is magically infused with love. When Russell is at his best, it's clear that what we are witnessing is some weird and wonderful show-business form of possession. He orchestrates his own pandemonium, and he gives the audience a good time.

Craig Russell became a star when his first film was released ten years ago; now at age thirty-nine he had a comeback vehicle. This fact is the subject of a Russell quip: "First they said it was a one-shot deal. 'He's just doing his life and his act.' Well, now they'll probably say it's just a two-shot deal."

Another new Canadian movie star was born at the 1987 Cannes Film Festival when *I've Heard the Mermaids Singing* was shown to wild acclaim in the Directors' Fortnight program, immediately turning a squeaky-voiced, unassuming funny girl from Toronto into an international sensation. Suddenly the name on everyone's lips along the Croisette was Sheila McCarthy.

Some people assumed that playing Sally Bowles in Stratford's *Cabaret* would complete McCarthy's ascent to superstardom, but the role turned out to be a trap. Audience expectations had been conditioned by the movie version of *Cabaret*, which was structured as a showcase for Liza Minnelli. The Sally Bowles of Christopher Isherwood's Berlin stories was not only English rather than American she was also a minor talent. That's why she was hanging out at the Kit Kat Klub. According to Isherwood, the whole point of Sally was that she *wasn't* Liza Minnelli. But in Stratford's production, the numbers built in such a way that when Sally turned out to be something other than a powerhouse belter, the audience felt let down.

McCarthy is shown to far better advantage in *I've Heard the Mermaids Singing*—a first feature written and directed by Patricia Rozema. It's a charming, low-budget fable set in the world of chic Toronto feminism, about a domineering gallery curator (Quebec actress Paule Baillargeon) who becomes boss, mother, mentor and wicked witch, all in one, to a confused, shy, "organizationally impaired" temporary secretary. Polly, the temp, turns out to be someone who should not be taken for granted—or crossed.

Living alone in a tiny apartment, seemingly inarticulate and aimless, this appealing, turnip-faced waif turns out to have surprising fantasies and aspirations. When she presents her photographs to the curator and they're rebuffed, she is devastated. But when she discovers the curator's secret, Polly loses her temper and her mentor winds up in hospital.

Comic delicacy is McCarthy's specialty, and it's the way she handles the emergence of the character's inner life that wins over audiences. There's nothing sentimental about her performance; she never begs us to feel sorry for Polly. Bits of business, such as Polly's fumbling at a Japanese restaurant, are so winning she makes us care about Polly on her own terms.

Even before *Mermaids* had its North American premiere at Toronto's Festival of Festivals, its ecstatic reception at Cannes had guaranteed it would recover its entire cost and that it would be seen all over the world. And the demonstration that the right film role could catapult a talented young Canadian actor into an international movie career provided some hope. Perhaps movie producers would show more respect now for the talent mine available to them on stages across Canada. Perhaps the years of waiting and neglect that Martha Henry and Jackie Burroughs went through before they were "discovered" would not have to be repeated by the next generation of talent.

PART III

SLOUCHING TOWARD CHINA

12

The Long March

Christmas week, 1986, was sunny and warm in southern California. But the number-one topic among Hollywood's Canadians that season wasn't the snow and freezing temperatures back home or the latest studio upheaval; it was *Bethune*. The hot rumor was that after all these years Ted Allan's story about the crusading surgeon was finally going to be filmed. John Kemeny had let his option run out, but a couple of hungry producers in Montreal, Pieter Kroonenburg and Nicolas Clermont, had raised some money and made a deal with the Chinese. Donald Sutherland was to star in the picture, the Chinese were building sets and the big question was whether Ted Kotcheff, who had been trying off and on for a decade to get this movie going, was going to direct it. The details weren't working out the way Kotcheff wanted, but Ted Allan, who had been collaborating with him on this venture for years, was urging, even begging, Kotcheff to accept the offer, however imperfect, for the sake of realizing at last the dream they had shared for so long.

Although Ted Allan had recently turned seventy and spent every winter in Los Angeles (living the rest of the year in Toronto), he was not exactly like those elderly Jews in Paul Mazursky's film *Harry and Tonto* who come to California to spend their last years in the sun. A writer who had moved around, living at various times in Montreal, Toronto, New York, Los Angeles and London, England, Ted Allan was above all a man who had spent the better part of his life writing obsessively about Norman Bethune. Allan had been only twenty years old when he worked alongside Bethune in the Spanish Civil War, but Bethune had cast a giant shadow across Allan's life. Not only had Allan written Bethune's biography; he had spent almost half a century writing a movie that Hollywood kept finding new reasons for not making.

Nor was Ted Allan alone in his obsession with a movie about Bethune. Almost from the beginning of the Canadian government's involvement in the feature-film business, from the creation of the Canadian Film Development Corporation in 1968 through its later metamorphosis into the TV-oriented Telefilm Canada, successive executive directors, with their scrambled mandate to be half Ottawa bureaucrat, half imitation-Hollywood tycoon, had made seemingly fruitless expeditions to Peking and L.A. trying to get the dream project off the ground. First Michael Spencer, then Michael McCabe, then Peter Pearson, the current Telefilm boss.

What was it about Bethune that drew all the titans of Canada's fragile show-biz industry to the same dangerous, impossible quest? It was as if all these people believed the surgeon saint could heal the nation's infected movie industry, purify it and effect some miraculous cure so that Canadian cinema could recover from its chronic malaise.

For a long time, they seemed to be banging their heads against the Great Wall of China. Bethune had been dreamed about and argued about and gossiped about as the impossible movie project, doomed never to be made. After so many dashed hopes and so many false starts, it seemed almost unbelievable that at long last Bethune actually *was* being made.

Considering his political development, it seems appropriate that Ted Allan was born in 1917, the year of the Russian Revolution. He had depicted the world of his childhood — the Montreal ghetto where he grew up poor — many times, but especially in his story *Lies My Father Told Me* and in the 1975 Canadian film version of it, which won a Golden Globe award as best foreign film and an Oscar nomination for Allan's screenplay.

The eldest of three children, Allan had to quit school to help support the family during the Depression. At fourteen, he joined the Young Communist League, despite the opposition of his parents. At eighteen he became Montreal correspondent of the *Daily Clarion*, the official organ of the Canadian Communist Party. Allan went to Spain as a volunteer fighter, but he was transferred to Bethune's blood-transfusion unit. Bethune appointed him political commissar. Allan had known Bethune in Canada, and they had a warm relationship. But Allan, who was by his own account a priggish young Communist at that time, was shocked by Bethune's heavy drinking, and they had a falling-out. Allan was not with Bethune during his final mission to China, but he developed a theory about it. He believed that Bethune was transformed in China and attained a kind of salvation before his death.

In 1941, two years after Bethune's death, Allan sold a film treatment about him to 20th Century Fox. A friend knew someone close to Daryl F. Zanuck. First, Allan wrote a twelve-page outline. Then Zanuck commissioned a 200-page treatment, for which Allan was paid $25,000. The actor Zanuck had in mind was Walter Pidgeon, who, like Donald Sutherland, had been born in New Brunswick. But the project didn't get very far; no screenplay was ever written. (Pidgeon, however, did play Bethune in a one-hour radio drama.) By the late 1940s, when Hollywood witnesses were interrogated by the House Committee on Un-American Activities about subversion in the movie capital, the political climate had changed so drastically it was unthinkable for any studio to be involved in a movie about a Communist hero.

Hollywood has no politics beyond the politics of what the audience will buy; but during the notorious age of the Hollywood Ten, characterized by blacklists, betrayals and treacheries of people who informed on their friends, as Orson Welles remarked, not to save their lives but to save their swimming pools, people like Ted Allan were personae non gratae in the United States. One of his friends, Reuben Shipp—a hugely successful radio and TV writer, especially of the hit series *Life with Father*—was hounded out of the country and ruined, personally and financially. Out of that experience Shipp wrote a devastating satire of McCarthyism, *The Investigator,* which caused an international incident when it was aired on a CBC radio series produced by Andrew Allan, who was one of Ted Allan's chief employers over the years. (Washington was furious, especially when a black-market recording became an underground hit in the United States.)

Allan moved to Toronto in 1950 after being asked to leave the United States. At the peak of the so-called Red Scare, Ted Allan was at work on a massive biography of Bethune. *The Scalpel, the Sword,* published in 1952, sold 1.5 million copies and was translated into nineteen languages, including Chinese. Allan's collaborator on the book was Sydney Gordon, another Marxist journalist who had been hired by Allan to help edit his Bethune material and who wound up doing so much of the writing that Allan decided to share credit—a decision he would regret.

After working extensively in CBC television drama for several years, Allan became disenchanted with politics at the CBC, and moved to England, where the community of Canadian expatriates, arts-and-media division, included Mordecai Richler, Ted Kotcheff, Sydney Newman, Reuben Shipp and Shipp's wife, the former CBC television host Elaine Grand.

Not until the late 1960s would leftist radicalism again become fashionable, and safe, in Hollywood. Once social protest and revolution went up for sale again in the mass media, the saga of Norman Bethune would become a hot property. In the meantime Ted Allan became a globe-trotting mid-Atlantic man.

In 1957, Waymin Situ, then head of the China Film Bureau, came to London to propose that Allan write a script about Bethune which the Chinese would produce. Allan and Sydney Gordon went to China in 1958 to look into the project. Allan decided that he was not the person to write the movie the Chinese wanted, because they didn't want to include anything that took place before Bethune's arrival in China. Gordon disagreed, and stayed on in China, but never did write the screenplay. (The Chinese, however, did produce a dramatic movie about Bethune, without the involvement of either Gordon or Allan. It didn't deal with Bethune's life prior to his arrival in China. The only Canadian exposure the film has had was one CBC showing on a Sunday morning.)

That trip to China marked the end of all cooperation between Sydney Gordon and Ted Allan. Gordon, who moved to East Berlin in 1958 and died in 1985, refused to cooperate with any movie deal involving Allan.

In 1969 a producer named Edward Lewis approached Allan, but the rights to *The Scalpel, the Sword* were muddied by the quarrel between Allan and Gordon. Lewis negotiated separately with the coauthors, each of whom was contracted to write a separate screenplay. Since Gordon never finished his, Lewis claimed to own Gordon's half of the rights. This might have created insurmountable difficulties for any future deal, but Allan solved the problem by buying back from 20th Century Fox the treatment Daryl Zanuck had commissioned nearly thirty years earlier. The buy-back price was $10,000. It was a brilliant manoeuvre, because Allan could then write a script based not on *The Scalpel, the Sword* but on his 1942 treatment, which he clearly owned and which predated the book.

Gordon sold his half of *The Scalpel, the Sword* to Otto Preminger, who at one point took out full-page ads in *Variety* to announce his Bethune production, and also went so far as to make overtures to Donald Sutherland and John Kemeny about it. Neither of the Canadians Preminger approached was interested. Preminger wanted to omit entirely Bethune's involvement in the Spanish Civil War — which Kemeny and Sutherland saw as pivotal. Allan refused to sell Preminger his half of the rights to the book.

Ted Allan's involvement with John Kemeny began in the mid-1970s, when Kemeny had just arrived in Hollywood on the wings of his triumph as the producer of *The Apprenticeship of Duddy Kravitz*. The Edward Lewis project had petered out, and Kemeny was able to pick up the option, making a deal with Columbia Pictures to finance a new screenplay.

It seemed ironic that Kemeny, who escaped from Communist Hungary while rocks were being thrown in the streets of Budapest in 1956, would be attracted to the saga of a Communist hero. But it was a 1966 hour-long National Film Board documentary about Bethune that rescued Kemeny from obscurity and positioned him to become one of the key players a few years later when the Canadian feature-film industry finally took off.

During the next decade *Bethune* was caught in the revolving doors of Hollywood's studio shuffles. It was an absurd extravaganza, with a cast including studio heads, major American movie stars, big-name directors and high-ranking government officials from Canada and China. Ted Allan wrote perhaps twenty versions of the script to satisfy the escalating and wide-ranging demands of a large number of interested parties. At Columbia Pictures between 1975 and 1978 there were four studio heads, and Allan wrote a new version of the script for each of them.

Norman Jewison became involved in the project in 1976, when he and Allan were both living in England. Bethune seemed like a natural project for Jewison, who was eager to reassert his Canadian identity. He and Allan started to work on the script together but never got it to a point that satisfied Jewison. When Jewison went to China with Kemeny and Michael Spencer of the Canadian Film Development Corporation, there were hardly any roads in the places he wanted to film, and conditions were so bad that Jewison decided he would have to bring in all the equipment from elsewhere. He also learned that the Chinese regarded Bethune as a saint and didn't want the movie to contain any suggestion of their hero's bourgeois background. Jewison encountered even more resistance when he approached his friends at the Hollywood movie studios. "To make a long story short," Jewison recalls, "what they said to me essentially was, 'We love you, Norman, but we can't spend a lot of money making a film about an obscure Canadian Communist doctor. It just won't fly.' "

Then in 1979 Ted Allan had a near-fatal heart attack. He underwent triple-bypass surgery. And he told those closest to him that his most fervent wish was to see his *Bethune* movie made before he died. Suddenly there was new hope. Ted Kotcheff, who had become a name the studios took very seriously, wanted to make *Bethune*, and was ready to join forces with Kemeny, his *Duddy Kravitz* collaborator.

In 1979 Ted Kotcheff spent an entire year trying to get *Bethune* off the ground. He went to China with Michael McCabe, who had succeeded Spencer as executive director of the CFDC, and they actually persuaded the Chinese government to let them make the film in China. But because they projected a large budget, they felt they would need the backing of a major Hollywood studio. And the making of Warren Beatty's idealistic epic, *Reds*, about another North American who became a Communist hero, was a signal that the time was right. *Bethune* seemed within the reach of a Hollywood studio.

But there was a big catch. No Hollywood studio wanted to take a chance on such a risky project without a very big star. Warner Brothers was willing to back *Bethune* only if Kotcheff and Kemeny could land one of the superstars on their list, which included Robert Redford, Jack Nicholson, Paul Newman, Dustin Hoffman and Warren Beatty. (Sutherland wasn't considered a big enough star to carry a $25-million movie.) The price of a superstar added about $4 million to the budget, but getting a star even at those prices wasn't easy. Each of these men was juggling a number of possible projects, and surrounded with an entourage of advisers and collaborators. Some balked at spending half a year in China. Others were waiting to see what happened with other deals.

Redford was more interested than the others, but he wanted to see a rewrite. Kemeny and Kotcheff couldn't finance another rewrite without Redford's commitment, but Redford wouldn't commit without a rewrite.

After a frustrating year, Kotcheff's interest waned for a while, but Jewison came up with the idea of doing Bethune as a TV series, and Kemeny made the rounds with him.

Jewison had been a hot TV producer before he switched to movies, handling such high-profile assignments as Judy Garland's TV series of the 1950s, but he had been unavailable for TV projects for two decades. Now he was making himself available to the TV networks for this one project. (At one point there was even a scheme for a TV series with Jewison directing some episodes and Kotcheff others.) But the networks weren't interested. Jewison knew *Bethune* was doomed when he wound up in the office of his old buddy Grant Tinker, one of the most powerful forces in U.S. network TV—and Tinker turned him down.

Shortly after Jewison bowed out, Kotcheff decided to give it another try. But by this time Kemeny's patience was wearing thin. He had spent a fortune on options, and he still wasn't happy with the script. He thought Kotcheff wasn't being tough enough with Allan about revisions; Kemeny would have preferred trying a new writer. He let the option run out but asked Kotcheff and Allan to stay in touch with him. If they were able to get the project moving again, he would come into it.

But when *Bethune* edged closer to reality, it was because Allan had made a deal with new producers, Pieter Kroonenburg and Nicolas Clermont.

The first time Kroonenburg realized that *Bethune* might be up for grabs was in May 1984, when he got a phone call from Gilles Carle, the Quebec director, who was at the Cannes Film Festival. Carle was calling about another project, but he happened to mention that Ted Allan and Ted Kotcheff were talking with Harold Greenberg, a Montreal producer who had ties with the Bronfman empire.

After starting in the photofinishing business, Greenberg, a large, white-haired man, had gone on in the film lab business and become the boss of Astral Bellevue Pathé, which had grown into one of the largest entertainment industry conglomerates in Canada. He had control of a major distribution company and of the pay-cable franchise First Choice. Greenberg had also produced a number of movies, almost all of them mediocre, including *Porky's*, which happened to be the largest-grossing movie in Canadian history.

Not long after his conversation with Carle, Kroonenburg received another Ted Allan script, *Love Is a Long Shot* (which was eventually produced as a made-for-TV CBC movie), and took the opportunity of inquiring about *Bethune*. Allan gave him a copy of the *Bethune* script but indicated that it was all but certain that Greenberg was taking it on. Later that summer, Kroonenburg met Kotcheff, who was in Montreal filming *Joshua Then and Now,* and Kotcheff reiterated that Greenberg was going to produce *Bethune*.

But suddenly everything changed. Kotcheff and Allan couldn't get Greenberg to return their calls. By this time, Julie Allan, the writer's daughter, was working for Filmline, and she served as a go-between. Kroonenburg and Clermont moved quickly. By February 1985, they had optioned *Bethune*. Julie Allan was to be the associate producer of the film.

Both Kroonenburg and Clermont were Europeans who had moved to Canada. Kroonenburg, who is in his mid-forties, had grown up in the Netherlands and attended film school there. He lived in Brussels, Rome and Paris, making commercials and TV films before moving to Canada in 1979. Since then he has been acquiring a track record as a producer, with such independent features as *The Lucky Star, Heartaches* and *Blue Boy*. Clermont, born in France, took up Canadian residence in 1968 and became involved in educational films before joining forces with Kroonenburg.

What made them think they could succeed with *Bethune* where others had been failing for more than forty years? Kroonenburg and Clermont came from a non-Hollywood school of moviemaking, and they counted on their connections in Europe. "I don't understand how people can make movies for $50 million," Kroonenburg says with wide-eyed innocence. "I'm flabbergasted to see budgets with ludicrous fees and millions of dollars wasted on lawyers and limousines and first-class travel."

His instinct on *Bethune* was that there must be a better way to do it than the Hollywood way. Hollywood, after all, was the place where this movie had failed to happen for forty years. He knew, too, that money from a Hollywood major would have a lot of compromises, catches and conditions attached. He preferred to find a way of raising the money without giving away control. But he seriously underestimated the problems and unforeseen expenses involved in shooting a major movie in remote areas of China.

The question was: could Filmline pull off a project of this magnitude without a Hollywood partner? The key partner in that case would have to be Telefilm.

Peter Pearson's initial response to *Bethune* was extremely tough-minded. Shortly after coming into his new job he met Ted Allan, who said he was reviving the project one more time with the collaboration of Ted Kotcheff.

Pearson drew a deep breath and replied: "If you want to do it, that's your business. I wish you luck. But don't expect any more money from us."

Telefilm and its predecessor, the CFDC, had already been burned by *Bethune*. In the early days of the organization, Michael Spencer, its first executive director, had gone to China, twice. He had even managed to get a personal appeal from Pierre Trudeau to the Chinese. Then in 1979 Spencer's successor, Mike McCabe, had made an expedition along with Kotcheff and Kemeny. Over the years the CFDC and Telefilm had sunk $300,000 into script development. And as far as Pearson could tell, *Bethune* was no closer to the screen now than it had ever been.

As far as Pearson was concerned, there were a lot of reasons for skepticism, if not cynicism. There was no way of knowing if the Chinese were really going to play ball. There was no way of knowing whether the people now involved were capable of mounting an epic movie. After Telefilm's experience with *Joshua Then and Now,* Pearson wasn't sure Kotcheff could operate within a budget as limited as *Bethune*'s. Pearson didn't like the idea of going into such a risky venture as the largest investor; he would have preferred living under the protective umbrella of a Hollywood studio.

Several factors changed his mind: the attitude of the

Chinese, the commitment of Donald Sutherland to play the title role and the demonstrated marketability of distribution rights. Buyers lined up for the privilege of paying several million dollars just for the U.S. pay-TV and cable rights; however, Pearson agreed with the producers that it would be better to make the film without outside involvement and sell distribution rights later.

And what of the enormous risks? Kroonenburg and Clermont were planning to make the movie plus a four-hour TV series on a budget of $10 million (Canadian) plus what the Chinese were willing to put up, which was estimated to be worth about another $6 million. (Of the $10 million, $4 million was coming from Telefilm, $2 million from CBC, $1 million from the French coproducers and $3 million from other private investors.) It was an extremely tight budget — far less than what Kemeny, Kotcheff and Warner Brothers had counted on. Kroonenburg and Clermont had done some very fancy footwork to get the budget down to this level, cutting out parts of the script and talking all the major players into compromises and deferrals. But what if the money ran out in the middle of shooting, as it had with *Joshua*? Might not Telefilm be blackmailed into making up the shortfall for the sake of preventing an international scandal?

As far as Pearson was concerned, *Bethune* was like any other production — though Telefilm has never put quite that much money into any other movie. "We have a completion guarantor in place who is responsible for the overage. We insist our investment be protected, and if there are any overages, we won't come up with any more money."

In the summer of 1985, Kroonenburg had a series of meetings with Leo Pescarolo, an Italian producer who had worked with Federico Fellini. Pescarolo's brother-in-law had just come back from China, where he had worked on the TV series *Marco Polo*, which was coproduced by Italians. Pescarolo got in touch with Kroonenburg because he had heard the Chinese were extremely keen on doing a film about a Canadian doctor named Bethune, and through official inquiries at the Canadian embassy, he'd learned that Kroonenburg and Clermont had bought the script. Although Kroonenburg was extremely interested in having European partners, the deal with the Italians didn't go ahead.

The decision of the Montreal producers to go ahead with the movie came as a surprise to John Kemeny, who was confident, even when he let his option expire, that if a movie about Norman Bethune was ever going to be made, he was the only producer who could do it. After all, he was an expert on Bethune, and he had been to China and had investigated the special problems of making a major movie in cooperation with a gigantic country whose doors to the West had been closed for so long. What other producer could combine a knowledge of the subject with Kemeny's track record with Hollywood's major studios and experience in making epic films despite overwhelming logistical and financial problems?

Allan felt a moral obligation to Kemeny, and he had an understanding with Kroonenburg and Clermont that Kemeny could be involved somehow in their production. Allan told Kemeny to call them, but he felt it was up to them to call him, and Allan couldn't get them to do so. For Kemeny, the long *Bethune* saga had a bitter ending.

Kroonenburg and Clermont, meanwhile, had picked up an important signal: the Chinese, reluctant to cooperate with Western moviemakers for decades, had changed their tune.

Since the Communist takeover in 1949, China had been virtually a closed set to all foreigners. China's moviemaking had been limited to kung-fu adventures or stern moralistic films modeled on those produced in the Soviet Union.

But with the beginning of economic reform in 1976 came new attitudes to moviemaking. Directors, writers and actors who would have been denounced as capitalist roaders under Mao re-emerged in the enlightened China of Deng Xiaoping and were being allowed to tackle controversial subjects.

And the Chinese also decided to welcome foreign filmmakers. Bernardo Bertolucci, the great Italian director, recently shot *The Last Emperor in China* with the help of British coproducers. *Marco Polo* had been made without a problem. In 1984 producer Shirley Sun and director Peter Wang, both Chinese American independents, made their low-budget, culture-clash comedy *A Great Wall,* about a San Francisco Chinese family visiting relatives in Peking, as the first feature coproduction with China. And early in 1987, Steven Spielberg closed the main streets of Shanghai to shoot *Empire of the Sun,* based on the novel by J.G. Ballard about the Japanese occupation during World War II.

Ironically, the European coproducer Kroonenburg and Clermont did get involved with was John Kemeny's French partner on *Quest for Fire,* producer-director Jacques Dorfmann. The Kemeny/Dorfmann alliance had ended disastrously, with each party suing the other. Dorfmann had another film he wanted to shoot in China, *A Woman of Shanghai,* and he needed coproduction financing. Kroonenburg and Clermont became minority coproducers on *A Woman of Shanghai,* raising one million dollars in Canada, and in exchange Dorfmann became a minority coproducer on *Bethune*. This provided a valuable trial run. *A Woman of Shanghai* was to be shot just before *Bethune,* with a Canadian assistant director, and it was a similar project—a theatrical movie plus a four-hour TV series.

The Chinese let it be known they were ready to talk, and in February 1986, a delegation from Peking arrived in Montreal. The Canadian producers talked frankly about their concerns. Norman Bethune had been a prodigious womanizer and heavy drinker, and they didn't want to be forced to whitewash him. The Chinese said they had no problem with realistic depictions of Bethune's life before he left for China, because what that would really show was how content he became in his work with the Chinese. They also stressed that times had changed; that Mao was human and had made mistakes; and that China's most important challenge now was to develop an opening to the West.

The Chinese were not only cooperative. They were also willing to be coproducers and make a huge investment of services and facilities — including studios, crews, film labs and thousands of Chinese troops as extras.

Ted Allan was finally going to make his own pilgrimage to the Great Wall. Two miracles had come to pass: Allan had survived his heart attack, and eight years later he was going to China for the filming of *Bethune: The Making of a Hero*. After forty-five years of courting Hollywood and living on its option fees, of being an outsider with his nose pressed to the glittering window of southern California fantasyland, Ted Allan was finally going to see his dream movie produced — without a penny from Hollywood. That was a punch-line revelation that would have made Allan's restless mentor, Norman Bethune, roar with laughter.

13

Donald in Wonderland

There may be something intrinsically ridiculous about a movie star who commands million-dollar fees wanting to play a Communist folk hero who gave up all his comforts and luxuries and sacrificed his life for a peasant revolution. Just imagine the hilarious comedy sketch SCTV could devise from this situation: a loud, pushy agent—played, of course, by Martin Short—takes a meeting, as they say in Hollywood, and cuts a deal (more Tinseltown lingo) with an egomaniacal tycoon—played by John Candy—on behalf of a pampered star who insists on all the usual perks and bonuses even as he is about to disappear into some of the more remote hills of China and transform himself into a self-sacrificing saint. But Donald Sutherland has never seemed the least bit embarrassed about his burning desire to portray Norman Bethune.

The first time I met Sutherland, the world's only male Canadian movie star (unless you insist on counting Michael J. Fox—but the audience is still waiting to find out what Fox wants to be when he grows up), he was talking about Norman Bethune. And over the years since then Sutherland has rarely stopped talking about Bethune. He felt some mystical bond with the turbulent doctor.

"He was fulfilled because he was doing the work he wanted to do," Sutherland told me. But when I asked about the connection between Bethune's personality and Sutherland's, he backed away from the comparison. "I'm not that daring," he confessed. "I don't confront people. I let things go by."

Playing doctor is nothing new for Donald Sutherland. Back in 1969, in M*A*S*H*, he originated the role of Hawkeye, a wizardly surgeon with the sad-sack face and the fraternity-boy spirit performing miracles at the Korean front. And the next year in the satiric movie *Alex in Wonderland*, Sutherland, playing a young, nouveau-hip Hollywood director, was offered a chance to do a movie about a heart-transplant doctor.

Alex inhabited a real wonderland, the wacky fun house of Hollywood in transition, populated by fashionable post–*Easy Rider* rebels in love beads. It's in this promised land gone haywire that an entertainingly crass producer (wickedly well-played by Paul Mazursky, the director and cowriter of *Alex*, who would have played Sutherland's role had MGM allowed it) offers Alex a chance to direct the movie about the transplant doctor.

Twelve years later, Sutherland actually did play a heart-transplant doctor in the Toronto-made *Threshold*, produced by Jon Slan and Michael Burns, directed by the American Richard Pearce. Though it failed to get widely distributed, the movie was one of the few decent Canadian productions Sutherland ever appeared in. Dr. Thomas Vrain, the noble surgeon/hero, is based on Dr. Denton Cooley, the controversial Texas surgeon who experimented with artificial hearts. The way Sutherland played him, Vrain was understated and self-mocking. Sutherland demonstrated his mastery of the understated style of screen acting, as he had a year or two earlier as Timothy Hutton's father in *Ordinary People*, that preposterous parable about WASP stiffs who can't feel until they encounter a warm Jewish shrink. In *Ordinary People* Sutherland's spindly hands seemed to express emotions the rest of his body kept bottled up; in *Threshold* it became obvious those hands were designed to perform surgical miracles.

Sutherland's commitment to *Bethune* represents more than a homecoming, more than a show of faith in Canada's film industry on the part of someone who has made it in Hollywood. Ever willing to give the Canadian film industry a boost, Sutherland has become a fixture at the annual Genie Awards. Once when he was interrogated by a customs officer at Toronto airport, he explained that he was flying in to present an award. "And what is the *value* of that award?" asked the suspicious customs man. Another year he got drawn into a controversy when the distinguished actress Roberta Maxwell was dropped from the Genie show because she was considered too short to appear alongside the gangling Sutherland.

At first glance, the life of Donald Sutherland might not seem to have a lot in common with Bethune's. But with the same Presbyterian imperatives in his background, Sutherland has always been a restless wanderer, like Bethune, and oddly insecure about his achievements.

Playing Bethune is a way of dramatizing Sutherland's own political development, which began when he met and married Shirley Douglas, an actress whose father was the late Tommy Douglas, leader of the CCF and NDP. After their marriage broke up in the 1960s, Sutherland's radical political activities continued through his involvement with Jane Fonda (his costar in *Klute*); together they campaigned and toured to support protest within the U.S. Army against the Vietnam war.

Bethune ancestors, Huguenots who moved to Scotland and then Canada, were mostly Presbyterian preachers and teachers; Sutherland, whose ancestry was Scots on all sides, had a maternal grandfather who was a Presbyterian preacher and a mother who taught math.

The Sutherlands came from Lockeport, Nova Scotia, where Donald's grandfather and great-uncle ran a general store that sold ropes and other supplies for ships. Donald has a much older half-sister and half-brother from his father's first marriage.

Sutherland's parents met in Medicine Hat, Alberta, and settled in Saint John, where his father became vice-president of the New Brunswick Power Corporation. As for religion, the family was officially United Church, which meant "we sang hymns and said grace." He remembers that his father was always taking off on impulse — on one occasion, to scalp tickets to Dodgers games at Ebbetts Field. Mostly, he remembers people singing in the back seats of cars.

The family moved to Bridgewater, Nova Scotia, in 1948, when Donald was thirteen. He spent only four years there (leaving home after high school to attend the University of Toronto) but Bridgewater remains in his memory as a magic, almost holy place, and whenever anyone asks him where he's from, he says Nova Scotia. It was in Bridgewater that Donald learned how to overcome his self-doubts.

His adolescence was hardly without pain. He had acne, he was frightfully awkward, and in spite of his size he was lousy at sports. He was an earnest student (who always called the teacher "sir") but not a brilliant one. His show-business career began at ten or eleven when he put on a puppet show. Trilby, his clown-tramp puppet, is believed to be still hanging in his sister's closet. He cried when his mother and sister went to see *King Lear* but refused to take him along because they thought it would be a bad influence on him.

He'd had polio and rheumatic fever and feared he was weird-looking. He asked his mother, who had an uncompromising honesty, "Mother, do you think I'm good-looking?"

There was a hurtful pause. Then she said quietly: "No, Donald, but your face has character."

He sulked in his room for days.

But in Bridgewater all things seemed possible. Henrietta Herkes, his high-school teacher, gave him a chance to practice drama. He played Scrooge in a school production of *A Christmas Carol*. And he gave the valedictory speech at his graduation. No one remembers what he said, but people still recall his delivery.

It was, of course, the voice that landed him a job as a radio announcer. He had gone to a local station to apologize for having asked a dumb question during a class visit. The manager said, "Never mind that, we've just lost an announcer. Would you like to do an audition?"

Sutherland did everything from Templeton TRCS commercials to news broadcasts, and he was a disc jockey as well.

The write-up in his school yearbook said: "'Suds,' who was born in Saint John, N.B., on April 17, 1935, wandered into our Grade 12 classroom and has been with us ever since. He has the unfortunate habit of losing his books and as he is going to Toronto University to study engineering we hope he will hang on to his instruments."

His father pressured him into taking engineering so he would have a profession, but Donald was mad for acting. He picked U. of T. because it was the only school he could find with both an engineering faculty and an important student theatre. He came last in his engineering class, but that hardly mattered. He switched to English at Victoria College, and by working with Robert Gill at Hart House discovered he really was an actor.

Sutherland left Toronto in 1958 and spent the next few years in repertory theatre in Britain. Someone spotted the ghoulish possibilities of his appearance and cast him in a cheapie Italian horror movie called *Castle of the Living Dead*. It was while he was in Rome doing this film that he met and married Shirley Douglas. Her father was the first person Sutherland held in awe. "When he walked into a room," he once told me, "I actually couldn't speak."

After four more Italian horror movies, Sutherland landed in Hollywood in 1967 to appear in *The Dirty Dozen*. He became a star almost by accident when he was cast as a prankish military doctor in what was expected to be a B-movie for the drive-ins. But Robert Altman's M*A*S*H*, a manic black comedy about how people hold on to their sanity in the face of war and death, was the surprise hit of 1970. That stroke of luck gave Sutherland a chance to show what he could do, and after that he didn't need luck.

Sutherland's specialty is a kind of gentle bewilderment. At six-foot-two, he is physically dominating on the screen but he's a giant with such a sweet, soft-spoken manner that in some roles he seems to drift away while you watch him.

He played the title role in *Klute* with admirable understatement, as a supporting role to Fonda's tough character study. But he can make a sensational impact in a small part, as he did in Bernardo Bertolucci's *1900*, playing a power-hungry Italian fascist who murders cats and children.

Sutherland persuaded the British director John Schlesinger to let him play Homer, the distinctly unglamorous bookkeeper who lives chastely with a predatory hooker in *Day of the Locust*. To prepare for the part, he ate his way through forty pounds of chocolates and cream puffs, "maybe because Homer seemed like an expression of all the guilt and repression I felt when I was fourteen." Yet in *Don't Look Now*, Nicholas Roeg's gothic occult thriller set in a very sinister Venice, he became, as Julie Christie's psychic husband, an erotic object; as the couple moved toward their doom in the watery city, their love scenes came at the audience in disconnected fragments. The movie cast a weird shadow. Sutherland named his next child Roeg after the film's director, but he was always uneasy in Venice, and years later, Roeg's younger brother almost drowned at the family's Quebec home in a spooky replay of *Don't Look Now*.

When Federico Fellini was asked why he wanted Sutherland, of all people, to play Casanova, he explained: "That moon face of his is completely alien to the image people have of Casanova, the dark-eyed, magnetic Italian with raven locks and dark skin. Since I want to turn the traditional model upside down, a face like that is exactly what I need. It was this indefinite face which seduced me. I could redesign it, make a new nose, chin, forehead, everything."

Fellini turned Sutherland into a celebrity vampire. Surrounded by dwarfs, monsters and perverts, and deprived of eyebrows, Sutherland was transformed into Fellini's most overbearing grotesque. Long before the symbolic denouement when Casanova copulates with a mannequin, it's clear that the film is an anti-erotic downer, with no distractions apart from Fellini's wig fetish; and the fact that it's intentional doesn't make it more palatable.

Fellini's *Casanova* was as much of a trial to sit through as some of the clinkers Sutherland made in Canada, such as *Act of the Heart*, Paul Almond's theological tearjerker, in which Sutherland played the priest for whose sake Geneviève Bujold put a match to herself. Then there was *Alien Thunder,* a fiasco about Indians and Mounties that was so bad W.O. Mitchell took his name off the script. *The Disappearance* did indeed disappear. *Nothing Personal* was a screwball comedy Sutherland had hopes for, until the day his wife, the Quebec actress Francine Racette, saw the movie and then appeared at the front door with a paper bag over her head.

There was a long period when Sutherland made so many movies that friends surmised he had a pathological fear of being unemployed for even five minutes. In 1978 he made *Invasion of the Body Snatchers* and *The Great Train Robbery* in England as well as playing cameo roles in *Murder by Decree* in London and *Bear Island* in the Arctic and *Ordinary People* in Chicago. Although he succeeded in Hollywood first and had a house there for years, he became a European figure by making *Don't Look Now* in Venice, *1900* in Parma and *Casanova* in Rome.

And all the while he kept coming back to Canada. Francine and the children live part of the year in the old Quebec farmhouse the family bought recently, and part of the year in an apartment in Paris they've hung on to. For a year or two, Sutherland spent as much time as possible in New York. But for most of the year, home is still L.A., where Sutherland owns a large apartment and his children attend a private French school. You could catch jetlag just from being in the same room with Sutherland.

It was in 1969 while sharing a platform with Fonda that Sutherland heard a reading of an essay called "Wounds" and was so moved by it that he broke his rule against appearing on TV and played Bethune in the TV series *Witness to Yesterday*, in which host Patrick Watson interviewed actors playing deceased historical figures. And he started trying to organize a movie about Bethune.

Then in 1976 Sutherland agreed to come back to Toronto to play Bethune in a CBC television drama. John Hirsch was the head of CBC drama at the time; Robert Sherrin was producing the program, and Eric Till was the director. For the role of Bethune's wife, Frances, from whom he was twice divorced, they had landed a young Canadian actress who had taken the theatre world of London, England, by storm — Kate Nelligan.

Once Sutherland said yes to the CBC project, it had to be worked into his frantic schedule. The CBC juggled its schedule to accommodate him. A month before rehearsals were to begin, Sutherland told the CBC he was unhappy with the script (by Rod Langley, from his own stage play), and a new script was written in a Las Vegas hotel room in four days. By the time Sutherland arrived in Toronto, Langley was seeking an injunction to stop the show. Eventually Langley dropped his legal action, but it added immeasurably to the tension of making *Bethune*. So did the pressure of time: Sutherland is used to having months to do a film, but *Bethune* had to be taped in less than two weeks. He would say, "I'd like to do that again," and they would say, "No, you can't—the allotted time is up, and we have to go on." That came as a shock.

Sutherland locked himself up in his hotel room and worked on creating a performance. Colleagues were overwhelmed by his fanatical attention to detail. As part of his research he arranged to observe surgical operations at a Toronto hospital. It was like being a doctor on call; the hospital would phone at 4:00 A.M. to ask whether he wanted to come on down.

All through the production there were dialogue changes and frantic long-distance phone conferences. Sutherland used his own power to ensure that Till got control of the final editing.

The CBC's *Bethune* for all that was no more than a dry run. It lacked dramatic shape, begged the interesting questions and had less epic sweep than a lunchtime stroll through one of Toronto's busier Chinese restaurants. Would it have turned out better if Langley had won his injunction, if Till had not had final cut? He would do better, Sutherland promised himself, if he ever got a chance to make the movie he'd been dreaming of. But the road to China was turning out to be almost as long and difficult for Sutherland as it had been for Bethune.

In 1985 when Pieter Kroonenburg asked Sutherland whether he would be interested in playing Bethune, Sutherland replied, "Not only am I interested, but I'll crawl all the way on my hands and knees to beg you to let me do it." When the producers took too long getting back to Sutherland's agent on a negotiating point, Sutherland worried that they might be considering another actor. "I'll kill you if you give this part to someone else," he warned, sounding like the murderous monster he played in *1900*.

Preparing for the role he had dreamed of playing for so

long, Sutherland went to New York to have his head shaved, Bethune style, and a photo of Sutherland with this look appeared in *People* magazine. Then it was back to Paris for a quiet interlude with his family while he transformed himself into Norman Bethune. Just before leaving for China, Sutherland spent a frantic week in Montreal. One day he had to go to Toronto for a costume fitting with a designer named Olga, and because he had suffered an ear injury, the producers thought it would be safer for him to make the trip by car. He decided not to stay in Toronto overnight, which made for an exhausting marathon along Highway 401. There was a driver, but he was so exhausted on the way back that Sutherland had to take over behind the wheel.

Only a week later did Sutherland realize that on the day of his quick visit to Toronto, the city was preoccupied with the Genie Awards, a rite of spring that serves as an excuse for an annual gathering of the Canadian film community. Among the special guests, indeed, was his son Kiefer, who had flown in from L.A. for the event, and whom the elder Sutherland would have dearly loved to see if he'd realized they were going to be in the same city for a change.

But by this time Sutherland had become so obsessively preoccupied with the character he'd been waiting to play for twenty years that he had spiritually moved into the world of the movie about to be made and was only dimly aware of events going on in the real world around him.

Why did Sutherland feel he had a sacred bond with Bethune? Maybe it was because Sutherland, like Bethune, always seemed to be on the way from one place to another, as if afraid to get too settled or too comfortable. Maybe it was because Sutherland, like Bethune, was haunted by the fear that he was unworthy of the luck and riches that had come his way. Maybe it was because Sutherland, like Bethune, was always willing to move to the far side of the world on a moment's notice if he had a chance to do the work he felt destined to do. Or maybe it was just that part of Donald Sutherland was still a painfully awkward adolescent from Bridgewater, Nova Scotia, trying to win the approval of Henrietta Herkes, the high-school drama coach.

14

Onward to the Great Wall

Even before Ted Kotcheff said no to directing *Bethune,* Pieter Kroonenburg and Nicolas Clermont had started sounding out other potential directors, just in case. They'd called Norman Jewison's office and got an official "Not available" without even reaching Jewison personally. (Jewison was in the middle of shooting *Moonstruck,* with Cher, and was contracted to complete editing and fine-tuning the movie for a fall release.) They also talked to Sidney Furie, a member of the Canadian contingent in L.A. whose latest project was *Superman IV.* Furie said he wouldn't be available unless the producers were willing to delay the filming of Bethune.

One of the most serious possibilities was Ralph Thomas, who had moved to L.A. a couple of years before along with his wife, Vivienne Leebosh, after spending several years in CBC television's drama department and then making a splashy feature debut with the 1981 movie *Ticket to Heaven.* Thomas was in the final stages of post-production on *Apprentice to Murder,* a movie he had made in Norway. Donald Sutherland was the star of the movie, and Sutherland and Thomas had become friends. Now Sutherland was saying that if Kotcheff wasn't going to direct Bethune, Thomas would be his next choice.

Thomas had been asked about his availability, but nobody had made him an offer. Meanwhile he had read the script and decided it would need major changes.

Almost everyone regarded Bethune as Kotcheff's project, which no one else should touch if Kotcheff was prepared to do it. Kotcheff told the producers of *Bethune* that he had a three-picture deal with Cannon Films, an independent international film company that had been making waves in Hollywood under its high-profile boss, Menahem Golan. Filmline began discussions with Cannon about getting together on *Bethune*, with Kotcheff directing as part of his deal with Cannon.

Kotcheff's Cannon deal specified a fee of $1.5 million (U.S.) for each picture he directed, which was in keeping with his status as a top Hollywood director. But Filmline was planning a relatively tight production with a director's fee of perhaps one-quarter that amount. If Cannon contributed $3 million (U.S.) to the film's budget as discussed, Kotcheff might have been able to command his Cannon fee. But no papers were ever signed between the two firms, and by the fall of 1986 Cannon's financial woes had become the hottest Hollywood gossip of the season. Eventually Cannon would have to be bailed out by Warner Brothers. But first Cannon began backpedaling on commitments that it no longer felt capable of fulfilling. Kroonenburg and Clermont realized that if *Bethune* was going to be made, it was going to be without Cannon. And Kotcheff, having his own problems with Cannon, told Kroonenburg he'd be better off without them.

Kotcheff was willing to take part of his salary as a deferral — meaning he'd collect it only if the film became extremely profitable — but the producers weren't prepared to offer that. There was some suggestion that extra money would be found for Kotcheff later on, but it couldn't be written into his contract yet; he would just have to trust the producers on that point.

For directing *Joshua*, Kotcheff had earned $500,000

(U.S.), and had the same amount in deferred salary, which, given the film's commercial record, he will never collect. He had considered that a great sacrifice, and he certainly had no intention of doing *Bethune* for less. After all, he had been working on *Bethune* for years without being paid a penny. In the case of *Joshua*, Kotcheff had managed to do a fair bit of negotiating. But the producers of *Bethune* were standing firm; Kotcheff was being offered $500,000 (Canadian)—less than he'd been paid for *Joshua*.

If it was just a matter of his salary, Kotcheff might have given way. But he had other grave misgivings. He feared that too many corners had been cut and that there just wasn't enough money to do *Bethune* on the scale he'd always wanted to. And if the money ran out, as it had on *Joshua*, he'd face the same kind of financial warfare that had turned out to be so stressful on that movie. On the Monday after Christmas, he gave his answer: No.

There was no indication this was anything but final, but part of him may have been hoping the producers would come back to him with a better offer.

They didn't. Months later, Kotcheff couldn't help feeling he had made the right decision when he heard reports about the nightmare problems *Bethune* was encountering during the shooting in China. Doing a coproduction with the Chinese was a tremendous ordeal. Hours had to be spent translating conversations. Equipment that was supposed to be available wasn't, and had to be flown in at the last minute. Catering arrangements fell through; there were no phones and no drinkable water on the set, and people started to get sick. Shooting fell behind schedule, there were huge disagreements about what script changes should be made. Although Hemdale, the company that distributed *Platoon*, bought U.S. rights for $2.5 million, there were still serious questions about what might happen if *Bethune* ran out of money before the film was finished. Everyone involved would have different accounts of what went wrong and who was to blame, but the one thing they could all agree on was that filming *Bethune* had turned into the ultimate Canadian movie nightmare.

Ted Allan was devastated by Kotcheff's decision. Suddenly he had to face going ahead without either of the people who had been his collaborators on this project for so many years.

Peter Pearson, Telefilm's executive director, was perplexed. All along, everyone had thought of *Bethune*, above all, as Ted Kotcheff's project. That was one of the main reasons Telefilm had put up $4 million.

Kotcheff's involvement provided a seal of approval and quality control. He was a tireless, totally dedicated pro. With Kotcheff at the helm, Pearson felt he could count on top-line production values. And he felt the movie was in the hands of someone who could handle with confidence the scale of production and budget involved in *Bethune.*

The news that Kotcheff had walked away from *Bethune* came as a huge shock to Pearson. He found it hard to believe that, after putting so many years into *Bethune*, Kotcheff could even consider letting it go.

Pearson called Kotcheff at his L.A. home.

"Of course, it's your decision," Pearson said. "But it's hard for us to think about doing it with another director. We've always thought of it as your picture."

To Kroonenburg he said: "You're going to let us know who the director is going to be before we wrap up this deal. We're in this project more because of Kotcheff than because of you guys. And if he is not going to do it, then you'll have to satisfy us that you can come up with a director who is acceptable to us. It has to be someone we know we can count on to handle a big production and a big budget. We can't take a chance fiddling around with someone we aren't sure can do it."

High up in the hills far to the left of the spot where the name HOLLYWOOD is spelled out in giant letters against the hillside, Kotcheff was sitting at his kitchen table taking in the view and sifting through a pile of scripts, trying to decide what movie to do now that *Bethune* was off his plate. He settled on *Switching Channels,* an update of the 1940 newspaper comedy *His Girl Friday,* which was itself a new version of the 1920s Ben Hecht/Charles MacArthur play *The Front Page,* only with the male reporter Hildy Johnson turned into a woman, played by Rosalind Russell, who got to trade wisecracks with her double-dealing editor, played by Cary Grant. Indeed, this would be the fourth movie version of the same material, and it was a real Hollywood project — starring two of the biggest stars of the mid-1980s, Kathleen Turner and Burt Reynolds. The producers wanted to make it in Toronto, to take advantage of substantially lower production costs. So Ted Kotcheff packed his bags once more and headed not for China but for his hometown.

At first when Kroonenburg and Clermont sounded out Phillip Borsos, Borsos appeared to be committed to another project. The same week that Kotcheff gave his answer, Borsos learned that his other project was falling through. Much to his elation; he was itching to do *Bethune.* And for the producers, he was a catch. He was young enough that they wouldn't feel intimidated by him, and young enough to be willing to work for a relatively modest fee in exchange for the chance to do the kind of work a young director rarely gets a chance to do.

Borsos had been interested in *Bethune* for years. He and Peter O'Brian, who had produced two movies directed by Borsos and was also his best friend, had looked into doing *Bethune* around the time that Kemeny's option ran out, but then they got committed to other projects. Borsos once discussed it with Kroonenburg when they ran into one another at a restaurant in L.A. Borsos said he'd love to read the script. Kroonenburg dropped it off, then called later to ask what Borsos thought of it.

"It isn't structured quite the way I'd do it," Borsos replied.

About a month before the end of 1986, Kroonenburg

sent Borsos another version of the script. Borsos was in L.A. for a meeting about another film — a low-budget horror picture — and indicated he thought he was going to be directing it. He read the *Bethune* script on the plane back to Toronto, even though he thought he had been hired for the horror picture.

A few days before Christmas, the producers of the horror picture backed out of the deal, plunging Borsos into a depression. He hadn't worked in eighteen months, and he was beginning to wonder how long it would take before he could direct another movie.

The movie he had been most enthusiastic about doing was *Millennium*, a $25-million movie to be produced in Vancouver by the American veteran John Foreman. He had agreed to the horror film only because *Millennium* was taking too long to get the go-ahead. Now things were looking up again for *Millennium* — briefly. On December 23, there was yet another meeting with yet another set of studio executives — and they decided to pass.

Borsos, meanwhile, had come down with viral pneumonia and decided to take the holiday week to ignore the world and lie in bed being depressed.

At 5:50 P.M. on New Year's Eve, his phone rang. It was Kroonenburg, asking whether Borsos was available to direct *Bethune*. The next Monday, Borsos went to Montreal. They discussed the two big problems — the script and the budget. Kroonenburg had already decided he wanted Borsos to direct *Bethune*.

O'Brian and Borsos met in Vancouver in the fall of 1979 during preproduction work on *Mr. Patman*. The producers were thinking of taking on Borsos as an apprentice. As things turned out, neither O'Brian (who was supposed to be associate producer) nor Borsos stayed around for *Mr. Patman*. But it was during this period that Borsos told O'Brian about his idea of doing a movie about Bill Miner, Canada's first train robber.

That movie, *The Grey Fox,* became something of a legend in Canadian film circles when it was released in 1982. It didn't make money, but it got great reviews and a suitcase-full of prizes, and it earned both Borsos and O'Brian a solid reputation.

Bill Miner was not your average outlaw. He was known as "the Gentleman Bandit," and historians credit him with inventing the phrase "hands up." Born in Kentucky in the mid-1840s, Miner held up the Arizona pony express in 1863 and became an accomplished stagecoach robber. But in 1901, when he got out of San Quentin, having served thirty-three years on and off, there were no stagecoaches left.

We see Miner riding a train from San Francisco to Seattle, as ill-suited as Rip Van Winkle to the new era into which he has stumbled. He lives briefly in Washington state with his sister and brother-in-law, but he knows he wasn't put on this earth to pick fruit. He toys with the notion of prospecting, but his sister breaks the news: the gold rush is over.

For the first twenty minutes or so, it appears *The Grey Fox* is going to be nothing more than a handsome, painstaking period piece—Canada's answer to those oh-so-civilized-and-respectable Australian pictures such as *We of the Never Never* and *Gallipoli.* (Indeed, Borsos was born in Australia and moved to Canada at age five; perhaps a little Australian sensibility seeped into his bones.) Luckily, Jackie Burroughs comes along to liven things up and snatch the movie from the jaws of artful lethargy.

What set Miner apart from other outlaws was his courtliness; well-mannered and benevolent, he epitomized the perfect old gentleman. The movie seizes on this aspect of Miner's character, not in a playful way.

Young Phil Borsos lived in the Fraser Valley only a few miles from the site of Miner's first train robbery. Miner was a local legend, and Borsos always wanted to make a movie about him. (At one point he tried to do it as a documentary, and at another time he planned a television series.) Borsos spent years trying to interest movie producers all over the world, and O'Brian was one of only two who responded positively. Borsos wanted to co-produce the movie with O'Brian, and he assumed that O'Brian would want some high-profile international director. O'Brian insisted that no one but Phil Borsos could direct *The Grey Fox*. The project went through nine rewrites and three writers before shooting began near Cranbrook, British Columbia, in the fall of 1980, with a budget of $4.3 million.

Borsos, who was trained in the visual arts, made a movie that provides a feast for the eyes right from the start. He achieved a complete, authentic re-creation of the Pacific Northwest around the turn of the century, but with the phony Hollywood mythology stripped away. Yet Borsos, a glutton for visual detail, seems to be a minimalist when it comes to human expression. It wasn't always clear whether Borsos meant to purify the genre by throwing out the lore and glamor and starting over, or whether he was just trying to show that even outlaws could be repressed members of a suffocatingly well-ordered society.

One of the amusing aspects of this yarn was that when Canada discovers a legendary outlaw in its history, it turns out that the outlaw was an import from the United States. In the movie, the Canadian sergeant who figures out Miner's identity is sympathetic; it's the villainous Americans who insist on having him hunted down. The Canadian responds the way Mike Pearson, say, responded to LBJ: against his better judgment, he lets himself be bullied.

The Grey Fox virtually turns Bill Miner into an honorary Canadian. His impulses are so deeply buried, he could be the Mackenzie King of crime. Miner never flaunts his notoriety the way an American outlaw would, and there's never any indication he enjoys it. The subliminal message is that in Canada, even a spectacularly daring bandit becomes a beautiful loser and a passive victim, his sweet dreams trampled by the rapacious American machine of retribution.

The rapacious American machine was something Borsos learned a great deal about in the next few years. *The Grey Fox* won seven Genie Awards, and Borsos wanted to go on working with O'Brian—a man of his own generation whose air of genial decency in a field overrun with con men, sharks and rough customers gave some people the impression he'd stumbled into the wrong occupation. Despite the awards, O'Brian had to sell his house to get out of debt. And in his Genie thank-you speech, he quipped, "I want to thank Bill Miner for robbing the train in the first place. As an independent producer in this economy, I can relate to that."

Articulate, diplomatic and boyishly good-humored, O'Brian had mastered the art of keeping his cool and getting out of tight spots. Born in Canada, he'd spent his early school years in England before his family moved back to Toronto's rarefied Rosedale district when he was twelve. That experience gave him a newcomer's sense of awe about Canada—and that sense has been his defining characteristic as a producer.

After dropping out of university to join a rock band, much to his family's consternation, then taking a degree in communications in Boston, O'Brian wound up serving an apprenticeship as second assistant director to Ivan Reitman on *Foxy Lady* in the early 1970s. Years later O'Brian remarked ruefully: "I thought if Ivan can do this, I can do it. I had no idea that fifteen years later he would be living in a mansion in Bel-Air and I'd be forced to sell my house in Cabbagetown."

In 1974, on a budget of $98,000, O'Brian produced *Me*, based on a landmark Toronto Free Theatre play; it was shown once at the Stratford Film Festival, then disappeared. During the 1970s he also produced *Love at First*

Sight, starring Dan Aykroyd, David Cronenberg's racing car film *Fast Company* and *Blood and Guts,* a potboiler about wrestling. He was also an associate producer on *Outrageous!*.

After *The Grey Fox,* Borsos and O'Brian spent four years planning *Father Christmas* (or *One Magic Christmas,* as it was eventually retitled) but the money kept falling through. Finally Borsos and O'Brian each went off to do a movie without the other.

Borsos went to the United States, where he had a nightmare experience working with a producer, David Foster, who was not at all like Peter O'Brian. The picture was *The Mean Season,* a trashy thriller with Kurt Russell as a Miami reporter who keeps getting hot phone tips from a mass murderer about where to find the latest corpse. The hefty six-foot-tall Mariel Hemingway plays the hero's girlfriend, whose helpless screaming becomes a kind of unintended running gag. It would be an understatement to say that *The Mean Season* wasn't a happy experience for Borsos. He more or less dissociated himself from the results, and Foster bad-mouthed Borsos in press interviews.

Borsos and O'Brian eventually got back together for *One Magic Christmas,* but this time they had an American boss, Walt Disney Pictures, which put up two-thirds of the $10-million budget and exercised the right to keep a tight hand on the production, with a vengeance. The new executives at Disney, Michael Eisner and Jeff Katzenberg, were defectors from Paramount, where they'd earned a reputation for riding roughshod over producers and for what was described by *New York* magazine as a policy of "beating people up."

The movie—a whimsical fable based on the Scrooge story—had been born one day at a bar in Vancouver while O'Brian and Borsos were making *The Grey Fox.* Borsos confided that he'd always wanted to do a movie about Christmas, and O'Brian said he had, too, and they'd shaken hands on the deal right then. They later got involved with Fred Roos, an American producer who helped Borsos develop the project, and Thomas Meehan, the writer of *Annie*, brought in by Roos.

The American actress Mary Steenburgen played the Scrooge role, and Harry Dean Stanton played a rather unsavory-looking angel. The picture was shot in Toronto and the town of Meaford, near Owen Sound. The shoot was, to put it mildly, a difficult experience, with a lot of frayed tempers and a crew close to mutiny, and the Disney executives breathing down everyone's neck. There was even a minor rift between Borsos and O'Brian. Disney wanted to get rid of any details, such as license plates, that would identify the setting of the film as Canadian. O'Brian fought for Canadian content; Borsos thought it was a silly issue to bother about.

Telefilm rules permitted only two non-Canadians in the cast, but after testing 4,000 prospects Borsos couldn't find the right Canadian girl. After much kicking and screaming, Telefilm allowed him to use Elizabeth Harnois, an American. (Her older brother was played by Toronto schoolboy Robbie Magwood.)

But that wasn't the end of the casting problems. The role of Father Christmas himself (aka S. Claus) had yet to be cast. It was a small but important role, involving two weeks' shooting. Borsos didn't want a bombastic, ho-ho-ho Santa; he wanted a real person. Borsos made a pitch for Laurence Olivier — he was also interested in Alec Guinness and Peter Ustinov — but O'Brian knew there was no way Telefilm would allow another import.

Meanwhile the costume department started to get downright rebellious. The character's scenes were to be shot in ten days, and the size of the Santa suit was still unknown.

At last O'Brian and Borsos found their Father Christmas — Toronto opera singer Jan Rubes, who had become a hot character actor as a result of *Charlie Grant's War* (in which he played the hero's old Jewish friend) and the hit Hollywood movie *Witness* (in which he played a stern Amish grandfather).

O'Brian was discovering just what was meant by the American producer who described life with the new bosses of Disney as working "in a bunker atmosphere, under constant threat of the guillotine." As an avowed Canadian nationalist who had nonetheless allowed himself to get into the clutches of a company that symbolized American cultural imperialism — all in the name of getting his dream movie financed — O'Brian had put himself into a ludicrous and impossible position. Disney had sent an executive overlord from California to make sure the Canadians didn't fall behind schedule. As Borsos and O'Brian were learning the hard way, there was a price to be paid for getting into bed with Mickey Mouse.

One Magic Christmas turned out to be a disappointment for those who expected great things from the Borsos/O'Brian team. It was an extremely safe, conventional, Capra-esque family drama, with a style that seemed calculated, tame and manipulative. The film got mixed reviews and did only moderate business in its broad release across North America.

Once Kroonenburg decided he wanted Borsos to direct *Bethune*, he needed Donald Sutherland's approval.

Sutherland had never met Borsos. Kroonenburg sent Borsos over to spend a day with Sutherland at the Ritz-Carlton Hotel in Montreal, where Sutherland was staying. Sutherland was favorably impressed by Borsos, and by the end of the day, their alliance was the hottest rumor in Montreal, Toronto and L.A. Borsos was the man who would be king.

Not surprisingly, Borsos wanted to go on counting on O'Brian to be his anchor. When he got the offer to do *Bethune*, he was torn. It sounded like one of the greatest opportunities a director could want. Yet he didn't know the producers, and he was wary of going into a huge, perilous venture with strangers. So Borsos conferred with O'Brian and came up with a proposition: suppose he said yes to *Bethune,* provided O'Brian be brought in as one of the producers? The scheme had some appeal for Telefilm as well. O'Brian's name had become synonymous with classy, prestigious productions. It would give Telefilm the kind of security they thought they had with Kotcheff.

After a week of phone calls, there was to be a summit meeting in Toronto on the afternoon of Friday, January 9. That happened to be the day of Peter O'Brian's fortieth birthday, which was being celebrated, along with the tenth anniversary of his company, Independent Pictures, by a dinner party for 300 people at Ontario Place, organized by O'Brian's wife, Dr. Carolyn Bennett.

At lunch time, O'Brian and Bennett were summoned to Ontario Place to deal with a crisis. There was no one to blow up the balloons for the party, and they had to do it themselves. The party was called for 6:30, and before going to Ontario Place, O'Brian had to drive to his home and change into his tuxedo. The *Bethune* meeting took place at 4:00 P.M. at the Park Plaza Hotel—not in a room, but in the lobby.

When O'Brian turned up, Kroonenburg and Clermont seemed ill at ease and weren't ready to start. They said they wanted to wait for Borsos, who was supposed to be arriving from L.A. O'Brian went to a pay phone and learned that the plane had been delayed.

Awkwardly, reluctantly, the Montreal producers put their cards on the table. Much as they respected O'Brian, they felt his involvement would prevent them from having their own relationship with Borsos. They felt *Bethune* was their project—they had developed it and brought it this far—and they didn't need another producer. And they couldn't come up with any money for O'Brian.

In a way, O'Brian was relieved. He'd been willing to get involved out of friendship for Borsos, but he wasn't sure what his role could or should be, and he had other pressing matters to attend to, which would be endangered if he took several months to go to China. As always, O'Brian extricated himself from an awkward situation with grace.

Changing into his tuxedo in a great rush at home, O'Brian took a call from Borsos, who had just arrived from L.A. and was on his way to Ontario Place to celebrate O'Brian's birthday. O'Brian broke the news to him.

"I'm sorry about this, Phil," said O'Brian, stumbling around his bedroom half-dressed and looking for his cufflinks, "but I think you should do the picture anyway."

Later that night, everybody who is anybody in the Canadian movie industry toasted Peter O'Brian. Peter Pearson made a humorous speech explaining that the real subject of O'Brian's movies was Canadian WASPs and their summer cottages, and Phillip Borsos said that Peter O'Brian was, above all, "my best buddy."

Long before the end of the night, Borsos had made up his mind. "I'm really sorry Kotcheff isn't going to be doing it," he told a journalist during the party. "But I'm really glad I *am* doing it."

He, too, had fallen under the spell of a movie that had drawn so many people into its strange, obsessive powers. Phillip Borsos, who was only thirty-four, knew very little about the political climate that had set the course of Norman Bethune's and Ted Allan's lives. And at this point he couldn't be sure whether making this movie was going to turn out to be the most triumphant venture of his career or Canada's answer to *Heaven's Gate*. All he knew for sure was that he was bound for China, with or without his best buddy.

Closing Shots

Pointing to the spectacular problems that plagued the production of *Bethune,* veteran observers felt sure the movie would stand in the end as proof that it was folly to attempt a project on this scale without having it backed by a Hollywood studio.

Clearly, Canada's dance with Hollywood was far from over. On the one hand, production was booming, even if Telefilm was under siege from its critics. *Bethune* was only one of dozens of movies before the cameras or in various stages of post-production. And the list of TV series and specials in the works was even longer.

Hollywood producers were happy to take advantage of the special advantages Canada offered — including excellent crews and technical facilities and the 75-cent dollar. Toronto became the third-largest film production centre in North America, behind L.A. and New York. Why, even *Amerika,* ABC's much-hyped miniseries about a Russian takeover of the United States, was made in Toronto. And visiting U.S. productions had to compete for available resources and talent with Canadian productions — many of which were activated with the help of U.S. partners.

The flurry of activity north of the border inevitably led to fits of paranoia south of the border. By the spring of 1987 the Canadian government was under pressure from

American free-trade negotiators who demanded that Canada stop the "unfair competition" of providing any form of subsidy to Canadian movies — be it through Telefilm Canada (its feature-film funding arm) or through tax incentives.

And in the summer of 1987 Canada's finance minister rocked the film industry by announcing he planned to curtail the very tax breaks that had created the production boom. Was the party over? Within weeks the industry had mounted a strong lobby aimed at delaying such a change, which threatened to bring the whole thing crashing down. Given a few more years, its protectors argued, the Canadian film industry should be able to hold its own without help from Ottawa.

Now, that's dancing!

Appendix

50 Notable Home Movies, 1978–1987

The Amateur (1981). In this conspiracy thriller—based on a novel by Robert Little, who collaborated on the script with Diana Maddox—American actor John Savage (of *The Deer Hunter*) plays the handsome revenge-seeker whose girlfriend has been executed by the terrorists holding a group for ransom, Iran-style. Naturally, it all turns out to be a CIA plot. The twisted path leads to Christopher Plummer, hiding behind a moustache and thick glasses. Among the other Canadians are Jan Rubes, Chapelle Jaffe, Lynne Griffin, George Buza and Lee Broker (formerly known as Larry Perkins). British veteran Charles Jarrot directs efficiently, but the material is strictly TV fodder. Implicitly it does raise one interesting question: couldn't a Canadian paranoia movie deal with the RCMP instead of the CIA? Produced by Garth Drabinsky and Joel Michaels.

Anne of Green Gables (1985). Kevin Sullivan's miraculous TV version of Lucy Maud Montgomery's famous book, with Megan Follows as Anne, Colleen Dewhurst as Marilla and Richard Farnsworth as Matthew. When it was shown on the CBC over two nights, more than five million people watched it. Pressed into doing another *Anne* film, Sullivan avoided the usual pitfalls of sequels with *Anne of Green Gables: The Sequel* in 1987.

Atlantic City (1981). There are delicious bits of manic invention that burst through the proceedings like arias in a comic opera, and they come from the mental universe of New York writer John Guare, the wittiest of all living American playwrights. Compared to director Louis Malle's best work, this picture is a trifle, but it has its share of happy surprises, including Burt Lancaster's comic deftness as Lou, an aging drift-dreamer on the fringe of gangland, and Kate Reid's breakthrough performance in the role of Grace, a gangster's widow who, propped up in bed in her Mae West getup, barks insults at Lou. Canadians in the cast include Hollis McLaren, Robert Joy, Al Waxman, Moses Znaimer and Robert Goulet. Moose Jaw is mentioned for a laugh. Chosen best movie of the year by the National Society of Film Critics in the United States. Produced by Denis Héroux and John Kemeny.

The Bay Boy (1984). Daniel Petrie's coming-of-age story set in Cape Breton during the Depression represents a homecoming for Canada's most enigmatic expatriate movie director. *The Bay Boy* isn't strictly autobiographical, but a number of details are close to the story of Petrie's boyhood. The sixteen-year-old hero is played with quiet authority by Kiefer Sutherland in his first major role. The boy is a dutiful "good son" in a Scottish Catholic family touched by tragedy. The film has striking images of Nova Scotia, but it also has serious flaws—notably Liv Ullmann, miscast as the hero's mother, and some clumsy thriller mechanics.

Les Bons Débarras (1980). The title means, roughly, "good riddance," and the setting is a squalid, small town in the Laurentians, but the film isn't depressing—it's elating. The audience is entranced by a compelling mother-daughter pair, played by Marie Tifo and Charlotte Laurier. The picture is a tour de force for the young Quebec director Francis Mankiewicz, who collaborated with writer Réjean Ducharme. No wonder it collected eight Genies, including the one for best film of the year.

By Design (1982). Claude Jutra's loopy comedy about two lesbians who want to have a baby was neither a critical nor a commercial success, but it's a lovely, surprising movie. Patty Duke Astin and Sara Botsford play the would-be parents; Saul Rubinek is the bewildered photographer chosen for stud service. Joe Wisenfeld shared script credit with Jutra and David Eames. Beryl Fox produced the film, shot in Vancouver.

Canada's Sweetheart (1985). In this outstanding TV film, Donald Brittain tells the saga of Hal C. Banks, the American thug who ruled Canada's waterfront in the 1950s and 1960s. Brittain mixes drama with documentary footage, and he's lucky enough to have baby-faced Maury Chaykin in the title role.

The Changeling (1980). This $7.5-million haunted-house movie, produced by Garth Drabinsky and Joel Michaels, is suitable for being told to eager nine-year-olds huddled around a beach fire. Doors creak, mirrors smash, and director Peter Medak (a Hungarian by way of England) keeps working the audience over while George C. Scott clomps around glaring, as if he blamed the public for the fact he could command a million dollars for appearing in a witless comic book when anyone could see he needed the challenge of great roles. Here he's John Russell, a distinguished composer and musician who leaves New York after his wife and daughter have been killed in an accident. Flamboyant, brilliant, charged with musical energy and with snarling, silver-haired egomania, Russell is like a gentile Leonard Bernstein. He takes off for Seattle, where, for reasons never explained, he decides to buy a mansion. Why would a fifty-five-year-old man living alone want a mansion? In Seattle? Because of the wonderful piano, of course. The house is held by the local historical society, and no one has lived in it for years. It has a mind of its own. Baths start running themselves, and a wheelchair becomes a treacherous runaway. Canadians in supporting roles come and go with unseemly haste.

Charlie Grant's War (1985). R.H. Thomson plays the plucky lad from Toronto who, according to legend, stood up to the Nazi thugs and smuggled Jews out of Austria with phony passports before landing in one of Hitler's camps. The facts about the real Charlie Grant remain shadowy, and Anna Sandor's script is problematic. But Martin Lavut, the director of this made-for-TV CBC movie, camouflaged the weaknesses and did a masterful job of creating subtext. And Thomson manages to make Grant into a character rather than a mouthpiece for noble ideals.

City on Fire (1979). An all-star Canadian disaster movie produced by Harold Greenberg, so ludicrously inept and full of howlers that it becomes perversely entertaining. The No-Name city rocked by explosions is Montreal. Among those scurrying about in the ruins are Ava Gardner, drinking, cursing and looking ruined; Shelley Winters as a doomed nurse who bravely mans the bedpans; and Susan Clark, who gets to flex her eyebrows while exchanging insults with Barry Newman. Leslie Nielsen plays the corrupt, idiotic mayor who is to blame for building a refinery in the middle of the city, and Henry Fonda turns up as the fire chief who must cope with the consequences. Mavor Moore harrumphs away and in his dying breath advises the mayor, "Never admit you were wrong." If Busby Berkeley had staged a dance number about Lourdes, it might look something like the "spray cure" finale here. Someone should try the spray cure on director Alvin Rakoff.

Dancing in the Dark (1986). Martha Henry gives new meaning to the phrase "kitchen-sink drama." As Edna McCormick, the enslaved Ontario housewife, she cleans and scrubs and polishes and vacuums with maniacal zeal. Henry delves so deeply into the bleak horror of Edna's life that you can't help succumbing to her spell. This picture, directed by Leon Marr from Joan Barfoot's novel, may not be fun to sit through. But Martha Henry's Genie-winning performance seeps into your pores.

The Decline of the American Empire (1986). This quirky, sardonic comedy about selective promiscuity among a group of smart French-Canadian academics is witty and entertaining, but also bloodless and bewildering. The jokey thesis, offered by one of the characters, is that we are living through a period of declining empire, and that's why people pursue purely hedonistic goals. Writer-director Denys Arcand's attitude is so droll and offhand that it takes a while before we realize he means this idea to be taken seriously. This is a sexy house-party movie, and a comedy for knowing adults that can be relished by everyone starved of sophisticated conversation. It's polished and assured; yet there's a thinness about it that keeps it from being fully satisfying. Winner of eight Genies and nominated for an Oscar in the foreign film category.

The Fly (1986). This darkly funny, gross-out parable about disgust is technically a U.S. production, but it was filmed on the outskirts of Toronto by that quintessential Toronto director, David Cronenberg. It's less campily amusing than the 1958 black-and-white cheapie cult film, which made us howl with laughter when the hero, having turned into an insect on the wall, squeaked desperately in falsetto, "Help me! Help me!" But Cronenberg's version is a fuller, more unsettling experience, and you can't shake it off. Jeff Goldblum, perhaps Hollywood's most likably funky actor, plays Seth Brundle, the obsessive scientist who invents a machine to teleport matter, and tests it on himself. A fly gets into the machine with him, and the fly's genes begin taking him over, spreading like a gradual, horrifying disease. There's an element of the Dr. Faustus legend here, and of Beauty and the Beast. Seth has a girlfrield (Geena Davis) who can't stop loving him even when he turns into a repulsive monster. The film is more like a remake of old Cronenberg films than a remake of *The Fly*; this time, he gets it right.

The Grey Fox (1982). This spectacularly well made first feature by Phillip Borsos tells the story of Canada's first train robber. As played by former Hollywood stuntman Richard Farnsworth, Bill Miner is not your average outlaw; he's a courtly, laconic old gentleman. But luckily, just when the audience is starved for flamboyance, Borsos serves up Jackie Burroughs, who bristles and simmers beneath her Victorian finery, as a renegade spinster surviving on the British Columbia frontier as a photographer. Together, they become beautiful losers. Produced by Peter O'Brian. Winner of seven Genies, including best picture and best director.

The Handyman (1981). Quebec actress Micheline Lanctôt turned writer-director and scored a small personal triumph with this beguiling vignette about a hopelessly romantic handyman (Jocelyn Bérubé) who falls in love with a bored Montreal housewife (Andrée Pelletier).

Heartaches (1982). Too few people saw this lovely comedy-drama. Don Shebib tells a lively, engaging story about two female misfits sharing an apartment and working at a Toronto factory together. As Rita, who talks too loud and walks like a truck driver, Margot Kidder does the best work of her life. Annie Potts is likable as her pregnant runaway roommate. The cast includes Robert Carradine and Winston Rekert, and the script is by Terence Heffernan. Toronto is the undisguised setting, and the city has never looked more appealing.

If You Could See What I Hear (1982). An inspirational as-told-to book about a blind man becomes an insufferably pert, comic lark, directed by Eric Till from a script by Stuart Gillard. Marc Singer has the role of Tom Sullivan, whose high spirits conquer sightlessness, and R.H. Thomson plays his happy-go-lucky sidekick who is always playing practical jokes on him. Sarah Torgov plays his caring girlfriend, and the cast also includes Helen Burns (as a lovably eccentric landlady), Jack Creley (as a long-suffering teacher) and Douglas Campbell (as the hero's dad). Tom not only drinks and plays golf but even sings at a bar (a regular Stevie Wonder). He's so normal, the film keeps exclaiming, why he even chases girls and gets laid. It's hard to decide which is ickier—Eric Till's notion of playful or Eric Till's notion of lyrical.

I Miss You, Hugs and Kisses (1978). Murray Markowitz's sleazy potboiler carries a disclaimer, but it is obviously based on the Demeter murder case. Markowitz doesn't have the sophisticated approach of George Jonas and Barbara Amiel, whose book *By Persons Unknown* examined the sociological nuances of the case. To him the case is just an excuse to run through the gory details and wallow in them. While pretending to explore doubt, he shows us all the ways the murder might have been committed—each more gory than the last. With Donald Pilon and Elke Sommer.

In Praise of Older Women (1978). By "older," producer Robert Lantos seems to mean twenty-six. Based on the famous novel by Stephen Vizenczey, the screen version, as directed by George Kaczender, has the innocence of soft-core porn, but with more polished performances. The Hungarian revolution, which brings the hero to Canada, is strictly a minor incident between orgasms while the young American actor Tom Berenger has a series of encounters with women played by the likes of Karen Black, Marilyn Lightstone, Helen Shaver, Alexandra Stewart, Louise Marleau and Susan Strasberg. It's hard to know why the Ontario censors wanted to snip it, but audiences psyched up by the publicity for something really dirty were disappointed. The film sells the harmless idea that good sex is healthy—and as easy to find as a new brand of detergent. Winner of Canadian Film Awards for Helen Shaver (best actress) and Marilyn Lightstone (best supporting actress).

I've Heard the Mermaids Singing (1987). Patricia Rozema's low-budget fable, set in the world of chic Toronto feminism, is about a domineering gallery curator and her "organizationally impaired" office temp, Polly. Sheila McCarthy's funny, winning performance as Polly is the main reason for seeing it.

Jacob Two-Two Meets the Hooded Fang (1979). This version of Mordecai Richler's playfully scary fantasy for children is by no means as stylish and witty as the stage version produced by Young People's Theatre, but it's amiable and eager to please. The special effects betray the low budget, but it looks better on a TV screen than a big screen. Produced by Harry Gulkin, directed by Theodore J. Flicker (an American).

John and the Missus (1987). John Munn, the hero of Gordon Pinsent's film—which Pinsent had previously written as a novel and a play—is a messianic Canadian monomaniac possessed by a fierce need to stay put. It's 1962, and the mine is being shut down in the Newfoundland coastal town where Munn's family has lived for hundreds of years, and the government is offering each family $1,000 plus $200 per family member to relocate. Other residents are resigned to leaving or giddy at the prospect of getaway money. But Munn is in a fury, and he comes to regard anyone who agrees to budge as a traitor. Cinematographer Frank Tidy provides clear, intense images, but there's really no one in this picture except Pinsent. As the Missus, Jackie Burroughs is almost mute; her part hasn't been written. But the final sequence, in which Munn's house is taken down to the water's edge, lifted on a barge and sent on its way to St. John's Harbor, has a lovely mythic quality. And whatever his shortcomings as writer and director, Pinsent earned the Genie he won for his performance as John Munn.

Joshua Then and Now (1985). Ted Kotcheff's screen version of the Mordecai Richler novel is the saga of a Jewish rebel who marries a WASP princess and conducts his own war with the Westmount establishment. It's exuberant but disjointed, perhaps a consequence of trying to make a feature and a TV miniseries at once. Luckily, James Woods has the right edge to be Richler's alter ego. But Alan Arkin steals the picture with his ribald performance as Joshua's father, the Bible-quoting crook Reuben Shapiro. The film's most dismaying flaw is Gabrielle Lazure's icy, vacuous performance in the role of Pauline. Produced by Robert Lantos and Stephen Roth.

The King of Friday Night (1985). For once a brilliant stage show was turned into a brilliant TV show. John Gray's autobiographical musical is about a rock band in the Nova Scotia outback in the 1960s. Gray wrote the songs, which are wonderfully fresh and energetic. Andrew Gosling contributed the wizardly video effects. And Frank MacKay, playing the band's fat boy, steals the show. Les Harris was the producer.

Louisiana (1984). A *Gone With the Wind* clone, starring Margot Kidder as a southern belle. John Kemeny, the producer, was plagued by disaster both natural and human. The idea was to turn out both a feature film and a six-part TV series.

Loyalties (1986). This first feature by Alberta director Anne Wheeler is carefully calculated to lead straight to a perfectly correct feminist manifesto. Susan Woolridge, who was unforgettably wonderful as Daphne Manners in *The Jewel in the Crown,* plays Lily Sutton, a trendy English doctor's wife, who for some murky reason has arrived with her family to make a new life in Lac la Biche, a former fur-trading outpost 175 kilometres northeast of Edmonton. At first we don't find out much about her husband, a seemingly charming fellow played by Kenneth Welsh, and we don't know why they left the comforts and civilities of England to rough it in the bush. They feel a keen sense of being apart from the local community, largely Indian and Métis. Woolridge is upstaged by Tantoo Cardinal, as a kind of Métis Mother Courage she hires to help with the house and children. The subject of the film is the bond that emerges between these two women; the plot mechanism is a rainy night, rape and a violent revenge attempt. The sisterly relationship between the two women is emotionally potent even if you notice how contrived it is, and the mouthy, down-to-earth Cardinal is an engaging new screen personality.

Meatballs (1979). Ivan Reitman had broken out of the B-movie circuit by coproducing *Animal House,* an American film that made him a genuine Hollywood millionaire. He followed up with this lightweight Canadian production about summer camp shenanigans—which he not only produced but also directed—and it turned into a spectacular hit. But the financial statements are more interesting than what's on the screen, which is witless and shapeless as well as innocent. You have to be willfully infantile to have a good time. With Bill Murray and Kate Lynch.

Mr. Patman (1980). This notable dud from the Hollywood North era was shot in Vancouver, but the audience is never told where we are. It's just as well. The film has a British director, John Guillermin, and an American star, James Coburn, as a male psychiatric nurse with a gift for healing lovable crazies.

Kate Nelligan appears as Nurse Peabody without giving any clues about the qualities that made her a phenomenal success on the London stage. The script was originally written by Philip Hersh, who took his name off it after a dispute with producer William Marshall. Tom Hedley, the Toronto magazine editor who wrote *Flashdance*, worked on the rewrite. The result is a feeble echo of *One Flew Over the Cuckoo's Nest*.

Murder by Decree (1979). In this expensive Anglo-Canadian coproduction, an ingeniously hokey script (by English playwright John Hopkins) pairs Sherlock Holmes off with Jack the Ripper in late-Victorian London. Toronto director Bob Clark works up too many Gothic fog effects, but he delivers lively, pulpy fun. Christopher Plummer is a dapper Holmes, but James Mason's deftly fussy Dr. Watson steals the movie (especially in a scene about the mashing of peas). The movie turns into a homecoming for Canadian celebrities. Donald Sutherland is a gaunt, Dickensian eccentric in the role of a wild-eyed psychic thought to have supernatural clues to the wave of prostitute murders. Geneviève Bujold acts her heart out in a madhouse tableau. And Susan Clark, playing an Irish tart, flashes her green eyes.

My American Cousin (1985). In this charming female coming-of-age memoir, written and directed by Sandy Wilson, the audience is captivated by a subject never before openly explored in a movie — Canadian ambivalence about Americans. We're in the Okanagan Valley, circa 1959. Sandy (Margaret Langrick) is twelve going on twenty-one when her cousin Butch (John Wildman) — a cool, uninhibited sixteen-year-old hunk — roars into town from California in a splashy red Cadillac convertible "borrowed" from his mother. *My American Cousin* is partly a requiem for the kind of small-town Canadian innocence that has perhaps vanished forever. Producer Peter O'Brian was rewarded for taking a chance on unknowns; the movie won six Genies.

9B (1986). This made-for-TV CBC movie has a fresh new face — that of Edmonton actor Robert Wisden, who brings energy and humor to the role of a bewildered British immigrant teacher coping with a high-school class full of mouthy troublemakers in the wilds of British Columbia. Based on a true story by Vancouver journalist Don Hunter, the film (produced and directed by James Swan from a script by Grahame Woods) is a happy surprise, full of outback charm.

90 Days (1985). This likably screwy comedy from the National Film Board is the story of two neurotic male casualties of the sexual battlefields. Alex (Sam Grana) is a failed womanizer. But one day he's approached at a bar by a stranger who wants to pay $10,000 for his sperm if . . . . Meanwhile, his buddy Blue (Stefan Wodoslawsky), an eccentric loner who is compulsively tidy, has flown over a pen pal from Korea (Christine Pak) who is sort of a mail-order bride, except that he can't make up his mind to marry her, and meanwhile they're sleeping separately in his apartment. This modest, disarming movie is directed by Giles Walker with the throwaway charm of an updated Lubitsch.

One Magic Christmas (1985). This safe, conventional family picture is a major disappointment for those who dreamed of what Phillip Borsos could do with material of his own choosing. Produced by Peter O'Brian and backed by both Telefilm and Disney, it's Capraesque Yuletime hokum, with Mary Steenburgen as a Scrooge-like mother who doesn't believe in Christmas, and Harry Dean Stanton as an angel who helps her see the light. Jan Rubes plays Santa Claus, helplessly. The style of the film is calculated, tame and manipulative. There's no magic in the storytelling or the performances; the picture's highest ambition seems to be to get by at the box office and satisfy the Disney executives.

The Plouffe Family (1981). Roger Lemelin, editor of *La Presse* for years, has written many books, but the one he's always remembered for is his second novel, *Les Plouffe,* the saga of a working-class Quebec City family of the 1940s. The Plouffes became Canada's favorite TV family in the 1950s. This marathon movie, directed by Gilles Carle (who collaborated with Lemelin on the script) has been hailed as Quebec's *Gone With the Wind.* Unlike the six-hour TV version, marred by dreadful dubbing, this subtitled feature, which runs twelve minutes short of three hours, is absorbing and resonant. Gabriel Arcand as Ovide, the opera-loving brother who fails at seduction as well as priestly self-denial, gives a marvelous performance that stays with you.

Porky's (1981). Bob Clark wrote and directed a self-consciously gross, adolescent comedy, in the *Animal House* manner, shot in Florida with a Canadian crew. It isn't much of a movie, but it was a huge box-office winner for executive producer Harold Greenberg.

Pouvoir Intime (1986). Quebec director Yves Simoneau pulls off something of a coup—a low-budget thriller that becomes an exercise in style. It's the unremarkable tale of a robbery that goes awry, with Jacques Godin as Theo, an ex-convict who is asked to hijack an armored truck. His client is a crooked government official so eager to reclaim a bag of incriminating evidence that he's willing to let Theo keep the loot. Theo's accomplices include his teen-aged son, a former cellmate and an old girlfriend (well played by that fine actress Marie Tifo). But something goes very wrong. One of the truck's guards winds up wounded and trapped in the back of the stolen truck, and at the robbers' hideout in an abandoned warehouse, the guard refuses to come out. The film turns into a tense, subtle mood piece about psychological warfare, waiting games, and the endless variety of dead-end traps. In French, with subtitles.

Quest for Fire (1982). A compelling epic about prehistoric man, produced by John Kemeny and Denis Héroux, and directed by Jean-Jacques Annaud, a Frenchman. It became a Canadian production more or less by accident when a strike forced 20th Century Fox to cancel its original plans. The cast of unknowns speaks a language invented by Anthony Burgess and uses body language developed by Desmond Morris. Much of the shooting was done in Canada.

The Rubber Gun (1979). Allan Moyle directed this affecting inside view of a Montreal drug commune. Moyle also worked on the script and appears in the film as an outsider—a sociology student researching a thesis. The actors all seem to be playing themselves, and the amateur quality works in the film's favor. In the role of a Jewish bisexual painter, Stephen Lack shows great sardonic charm.

Running (1979). This slick, empty-headed, jock soap opera is allegedly Canadian, though its characters are located in Middle America. The script, by Steve Stern (an ex-Torontonian who moved to Hollywood) is about a loser-drifter who can't seem to stick to anything—until he decides to enter the Olympic marathon. Stern also directed the film, and brings out all his own banal intentions. Michael Douglas plays the runner who not only has failed to make a decent career for himself or a living for his family but has also choked in previous sporting endeavors. No wonder Susan Anspach tosses him out and starts dating a used-car salesman. But all that changes once he gets to Montreal and the 1976 Olympics. The film cleverly intercuts footage from TV coverage of the Olympics, which provides ersatz excitement. Anspach does her noble feminist bit, and tearfully waits to take him back as he crosses the finish line all bloodied and limping. It seems she only kicked him out for his own good.

Silence of the North (1981). Playing Olive Fredrickson, Canada's woman in the wilderness, Ellen Burstyn suffers and suffers but always plunges bravely on, smiling radiantly in the manner of one who is fully aware of having attained sainthood. Gordon Pinsent, as the heroine's second husband, brings a bit of energy and charm to the proceedings, and cinematographer Richard Leiterman gets some marvelous footage on the breakup of the ice on the Athabasca River, but mostly this is deadly stuff. Allan King directs, helplessly.

The Silent Partner (1978). Elliott Gould is uncharacteristically restrained as a bank clerk drawn into a plot in this expensive made-in-Toronto production about the holdup of a bank at the Eaton Centre. The crime occurs during the Christmas season, and the gunman is Christopher Plummer being entertainingly maniacal in a Santa Claus suit. Celine Lomez, the Quebec actress who played the title role in *Gina,* is the femme fatale who gets involved in Plummer's cat-and-mouse game with Gould, and the international cast also features Susannah York. Director Daryl Duke gives the enterprise some class; this movie swept the Canadian Film Awards, and if you consider the other entries for 1978, you'll know why.

The Terry Fox Story (1983). In this made-for-TV movie about the one-legged runner who raised millions for cancer research, director Ralph Thomas and his writers back away from the interesting questions about Fox's Marathon of Hope and make him so normal he's boring. Eric Fyer is likable in the title role, but he's no actor, and it's clear his main qualification is that he's a one-legged athlete (eliminating the need for a double or trick photography).

Threshold (1981). Donald Sutherland plays Thomas Vrain, the world's greatest heart surgeon. The story, the director (Richard Pearce) and the writer (James Salter) are American, but this is a Canadian movie, produced by Jon Slan and Michael Burns, and filmed mostly in Toronto. The hero is based on Dr. Denton Cooley, the controversial Texas heart-transplant surgeon, who makes a cameo appearance in the film and provided technical advice. Jeff Goldblum as the miracle doctor's mouthy sidekick provides a needed touch of comedy. The style of the movie is high-tech, cool and sleek. The picture got good reviews but died at the box office.

Ticket to Heaven (1981). A scary psychological thriller, ably directed by Ralph Thomas, about a religious cult. Nick Mancuso gets sucked in and brainwashed; Saul Rubinek helps kidnap him, and R.H. Thomson is the deprogrammer who unscrambles his mind. The hot subject carries it.

The Tin Flute (1983). Gabrielle Roy's novel about a French-Canadian family suffering through the Depression may not have been the highest kind of literature, but it deserved better than this dreadful adaptation, which has no redeeming qualities.

Too Outrageous! (1987). Craig Russell, an ex-hairdresser who does entertaining impressions of female performers, became an underground star when he played himself in *Outrageous!* in 1977. Ten years later the sequel provides a comeback vehicle for Russell, and he seizes it exuberantly. When Russell puts on his Tina Turner wig and stomps around with mock-insolent zest, he breaks free of the pieties in the conception of writer-director Richard Benner, who concocts a fairly maudlin victim fantasy.

Tribute (1981). In this screen verison of Bernard Slade's shameless play, terminal cancer is used to push the audience into loving Jack Lemmon for his weakness. Lemmon plays the wisecracking show-biz agent Scottie Templeton, who turns his own impending death into a masochistic gag. With Colleen Dewhurst as the big-mama doctor, Robby Benson as the snotty son, Lee Remick as the forgiving ex-wife and Gale Garnett as the warm-hearted hooker. Produced by Garth Drabinsky and Joel Michaels.

Two Solitudes (1978). Jean-Pierre Aumont (from Paris) plays a French-Canadian seigneur, and Stacy Keach (from Los Angeles) plays the Anglo-Canadian businessman-politician who dupes him. Aumont smiles wanly and says, "I meant well." That phrase could serve as an epitaph for writer-director Lionel Chetwynd, who tries to get by on good intentions. Based on the Hugh MacLennan novel, the movie may be taken seriously by people who feel they are doing something patriotic by sitting through a solemn movie about the violation of a trust between Francophone and Anglophone Canadians. The cast includes Claude Jutra, Raymond Cloutier, Gloria Carlin and Mary Pirie, but Chris Wiggins is the only one who finds a character to play.

The Wars (1983). The background of Timothy Findley's novel and this Robin Phillips film adaptation is World War I, and we are among the prosperous WASPs of Rosedale. Robert Ross, played by Brent Carver, goes off to war against the wishes of his mother (Martha Henry) and learns about life. The bizarre climax involves his decision to release horses from a burning barn in contravention of his officer's orders. We're meant to feel that somehow his needless death is caused by the coldness, bitterness and general hatefulness of his family. Phillips has caught the tone of the book, but he's unable to go beyond its limitations. The cast includes many of the actors Phillips worked with at Stratford, including Jackie Burroughs, Alan Scarfe, Barbara Budd, Domini Blythe and Clare Coulter. Daphne Dare was art director. Produced by Richard Nielsen.

Your Ticket Is No Longer Valid (1982). Romain Gary's novel about an aging tycoon facing two crises—financial collapse and sexual impotence—was turned into an accidentally hilarious movie. Who can keep a straight face when Richard Harris solemnly tries to rally his penis to its former glories? "Do not underestimate the value of a partial erection," advises a wise doctor. Produced by Robert Lantos. Also known as *Finishing Touch*.

Index

Page numbers in **bold** refer to capsule reviews in the Appendix.